# INTERNATIONAL FUTURES

# DILEMMAS IN WORLD POLITICS

## Series Editor

George A. Lopez, University of Notre Dame

Dilemmas in World Politics offers teachers and students of international relations a series of quality books on critical issues, trends, and regions in international politics. Each text examines a "real world" dilemma and is structured to cover the historical, theoretical, practical, and projected dimensions of its subject.

# FORTHCOMING TITLES

V. Spike Peterson and Anne Sisson Runyan
**Global Gender Issues**

☐ ☐ ☐

Sarah Tisch and Michael Wallace
**Dilemmas of Development Assistance:
The What, Why, and Who of Foreign Aid**

☐ ☐ ☐

Bruce E. Moon
**International Trade in the 1990s**

☐ ☐ ☐

Ted Robert Gurr and Barbara Harff
**Ethnic Conflict in World Politics**

☐ ☐ ☐

Frederic S. Pearson
**The Spread of Arms in the International System**

# INTERNATIONAL FUTURES

■　　■　　■

## Choices in the Creation
## of a New World Order

### Barry B. Hughes
UNIVERSITY OF DENVER

**Westview Press**

BOULDER □ SAN FRANCISCO □ OXFORD

To Stuart Bremer
My Berlin connection, bookstore guide,
modeling colleague, and friend

*Dilemmas in World Politics Series*

Copyright © 1993 by Westview Press, Inc., except for the accompanying computer program, which is copyright © by Barry B. Hughes

Published in 1993 in the United States of America by Westview Press, Inc., 5500 Central Avenue, Boulder, Colorado 80301-2877, and in the United Kingdom by Westview Press, 36 Lonsdale Road, Summertown, Oxford OX2 7EW

Library of Congress Cataloging-in-Publication Data
Hughes, Barry, 1945–
   International futures : choices in the creation of a new world
order / Barry B. Hughes.
      p.   cm. — (Dilemmas in world politics)
   Includes bibliographical references and index.
   ISBN 0-8133-1650-2. — ISBN 0-8133-1651-0 (pbk.)
   1. Forecasting.   2. Policy sciences.   3. Forecasting—Mathematical
models.   4. Forecasting—Data processing.   I. Title.   II. Series.
H61.4.H828   1993
003'.2—dc20
                                                                    93-7227
                                                                    CIP

Printed and bound in the United States of America

(∞)   The paper used in this publication meets the requirements
      of the American National Standard for Permanence of Paper
      for Printed Library Materials Z39.48-1984.

10   9   8   7   6   5   4   3   2   1

# Contents

□ □ □

# Tables and Figures

## Tables

## Figures

# Preface and Acknowledgments

This book seeks to immerse you in thinking about global futures. It is not a book for passive readers. Unlike most books on the future, the volume does *not* communicate a specific vision of global developments. Instead it asks you to participate in the development of your own understanding and vision.

The book involves you in thinking about the future in two ways. The first is by means of traditional text. Chapter 1 argues that we understand the future (1) through extrapolation of trends and (2) through causal understandings of the world. Chapter 2 assists you in the exploration of trends, and most of the rest of the volume helps you to investigate competing causal understandings of global systems. In addition, we each combine our own values with analysis of trends and causal relationships in the creation of our own prescriptions. The text therefore also helps you to identify common value orientations and to think about your own.

The second tool, and one intended to involve you even more fully, is a computer simulation model called International Futures (IFs).[1] IFs is a global model that simulates population, food, energy, environmental, economic, and political developments from a base year of 1990, allowing forecasts extending as far into the future as the year 2035. It divides the world into 10 geographic regions—four are individual countries (the United States, Russia, China, and Japan), one is an increasingly close-knit grouping of countries (the Western Europe of the European Community), and five are broad groupings of countries (other economically developed countries, members of OPEC, other Latin American countries, other African countries, and other Asian countries).

This book and the accompanying computer simulation help the reader grapple with a fundamental problem in human affairs: We cannot foresee the future, but we must act in the face of that uncertainty in ways that we know can dramatically affect our well-being and that of future generations. The first chapter elaborates that problem and argues that we do well to approach action in the face of uncertainty in three steps: investigating where change appears to be taking us, specifying as carefully as possible the kind of future we would like to have, and studying the nature of the leverage we have upon events.

---

**Important Note**

**Note to Instructors:** In a classroom environment you can make the use of IFs optional. You might allow the students who are so motivated to base their term papers on the use of IFs while others engage in more traditional research.

---

The second chapter initiates the first of those three steps, the investigation of global change. Chapter 3 then introduces the computer simulation, IFs, as a tool for further examining change. Chapters 4 through 6 focus our attention simultaneously on the value-based debates over the kind of future we want and on the leverage that we might have in bringing it about. Each of those chapters includes general discussion and analysis and then proceeds to explain how IFs can add to the analysis. The three chapters devote most attention, respectively, to political, economic, and environmental issues. Finally, Chapter 7 asks the reader to consider all three types of issues simultaneously and to ponder the future he or she wants and believes might be possible. The seven chapters of this volume obviously do not eliminate the basic necessity of acting in the face of uncertainty, but they should facilitate serious consideration of choices in the creation of the new world order.

A few design features make the book more readable and the computer model easier to use. First, a number of boxes highlight "Important Notes," attention to which should greatly reward the reader (see boxes on this page). Second, indentation and the symbol ▶ set off more technical computer information and tips so that you can more easily page back to them later. For instance, on p. 49 you'll see

▶ **Starting IFs and Using the Main Menu.** Before you can examine the workings of the seven forces, you need to know how to use IFs. Assuming that the model is installed on your computer (see Appendix 3 for installation instructions and requirements), you need only be located in the directory named IFs90 to initiate interaction with the model. At the DOS (operating system) prompt, type IFs90 (uppercase and lowercase letters are always interchangeable) and then touch the <Enter> key.

Third, three appendixes concentrate the most technical information on the model, including installation instructions, so that it interrupts the text less and can provide easy reference.

---

**Important Note**

**To Install and Use IFs:** Appendix 3 to this volume includes installation instructions and a brief discussion of IFs.

---

I hope you will find this book of considerable use in thinking about the future, whether or not you also use the IFs model. If you do not use IFs, it is reasonable to skip portions of the text that focus on it (especially Chapter 3 and the last section in each of Chapters 4 through 7).

Although this book and the IFs model are fully self-contained, they can also usefully serve as a supplement in the study of world politics to Barry B. Hughes, *Continuity and Change in World Politics*, 2d ed. (Prentice-Hall, 1994). The structure of presentation in the two books is complementary.

This volume and model build upon the work or have benefited from the help of so many over a period of nearly 20 years that it is impossible to acknowledge those individuals fully. I gratefully acknowledge the long-term, generous support and encouragement of Harold Guetzkow and Karl Deutsch. It is especially important to recognize the modeling debts this effort owes to Mihajlo Mesarovic, Thomas Shook, John Richardson, Patricia Strauch, Juan Huerta, and other members of the team who developed the World Integrated Model and to recognize Stuart Bremer, Peter Brecke, Thomas Cusack, Wolf-Dieter Eberwein, Brian Pollins, and Dale Smith of the GLOBUS modeling project. Over the years individuals who have used or tested earlier versions of the model, including Jonathan Wilkenfeld, Gerald Barney, Donald Borock, Donald Sylvan, and Richard Chadwick, have contributed much to its continued development. Peter Brecke, Phil Schrodt, and Douglas Stuart provided very useful reviews of this volume as they tested IFs. Michael Niemann, Terrance Peet-Lukes, Douglas McClure, and James Cole assisted in the process of developing microcomputer adaptations of IFs. Many, many others have helped in the production of a model and a volume that inevitably have more flaws than the author would care to admit but that would have been impossible at all without their ideas and encouragement.

*Barry B. Hughes*

## NOTES

1. The National Science Foundation, the Cleveland Foundation, the Exxon Education Foundation, the Kettering Family Foundation, and the Pacific Cultural Foundation provided much-appreciated financial support for earlier versions of IFs and thereby indirectly for this edition. The United States Institute of Peace has provided essential support for this release. None of these organizations bears any responsibility for the content or remaining failings of International Futures.

# Acronyms

| | |
|---|---|
| CFCs | chlorofluorocarbons |
| CFE | Conventional Forces in Europe |
| CSCE | Conference on Security and Cooperation in Europe |
| G-77 | Group of 77 |
| GATT | General Agreement on Tariffs and Trade |
| GDP | gross domestic product |
| GNP | gross national product |
| GSP | Generalized System of Preferences |
| IBRD | International Bank for Reconstruction and Development |
| IEA | International Energy Agency |
| IFI | international financial institution |
| IFs | International Futures |
| IFs90 | International Futures 1990 |
| IGOs | intergovernmental organizations |
| IMF | International Monetary Fund |
| INF | Intermediate-range Nuclear Force |
| INGOs | international nongovernmental organizations |
| ITO | International Trade Organization |
| LDCs | less-developed countries |
| NAFTA | North American Free Trade Agreement |
| NATO | North Atlantic Treaty Organization |
| NIC | newly industrialized country |
| NIEO | new international economic order |
| OECD | Organization for Economic Cooperation and Development |
| R&D | research and development |
| START | Strategic Arms Reduction Treaty |
| UNCED | United Nations Conference on Environment and Development |
| UNCTAD | United Nations Conference on Trade and Development |
| WIM | World Integrated Model |

# ONE

□ □ □

# Action in the Face
# of Uncertainty

Most early European explorers believed the earth to be round, so that one could eventually return to Europe by sailing far enough to the west. Successive expeditions chose to push farther and farther to the west in the search for a route around the world, a search that others viewed as foolhardy and dangerous. In 1519 Ferdinand Magellan sailed west from Europe with five ships and 265 men. In 1522 one ship returned to Spain from the east with 18 men, completing the first voyage around the world. Magellan himself died in the Philippines. His expedition and those of others established new contacts among the peoples of the globe, the consequences of which we are still watching evolve.

In the early 1980s the USSR exhibited increasing economic weakness, compounded by a succession of short-term and weak leaders. In 1985 Mikhail Sergeyevich Gorbachev became general secretary of the communist party. He quickly chose to enunciate new doctrines for the society and economy of the country, including *perestroika* and *glasnost* (restructuring and openness). In approximately six years of his leadership, the Soviet Union dramatically transformed its international relationships by withdrawing its control over much of Eastern and Central Europe and by moving toward accommodation with the Western powers. In 1991 the country dissolved into 15 independent republics, each seeking its own path to economic and political reform. Gorbachev lost power. The consequences of Gorbachev's choices were dramatic and are also still unfolding.

Humanity now confronts a future as uncertain as the ones that faced these two decisionmakers. We devote about 5 percent of our total eco-

1

nomic output to the pursuit of military security, and we have simultaneously created an insecure world with nearly 60,000 nuclear weapons in the hands of a growing number of separate political entities. The economic product of the average human has attained levels surpassing any in history, whereas the economic performance of most of the world's economies in the last decade was weak and income disparities grew in large numbers of them. The technological sophistication of scientists and engineers has created new marvels in electronics, biology, and other fields, but many aspects of our shared environment have deteriorated. Many of the choices that individuals and organizations make in the next decade will have consequences as important as the decisions made by Magellan and Gorbachev. Those who make such decisions will never be able fully to anticipate their consequences. They will act in the face of uncertainty. Yet they will make choices; collectively they will bring into being a new world order.

*What will be the future of human environmental, economic, and political-social systems?* That is the central question of this volume. The easy and correct answer is that no one knows. If we were so fatalistic as to believe that we had no control over the future, we might simply accept that response and return our attention to daily life. Most of us believe, however, that our actions substantially shape our future and those of our descendants. Many of us fear that misguided action, whether it be environmental despoliation or nuclear war, could lead to catastrophe. Many hope that thoughtful behavior can instead assure a peaceful and prosperous world. We therefore find ourselves in *a very real dilemma: We cannot know the future, but it is important to act in the face of that uncertainty.*

The question that motivates this volume takes on special importance today because many features of the world order defined in the late 1940s have changed dramatically in the last few years. It is clear both that we face critically important political, economic, and environmental issues and that the structures and institutions with which we will address them are in great flux. A new world order will come into focus over the next decade. Any established world order constrains many choices and makes the consequences of action somewhat predictable. In contrast, a period of new world order creation requires that we reconsider even the most fundamental of choices, and it simultaneously reduces predictability. We must now act in the face of the greatest uncertainty.

In order to reduce the dilemma to manageable proportions, we must make at least reasonable estimates about what the future holds, with and without our action. In order to make such estimates, we can decompose our general question about the future into three more specific ones. First, *where do current changes appear to be taking us?* Second, *what kind of future would we prefer?* Third, *how much leverage do we have to bring about the future we prefer?* Each of these questions is more manageable (although hardly simple), and collectively they help us grapple with the necessity of choice in the face of incomplete knowledge. The task of this book is to assist you in investigating these three questions and thereby to address the dilemma we collectively face. In the process you will organize your own thoughts about the new world order.

## THE EXAMINATION OF CHANGE

The two standard techniques for studying where change might be taking us are **extrapolation** (trend projection) and **causal analysis** (a consideration of cause-and-effect relations). If global population is growing at 1.7 percent this year, a simple extrapolation of the future assumes that it will grow at 1.7 percent each year in the future. A more sophisticated extrapolation might recognize that annual population growth rate has declined from 2.0 percent each year in the late 1960s to 1.7 percent now. Therefore, the rate of growth may decline further in the next few decades. Even more sophisticated analysis might recognize cyclical behavior in a phenomenon (such as business cycles in the economy) and extrapolate the cycles into the future.

Extrapolation might allow its user to make a fortune on the stock market ("technical" analysts or "chartists" rely on it heavily) and might also provide some very good guesses about global futures. It has, however, significant limitations. There is an old story about a person falling from the top of the Empire State Building. As she passes the 51st floor, a friend at a window asks how it is going. The response is "So far, so good." The reason that most of us see a little black humor in this is that we automatically supplement extrapolative reasoning with causal analysis. We know the effect on the human body of hitting the ground at high speed.

In theory, causal analysis is much superior to extrapolation. In the stock market, for instance, "fundamentalists" direct their attention to the presence or absence of underlying strengths of companies that might eventually cause their earnings and stock prices to rise. Weather forecasting provides another example of how causal analysis differs from and may improve upon extrapolation. If it has been raining for four days, simple extrapolative analysis tells us to predict rain tomorrow; that might be a reasonably good forecast. In contrast, however, a meteorologist who knows that the low pressure area over us now will give way to high pressure by midnight and that high pressure areas generally provide (cause) clear skies will continue to predict sunshine. Similarly, extrapolative analysis might lead us to predict that the world will use ever larger amounts of oil in supplying its energy needs. Causal analysis might consider estimates of the amount of oil in the earth's crust and predict that the oil use will peak and then decline.

In practice, however, causal analysis is extremely difficult and complex and may not always be superior to extrapolation. The central problem is one of specification of the appropriate causal relationship. Students of international politics face this problem with respect to war. Extrapolations of the amount or intensity of warfare, even those that attempt to look at cycles of war, generally do not provide a very solid basis for forecasting because past patterns of warfare appear very irregular. Instead, most scholars search for the causes of war: power differentials among countries, incompatible interests, ethnic rivalries, economic difficulties, the nature of government decision-making mechanisms, miscalculations by leaders, human aggressiveness, and so on. Among the problems with causal analysis of war are that there seem to be a very large number of causes, they often interact with one another in extremely complex ways, and the relationship between identified causes and warfare may even vary over time.

To make forecasting of warfare even more difficult, it is a discrete variable. Like pregnancy, and unlike the amount of oil produced in the world, it either occurs or does not, with rather sudden breaks between the two conditions. Frequently with discrete variables (such as warfare, pregnancy, or rain), analysts replace specific forecasts with probabilities and seek to understand when probabilities increase or decrease.

In most causal analysis, the specification of the causal variables becomes quite complex. It often becomes difficult for analysts to calculate all of the relationships and to produce a forecast. They therefore sometimes turn to a computer representation (computer simulation) of the relationships that allows them to make changes in the **independent variables,** or causes (either on an experimental basis or based on data) and to recalculate quickly the implications for the **dependent variable,** or effect, of interest. For instance, our student of warfare could change the value of ethnic tension and compute the implications for the outbreak of war.

This book will analyze global change using both extrapolation and causal analysis. Moreover, the IFs computer simulation that accompanies the book will allow the reader to undertake his or her own analysis using both techniques for investigating change.

## VALUES AND THE FUTURE

What kind of future would you like to see? The second of our two questions is also not a simple one. There is an old saying that the only thing worse than not getting your heart's desire is getting it. We probably have all had the experience of wanting something desperately and then finding that obtaining it did not make us happy. Often the problem is a failure to clarify our own values in advance.

Let us consider three value issues. These correspond to three complexes of issues on which this volume focuses: the broad environment (issues of ecological survival), the economy (issues of material well-being), and the international political system (issues of physical security). With respect to the broad environment, there is a general and partly value-based debate between those who see the key to survival of humans over time in their mastery of the environment and those who see it in building sustainable relationships with the environment. The former value **progress** and are likely to desire ever-improving technology. They often see that progress as providing a cushion against the vagaries of nature. The latter value **sustainability**; they frequently propose accepting a basic standard of living compatible with human health and focusing further efforts on greater spiritual or cultural achievement. They often argue that humans are part of nature rather than superior to it and that humanity must recognize the limits that nature sets.

You might recognize that this disagreement over values interacts with a difference in understanding of the world. Those who value progress believe that it is possible for humans to extend control or mastery over the environment; those who argue for sustainability often express skepticism concerning humanity's ability to place itself above the environment.

With respect to the economy and issues of material well-being, one group tends to emphasize **economic growth**. "A rising tide lifts all boats" could be their rallying cry; economic growth will improve the condition of all. They seek greater investment and improvements in economic efficiency. A second group may also desire economic growth but places greater importance than the first on **equality** (sometimes greater equality is seen as part of a broader phenomenon called development, involving widespread improvements in the quality of life, not simply increases in income). They often argue that individuals or even entire countries are at a relative disadvantage in reaping the benefits of growth because of their starting position in the economic system. They therefore prefer futures in which some compensation or even restructuring occurs to redress imbalances. The poor need not always be with us, at least not in such large numbers. And poverty is not simply a matter of absolute condition but also of relative deprivation.

Again, differences in value orientation interact with differences in understanding. Those who argue for economic growth frequently assert that an emphasis on equality will retard that growth, whereas those who place equality higher argue that doing so can facilitate growth.

When we turn to the international political system and issues of physical **security,** we find similar value-based disagreements. Some emphasize the virtue of protecting one's own security because, they argue, no one else will value it equally or sacrifice on one's behalf. In some cases, war will be a necessary instrument of policy in that search for security. The price of security and peace is eternal vigilance. Others argue that our greatest attention should be on the preservation of **peace** and that only collective efforts in the world will ultimately provide both peace and security. Eternal vigilance gives rise not to peace but to arms races and periodic wars. Therefore, we should collectively beat our swords into plowshares.

Once again, competing value orientations often reflect different understandings of the world. Those emphasizing security doubt the achievability of peace without such an emphasis; those stressing peace will sometimes argue that a fixation on security is inimical to peaceful interaction.

This discussion reminds us that our effort to understand the future must also incorporate an exercise in value clarification. Although this volume will provide some assistance in that exercise, the burden of doing it lies overwhelmingly with the reader.

## HUMAN LEVERAGE

The previous discussion made clear that value disputes interact strongly with competing understandings of systems in which humans find themselves. That takes us to the third (sub)question of this volume: What leverage do we have in shaping our future? Those who value progress and mastery of the environment understand the relationship between humanity and the environment as one that allows humanity to rise above the environment and to improve the condition of each succeeding generation. This view of the modern world originated in Europe within the last few centuries and gradually spread around the world; we will call those who hold it **modernists**. Those who advocate sustainability argue that what the modernists see as progress is often only unsustainable overexploitation of the environment. It relies upon using resources, such as fossil fuels, that are not replaceable and upon dumping pollutants onto the land and into the air and water faster than these environments can cleanse themselves. Technology may support that overexploitation in the short- and even mid-term, but ultimately the economic systems based upon it are built on sand and will collapse. These individuals are **ecoholists** (see Pirages, 1983; Hughes, 1985c; Haas, 1990) and look for leverage in population control and more careful husbandry of resources.

Many of those who value growth have a strong faith in the market. They generally believe that if governments let it function in as unfettered a manner as possible, it will generate growth of value to all participants.

Traditionally (and still today in Europe), those who valued free or liberated markets and who believed in their benefits were called **liberals**, and we adopt that terminology here. Many liberals also value some measure of equality. They often believe, however, that active participation in the market is the best mechanism for improving the lot of the poor. In contrast, those who focus our attention sharply on equality frequently believe that so-called free markets reward those who enter them with the strongest position. Those who control capital have a stronger bargaining position than those who can offer only their labor. Moreover, those who control capital often also have the means to influence the political system and can use it to reinforce their market position. **Structuralists** argue that these structural characteristics of the market environment make it very difficult for the disadvantaged to redress the inequalities of initial positions in the economic system and that society must act consciously to do so.

Those who value security often look to the traditional state (country) as the most reliable guarantor of that security. States use police to maintain order internally and rely upon military forces to pursue it externally. **Realists** recognize that the system is imperfect but argue that a world without central government is fundamentally a world of anarchy. In such an environment, protecting the power of states remains our best hope. Critics of that understanding point out that the security of the state system has always come at the cost of intermittent warfare. The weapons of the modern era, especially nuclear weapons, have raised that cost far too high. Moreover, the pressures for interstate cooperation on environmental, economic, and security issues have grown at the same time that communications and transportation technology make such global cooperation increasingly possible. **Globalists** therefore understand the fundamentals of world politics very differently and conclude that we must pursue cooperation and peace rather than the balance of power.

We thus face a complicated task in addressing the second and third of our three questions, those asking what future we would prefer and what leverage we have. Value orientations and understandings of the world tend to shape and reinforce one another. In fact, values tend to shape discussions of even our first question, concerning where current changes appear to be taking us. We will see that the six different value-understanding orientations (we call them **worldviews**) emphasize different trends and interpret some in quite different ways.

## HOW SHOULD OUR STUDY PROCEED?

To repeat, our central dilemma is that we cannot know the future, but we must act as if we did. A good place to begin our assault on that dilemma is with an attempt to extrapolate trends and to investigate with fairly simple tools where the future may be taking us. Chapter 2 provides you with information concerning major global trends. It draws your attention to trends of interest to each of the worldviews and will note some differences of interpretation. In addition, it will provide a more extensive discussion of different extrapolative techniques. In short, the primary purpose of Chapter 2 is to make a preliminary effort at answering our first question: Where is global change taking us?

Chapters 4 through 6 will shift our attention to causal analysis and increase our ability to address the first question. Even more important, they extend the brief discussions in this chapter of the understandings of the global system incorporated in the various worldviews. Those chapters therefore begin to address the questions, What future do we want? and What leverage do we have?

As the causal-analysis discussion of global change in those chapters deepens, however, the question of human leverage becomes quite complex. The issue of secondary and tertiary consequences of actions becomes critical. There are, for instance, considerable disputes over the implications of giving food and other aid to less-developed countries. Often those disputes do not center on the primary impact of aid on recipients but instead on the secondary implications of the aid for changes in the economic and political systems of the recipients and the tertiary, or third-order, implications of those changes in turn upon the long-term well-being of the recipients.

Such secondary and tertiary consequences make it very difficult to study issues in isolation. Everything becomes connected to everything else, and tracing through consequences of action becomes very difficult for any analyst. One approach to overcoming that difficulty is to use computers. If we can represent these complex interactions in a computer simulation, or model, we can then let the computer trace through the implications of our actions.

Such a computer simulation is available as a supplement to this volume. The IFs model will allow you to engage in your own experimentation with human intervention and to undertake your own assessment of the extent of human leverage (and of secondary and tertiary consequences). Chapter 3 presents that model and introduces you to its use. If you do not intend to use the model, you can skip that chapter.

Although that model will assist you in better addressing our three questions, it is no panacea. Even with the best of computer simulations, the future remains essentially unpredictable. Some bold predictions will inevitably be correct, whether based on astrology or on computer simulation. A few of those based on computer simulation may even be correct for the right reasons—they will reflect an accurate causal understanding of the way the world works. As the Danish physicist Niels Bohr put it, however, "Prediction is very difficult, especially about the future" (Watkins, 1990: 152).

## CONCLUSION

This chapter has begun to investigate choice in the face of uncertainty about the future of key global issues. It has suggested that we look first at where global change is taking us. To do so, we can use either extrapolation of trends or causal analysis. Causal analysis presents problems because of the need to carefully specify independent and dependent variables and the nature of key causal relationships. In part for that reason, Chapter 2 will initiate our consideration of change with the use of extrapolation.

In addition, however, we must undertake some difficult soul-searching with respect to our own values and the kind of future we really would like to see develop. That requires that we consider values such as progress, sustainability, economic growth, equality, security, and peace. In some cases, emphasis on one or more of these values will conflict with emphasis on others. We obviously seek policy decisons that can satisfy multiple values, but we must be prepared to make trade-offs.

Finally, we need to invetigate whether or not we have any real leverage in bringing about our desired future(s), and if so, how much. Competing worldviews, such as modernism, ecoholism, liberalism, structuralism, realism, and globalism, draw our attention to different values or rankings of them and also carry theoretical understandings of the world that offer sharply different conclusions on leverage available.

# TWO

□   □   □

# Global Change

Where does change appear to be taking us? Chapter 1 proposed that we address that question before asking what futures we prefer and what leverage we have in shaping our future.

At what specific trends should we look? Some general thoughts about human activity might help. Human beings organize themselves into political and social communities. Those communities interact with each other and with the broader physical and biological environment through economic and technological activity. In the process of interaction with that environment, we extract food and energy from it. We also produce wastes that we return to the environment. Although any list of categories is somewhat arbitrary, such a simple sketch of the **human development system** (Mesarovic and Pestel, 1974: 29) suggests a set of broad issue areas on which to focus.

Specifically, we begin with demographics because it is fundamental to know how many of us there are, how fast we are growing, and how many of us there might be in the future. We move next to our ability to feed ourselves. Is the food supply keeping up with our growth in numbers? Then we turn to energy. Energy is the "master resource"; it has been said that with sufficient energy, we can grow food on the top of Mount Everest and extract all necessary raw materials from sea water. What are the patterns in our use of energy, and what can we say about its long-term availability? Next we move to the environment. We know that our impact on the environment has increased; how great is that impact? Technology greatly influences our patterns of resource extraction, waste creation, and interaction with each other. Are there recognizable patterns of technological innovation? Our economic system brings together humans as both producers and consumers; it uses energy; and it creates pressures on the environment. Changes in the economic structure therefore suggest much about the interaction of demographics, food and energy supply, the broader environment and technology. Can we identify such restructuring? Finally, our political and social structures stand at the peak of this human development system. What political-social trends and transformations can we recognize?

## TYPES OF CHANGE

Before we turn to an examination of specific trends, however, it is important to understand that there are several common patterns of change. The first is **linear**. A linear growth process adds equal increments year after year. If a relative gave you $100 for your birthday each year and you hid it away, your funds would grow linearly and at the end of 10 years you would have $1,000. If loggers, ranchers, and homesteaders in the Amazonian rain forest cleared 4,286 square miles each year, the forest size would decline linearly.[1]

Many processes grow **exponentially** rather than linearly. Instead of growing by a fixed amount in each period, they grow by a fixed percentage. For instance, if you received a one-time gift of $100 from your relative, put it in a savings account earning 7.0 percent annual interest, and left the account undisturbed, your money would grow exponentially. Your money would earn $7.00 the first year and produce a balance of $107. In the second year, your money would earn 7.0 percent of the new balance, a total of $7.49, and you would have a balance of $114.49. At the end of 10 years, your money would have grown to $196.72. Because the interest that you leave in your account also earns interest, an exponential growth process of this kind produces an upward-sloping curve (see Fig. 2.1). If the United States were to increase its nuclear arsenal by 14.0 percent each year (roughly the rate of increase between 1950 and 1990), that arsenal would exhibit the same type of upward-sloping growth curve.

In the example of a bank account growing at 7.0 percent, an initial investment nearly doubled in 10 years. We often characterize exponential growth processes by their **doubling time** (the number of years or other periods over which a growth process doubles an initial value). The **rule of 72** provides an easy way of estimating that doubling time. Dividing 72 by a percentage growth rate provides a quite good estimate of the number of periods required for doubling. Money at 7.0 percent interest will double in just a little over 10 years. A nuclear arsenal growing at 14.0 percent will double in just a little over 5 years.

Sometimes the growth rate of a process accelerates. If the United States became ever more proficient at producing nuclear weapons, so that at the

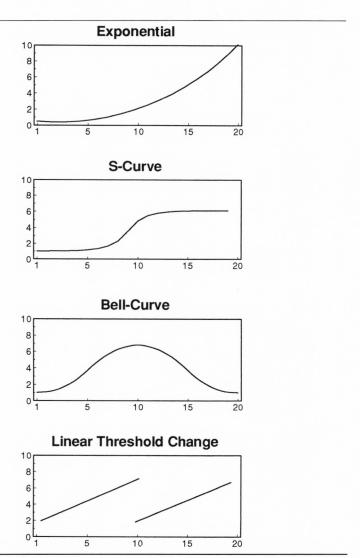

FIGURE 2.1   Types of growth

beginning of the decade the growth of its arsenal was 10.0 percent annually and at the end it was 18.0 percent, the curve representing its stockpile would grow even more sharply, in a **superexponential** process.

Both linear and exponential growth implicitly assume that a process goes on indefinitely. We know, however, that there are often limits that constrain growth processes. Sometimes those limits cause an abrupt cessation of growth. For instance, your relative may decide that when you reach a certain age you no longer require financial assistance. Similarly, the end of the cold war has caused the United States to halt the trend of growth in its nuclear arsenal.

Very often, however, growth processes do not simply reach a limit and then abruptly cease. Instead, they generally follow one of two patterns with respect to limits. The first is a pattern of exponential (or even superexponential) growth up to a turning point and then a pattern of slowing growth up to the limit. The growth of most organisms traces such an S-curve. When a sapling is very small, it grows only a few inches in a year. As it grows, it adds a greater increment each year throughout its early life. Eventually, however, that growth increment declines and then ceases. This growth pattern traces an **S-curve** like that in Figure 2.1. Whereas the bottom half of the S-curve is exponential growth, the top half is called **saturating exponential growth**—the process eventually reaches a saturation or cessation point.

The second growth pattern involving a limit also traces an S-curve but extends the upward growth by tracing another S-curve back down. The overall pattern becomes a **bell-shaped curve** (see Fig. 2.1) and may indicate the phenomenon of **overshoot and collapse**. For instance, population growth in many historical empires followed approximately an S-curve pattern to a maximum value and then subsequently tracked an inverted S-curve back down. Some of those empires probably outgrew the ability of the environment to supply food or energy and then collapsed. If the United States and Russia avoid rekindling of the mutual fears that stoked the cold war, their nuclear arsenals may well decline over time in much the same way that they earlier grew.

A final basic pattern of growth involves **threshold change.** Instead of continous change, some processes exhibit abrupt increases or decreases to new levels (see Fig. 2.1). The earlier example of an annual gift by a relative illustrates this. If we tracked the bank account of a thrifty recipient on a daily basis rather than an annual one, we would see a pattern of large jumps annually (the birthday gifts) combined with smaller and smoother increases from the reinvestment of daily interest. Interstate war is another threshold event. Because of its irregularity, threshold change is probably the most difficult type of growth on which to build forecasts.

These five basic growth and decline patterns (linear, exponential, S-curve, bell-curve, and threshold change) can combine in complex ways. For instance, the repetition of bell-shaped growth over time can create a cyclical pattern (consider the repeated growth and collapse of an empire). Or a cyclical pattern might combine with an underlying pattern of long-term linear or exponential growth. For instance, the U.S. economy has exhibited exponential long-term growth, but roughly four-year business cycles have snaked around that underlying trend.

The tremendous complexity of possible patterns is, of course, what makes forecasting with extrapolation (projecting a growth pattern beyond the period for which we have data) dangerous. As obvious as it is, the most common error in forecasting is simple extrapolation of linear or exponential growth without considering the possibility of changes in the pattern.

For instance, in Chapter 1 we noted the forecasting flaw of the individual falling from a building and declaring halfway down, "So far, so good." Consider a similar story about exponential growth. Passengers on an airplane with four propellers depart Hawaii for an 8-hour trip to Los Angeles. When the plane loses power in one engine, the captain announces that there is no problem, but the flight will last 9 hours. When it loses another engine, the captain extends the forecast of flight time to 11 hours. After the third engine burns, a more nervous captain reassures passengers of the crew's ability to continue and to land but forecasts a total trip duration of 14 hours. One passenger turns to another and says, "You know, if that fourth engine goes out, we could be up here all night!"

Many people have lost fortunes in the stock market by investing in the belief that the market was following a pattern of exponential growth, only to discover that it was at the top of a bell-shaped curve. A linear extrapolation of the growth in earnings of Arnold Schwarzenegger between 1988 and 1989 would forecast an income for him of $360 million in the year 2000. An exponential extrapolation of the growth in the national debt of the United States during the 1981–1991 period would put that debt at $8.0 trillion in the year 2000, about twice the projected size of the economy for that year.[2] Mark Twain poked fun at such extrapolation.

> In the space of 176 years the Lower Mississippi has shortened itself 242 miles. That is an average of a trifle over one mile and a third per year. Therefore, any calm person, who is not blind or idiotic, can see that in the old oölitic Silurian period, just a million years ago next November, the Lower Mississippi River was upward of one million three hundred thousand miles long, and stuck out over the Gulf of Mexico like a fishing-rod. And by the same token any person can see that 742 years from now the Lower Mississippi will be only a mile and three-quarters long, and Cairo and New Orleans will have joined their streets together, and be plodding

comfortably along under a single mayor and a mutual board of aldermen. There is something fascinating about science. One gets such wholesale returns of conjecture out of such a trifling investment in fact. (Buchanan, 1974: 17)

How are we to know when extrapolation is useful and when it is ludicrous (or dangerous)? Linear extrapolation of the percentage of its economy that the United States spends on health care (about 7.0 percent in 1970 and 11.0 percent in 1990) would lead to a forecast of 13.0 percent in the year 2000. That might be a good forecast (although some data suggest that spending already reached 14.0 percent of GNP in 1992). Continued linear extrapolation would provide a forecast of 17.0 percent in 2020 and 21.0 percent in 2040. Even those might be good forecasts, but the longer time horizon makes them riskier. None of us would be so foolish as to extend that horizon to 2450 and produce a forecast of 103.0 percent.

Forecast risk obviously increases with length of time horizon; it also generally increases with the rate at which a process is growing or declining, and it often decreases somewhat with the length of the base period from which we are forecasting. The best rule of all is to combine extrapolation with at least a rudimentary consideration of the causal dynamics of the system under consideration. That helps identify the existence of limits on a process and can even help in spotting likely turning points. We will try to keep these rules in mind as we turn to historical data and forecasts.

## DEMOGRAPHIC CHANGE

Global population has grown exponentially, in fact superexponentially, over a very long period of time (see Fig. 2.2). Humanity populated most of the globe by 8000 B.C. and numbered about 5 million (Ehrlich and Ehrlich, 1972: 12). By A.D. 1000 population had reached approximately 250 million, and it attained a level of 500 million in roughly A.D. 1600. The growth rate over that nearly 10,000-year period was less than 0.05 percent annually. By the end of the eighteenth century, however, population growth rate had accelerated substantially (to about 0.5 percent), and in the nineteenth and twentieth centuries the rate rose quite steadily.

Simple exponential extrapolations of world population growth made in the 1960s began to create considerable anxiety. Were global population to continue growing at the 2.0 percent annual rate of that decade, it would double from 3 to 6 billion people before the year 2000, rise to 12 billion by 2030, and reach 24 billion in 2065 (the rule of 72 makes such estimates easy).

In fact, the level probably will reach 6 billion in about 1998. Most forecasters believe, however, that population growth will increasingly exhibit

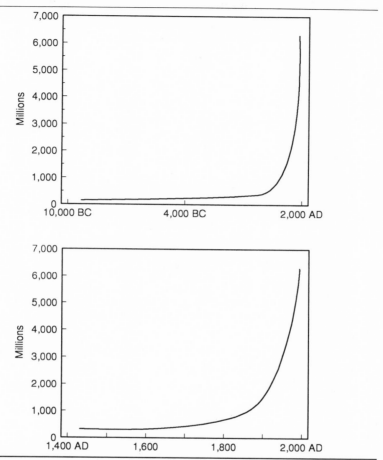

FIGURE 2.2 Global population growth. *Sources:* Paul R. Ehrlich and Anne H. Ehrlich, *Population, Resources, Environment* (San Francisco: W. H. Freeman, 1972), 12; Population Reference Bureau, *World Population Growth and Response* (Washington, D.C.: Population Reference Bureau, 1976), 4.

the pattern of an S-shaped curve rather than continuing in superexponential form. Moreover, it appears that we passed the turning point of that S-shaped curve in the late 1960s and that the global population growth rate has since declined somewhat (see Table 2.1). Thus instead of a steady climb to 12 billion, 24 billion, and even higher levels, global population will perhaps level off at about 10–12 billion people near the end of twenty-first century.

TABLE 2.1   Global Population and Population Growth Rate

| Year | Population (millions) | Growth Rate (preceding period) |
|------|------|------|
| 1750 | 791 | |
| 1800 | 910 | 0.4 |
| 1860 | 1,262 | 0.5 |
| 1900 | 1,600 | 0.5 |
| 1920 | 1,800 | 0.6 |
| 1930 | 2,000 | 1.0 |
| 1940 | 2,250 | 1.1 |
| 1950 | 2,510 | 1.0 |
| 1960 | 3,008 | 1.8 |
| 1970 | 3,683 | 2.0 |
| 1980 | 4,433 | 1.9 |
| 1990 | 5,321 | 1.8 |

*Sources:* 1750–1900 values from John D. Durand, "The Modern Expansion of World Population," *Proceedings of the American Philosophical Society* 111(1967): 137; 1900–1950 values from United Nations, *Demographic Yearbook* (New York: UN, 1961); 1960–1980 values from Ruth Leger Sivard, *World Military and Social Expenditures 1991,* 14th ed. (Washington, D.C.: World Priorities, 1991), 50; 1990 values from Population Reference Bureau, *World Population Data Sheet* (Washington, D.C.: Population Reference Bureau, 1991).

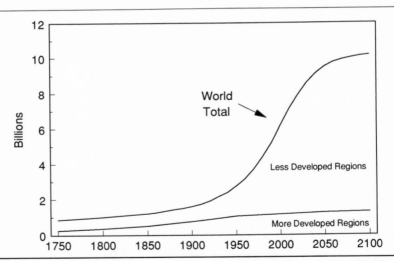

FIGURE 2.3   World population growth by development level. *Source:* Thomas W. Merrick, "World Population in Transition," *Population Bulletin* (Population Reference Bureau) 41, no. 2 (April 1986):4.

In addition to indicating the probable leveling of growth in world population, Figure 2.3 shows the substantial differences in population growth patterns of economically more- and less-developed regions of the globe. The latter regions are growing much more rapidly. Population growth rates began declining in the more-developed regions about a decade before they began slowing in the less-developed regions. More significantly, annual rates in developing countries average about 1.0 percent more than rates in the developed countries. In Africa annual population growth rates are a full 2.7 percent higher than those in Europe and actually continue to increase. Table 2.2 shows the pattern of regional population increase over time.

Population forecasts, at least over a period of 20 to 30 years, tend to be more accurate than those in the other issue areas that we will review here. Most of the humans who will have children in the next 20 years have already been born, and fertility and mortality generally do not change rapidly. Nonetheless, there are great uncertainties about population forecasts, particularly over the longer term. Some argue, for instance, that the human population has reached or exceeded the ultimate limits imposed by its food and energy supplies (Brown, 1981; Meadows et al., 1972). If so, population growth might unfortunately be more likely to follow the pattern of a bell-shaped curve (overshoot and collapse) than that of an S-shaped curve.

Such debates correctly take us beyond extrapolation, however, and into causal analysis. We will turn to such analysis in subsequent chapters.

## CHANGE IN AGRICULTURE AND FOOD

There is a great deal of confusion about the growth of global food supplies relative to the growth in population. Repeated famines in Africa and regular expressions of concern about long-term food availability elsewhere have convinced many people that food production has not kept up with population growth. The reality is that in the 40 years between 1950 and 1990, global food production *per capita* grew by approximately 38.0 percent. That is, the amount of food available to the average human increased by almost 1.0 percent annually. Figure 2.4 shows that phenomenal record of achievement. Moreover, many regions of the world have shared in that achievement. Europe, Asia, and the United States have reported the most substantial advances, increasing production per capita by 79, 37, and 22 percent, respectively. On the other hand, Latin American gains have been modest, and African production per capita is 15 percent less than in 1950.

TABLE 2.2   Regional Population, 1750–2025

| | Population (millions) | | | | | Growth Rate |
|---|---|---|---|---|---|---|
| | *1750* | *1850* | *1950* | *2000* | *2025* | *(1991)* |
| Asia (without USSR) | 498 | 801 | 1,381 | 3,718 | 4,976 | 1.8 |
| Africa | 106 | 111 | 222 | 844 | 1,641 | 3.0 |
| Latin America | 16 | 38 | 162 | 535 | 740 | 2.1 |
| Europe (without USSR) | 125 | 208 | 292 | 266 | 518 | 0.3 |
| North America | 2 | 26 | 166 | 298 | 367 | 0.8 |
| Former USSR | 42 | 76 | 180 | 312 | 363 | 0.8 |
| Oceania | 2 | 2 | 13 | 31 | 41 | 1.2 |
| Total | 791 | 1,262 | 2,515 | 6,292 | 8,645 | 1.7 |

*Sources:* 1750–1950 values from John D. Durand, "The Modern Expansion of World Population," *Proceedings of the American Philosophical Society* 111 (1967):137; 2000–2025 values from Population Reference Bureau, *World Population Data Sheet* (Washington, D.C.: Population Reference Bureau, 1991).

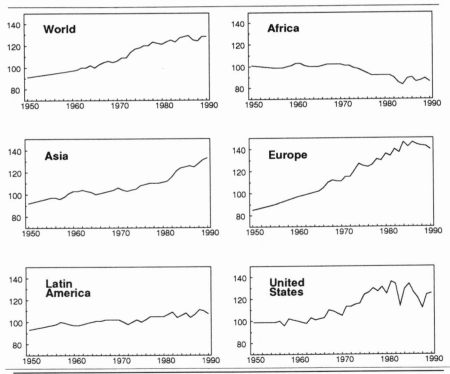

FIGURE 2.4   Food production per capita: Percent of 1961–1965. *Source:* United Nations FAO, *FAO Production Yearbook* (Rome: United Nations Food and Agriculture Organization, 1965, 1975, 1981, 1985, 1987, 1991).

As always, there are dangers in simple extrapolation. The most significant is that the rate of global increase may be slowing or even stopping. In contrast to a global per capita increase of 11 percent in the 1970s, the increase in the 1980s was only 3 percent, and there were no gains in the last half of the decade. One interpretation of this is that we have reached the top of a bell-shaped curve and that forecasts that population growth would eventually outstrip our ability to increase food supplies have finally come true. Another interpretation is that the slowdown of gains in the 1980s was a cyclical downturn around a long-term upward trend. Reasons might include stagnant economies in many less-developed countries during that decade, a number of bad harvest years in the United States during the last half of the decade, and ongoing efforts by both the United States and Europe to solve long-term problems of overproduction.

Figure 2.5 draws our attention further to the possibility that food production per capita is peaking by looking at the global production per capita of specific biological resources. It appears that we may have already reached or passed per capita production peaks in many of those.

The debate over the relative growth of population and food has deep historical roots. For example, at the end of the eighteenth century, the Reverend Thomas Malthus argued that population, left unchecked, grows geometrically (exponentially) and that food supply increases only arithmetically (linearly). He therefore concluded that it was inevitable that population would outstrip food and that starvation would ravish humanity. Similarly, at the beginning of the twentieth century, Sir William Crookes reported in his Presidential Address to the British Association of Science that "there remains no uncultivated prairie land in the United States suitable for wheat growing. The virgin land has been rapidly absorbed, until at present there is no land left for wheat without reducing the area for maize, hay, and other necessary crops. It is almost certain that within a generation the ever increasing population of the United States will consume all the wheat growing within its borders and will be driven to import and ... scramble for a lion's share of the wheat crop of the world" (Wortman and Cummings, 1978: 86). It is therefore not surprising that many contemporary analysts voice suspicions of negative forecasts and interpret recent stagnation of food supply per capita as a temporary phenomenon.

Moving from the global to the local level, there are major differences in the food available to humans in different world regions. Figure 2.6 illustrates these differences by showing per capita caloric consumption for various regions. Whereas citizens of the United States consumed an average of 3,671 calories per capita daily in 1989 (World Bank, 1992: 273), caloric consumption in the poorest countries of the world ranged generally between 1,700 and 2,600. It is obvious from that figure that global produc-

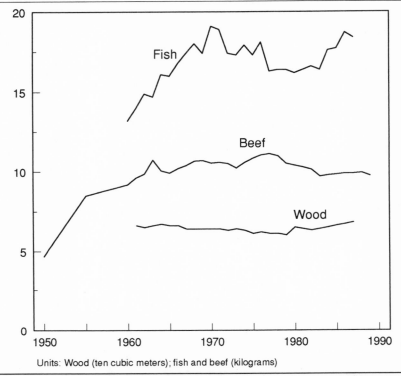

Units: Wood (ten cubic meters); fish and beef (kilograms)

FIGURE 2.5   Global production per capita of biological resources. *Sources:* Barry B. Hughes, *World Futures* (Baltimore: Johns Hopkins University Press, 1985); United Nations FAO, *FAO Production Yearbook 1989* (Rome: FAO, 1990).

tion per capita will have to increase a great deal more if the poor of the world are to have diets comparable to those of the rich.

The differences in caloric consumption across regions would be even greater were it not for increases in the trade of grain. In contrast to the first half of the century, substantial volumes of grain now flow from regions of surplus (primarily North America and Western Europe) to the rest of the world. Table 2.3 traces those flows.

The historical pattern of food production, consumption, and trade provides a less-ready base for extrapolation than did that of population size. In fact, most forecasts quickly abandon the historical patterns and move to causal analysis. Some are pessimistic. They point to the unavailability of additional land for the expansion of production, relative to historical eras, and to environmental degradation (for example, deforestation and desertification) of land already under production. Some are optimistic. They direct our attention to new technologies for manipulating plant and

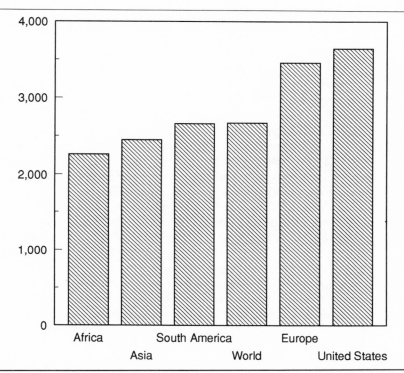

FIGURE 2.6 Per capita daily calorie consumption. *Source:* United Nations FAO, *FAO Production Yearbook 1989* (Rome: FAO, 1990), 289–290.

TABLE 2.3 Annual World Grain Trade (million metric tons of net exports)

|  | 1934–1938 | 1950 | 1960 | 1970 | 1980 | 1988 |
|---|---|---|---|---|---|---|
| North America | 5 | 23 | 42 | 54 | 131 | 119 |
| Latin America | 2 | 1 | (1) | 4 | (10) | (11) |
| Western Europe | (10) | (22) | (25) | (22) | (16) | 22 |
| Eastern Europe/USSR | 1 | 0 | 1 | (1) | (46) | (27) |
| Africa | 0 | 0 | (5) | (4) | (15) | (28) |
| Asia | (1) | (6) | (19) | (37) | (63) | (89) |
| Oceania | 3 | 3 | 6 | 8 | 19 | 14 |

Parentheses indicate imports.

*Sources:* Barry B. Hughes, *World Futures* (Baltimore: Johns Hopkins University, 1985), 133; Lester R. Brown, "Reexamining the World Food Prospect," in *State of the World 1989*, ed. Lester R. Brown (New York: W. W. Norton, 1989), 45.

animal life. We will return to these issues of causal analysis in subsequent discussions.

## CHANGE IN ENERGY

Whereas food is energy for the human body, physical energy fuels the human economy. The amount of physical energy available to the average human has increased dramatically in the last 200 years. Watt's steam engine generated 40 horsepower in 1800, a dramatic advance over earlier models and over water mills and windmills. A modern electric generating plant delivers 1.5 million horsepower (Cook, 1976: 29). Figure 2.7 shows an almost 10-fold increase in per capita energy use since 1850. That figure, like others we have seen, could be extrapolated in more than one way. To some it may look clearly like an exponential, even superexponential, curve that promises to continue sharply upward. To others it may appear that there is a hint of a turning point at the end of the curve that portends slower growth in years ahead and converts the overall form to an S-curve. To still others, it could be one side of a bell-shaped curve that is poised near the top and threatens to begin a descent.

Those who are less optimistic about future growth often direct our attention to oil, the largest single source of primary energy for the economy. Figure 2.8 shows that global oil production increased very sharply and quite steadily from neglible amounts in the 1920s to a peak of nearly 3.3 billion metric tons in 1979. It stabilized near that peak in the early 1980s as a result of substantial increases in prices by OPEC and other producers. As the makers of that figure correctly foresaw in 1982, global oil production ended the decade at close to its peak (British Petroleum, 1991: 4).

The forecast in Figure 2.8 by the Organization for Economic Cooperation and Development (OECD) assumes that there is a fixed amount of oil in the earth available to humans and that oil production and consumption therefore will eventually decline and almost cease. By estimating that limited amount, they have been able to match the area under the curve to it (a total of 327 billion metric tons) and draw a bell-shaped curve that forecasts the life cycle of global oil production. This procedure moves well beyond simple extrapolation and into causal analysis; we will return later to the approach.

It should be obvious that the estimate of the area under the curve is critical. It should also be obvious, however, that larger and smaller estimates will only shift the peak years and the amount and will not change the overall shape of the curve. M. King Hubbert made one of the most successful forecasts ever produced on the energy issue in the late 1950s using the same approach, matching the area under a bell-shaped curve to an es-

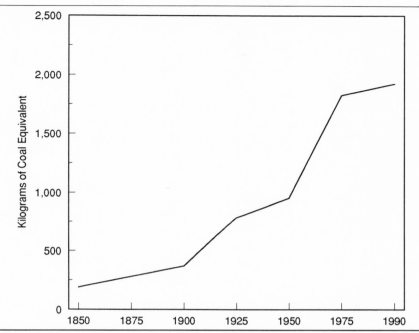

FIGURE 2.7   Energy consumption per capita. *Sources:* Joel Darmstadter, *Energy in the World Economy* (Baltimore: Johns Hopkins University Press, 1971), 10; United Nations, *Energy Statistics Yearbook* (New York: United Nations, 1986); British Petroleum, *BP Statistical Review of World Energy* (London: Ashdown Press, 1991), 33.

timate of ultimate oil resources within the United States. He forecast that U.S. oil production would peak about 1970 and begin a long, slow decline (Wildavsky and Tenenbaum, 1981: 233). U.S. oil production did, in fact, begin a decline in 1970, and the decline continues. Geologists have explored most of the rest of the world for oil much less thoroughly than they have the United States, however, so there is less basis for estimating the precise peak of the curve that portrays world oil resources. We should remember that in 1891 the U.S. Geological Survey estimated the chance of finding oil in Kansas or Texas at near zero and that in 1939 the Interior Department declared that U.S. oil supplies would last only thirteen years (Kahn, Brown, and Martel, 1976: 94–95).

We generally refer to the projected decline of global oil production as an **energy transition** because most observers expect other energy forms to replace oil and natural gas, much as oil earlier replaced coal. Table 2.4 shows the pattern of actual transition though 1990 and provides a forecast for the year 2000. However, energy forecasts regarding the availability

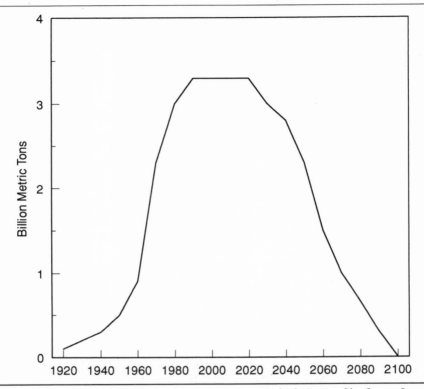

FIGURE 2.8   Hypothetical oil production and resource depletion profile. *Source:* International Energy Agency, *World Energy Outlook* (Paris: Organization for Economic Cooperation and Development, 1982), 215.

and use of other energy forms become particularly murky (note that the forecast does not even include solar energy). In the 1950s the Atomic-Energy Agency forecast installed nuclear capacity in the United States alone at two thousand gigawatts by the year 2000 (Hughes, 1985c: 104), which would require approximately two thousand very large nuclear generating plants; in 1990 the country had approximately one hundred gigawatts of capacity (World Almanac, 1992: 196).This discussion has already touched upon some of the issues to which we will need to return in our discussion of causal logic. These include the resource base of fossil fuels and the promise (and cost) of alternative energy technologies. They also include the prospects for economic growth and the relationship between economic growth and energy demand.

TABLE 2.4   World Energy Supply by Energy Type

| | Percentage Contribution to Global Supply | | | |
|---|---|---|---|---|
| Energy Type | 1965 | 1980 | 1990 | 2000 |
| Oil | 42 | 47 | 38 | 31 |
| Coal | 37 | 26 | 27 | 28 |
| Gas | 15 | 19 | 22 | 19 |
| Hydroelectric | 6 | 6 | 7 | 8 |
| Nuclear | 0 | 2 | 6 | 10 |

Sources: Exxon Corporation, World Energy Outlook (New York: Exxon Corporation, 1980), 10; British Petroleum, BP Statistical Review of World Energy (June) (London: Ashdown Press, 1991), 34.

## ENVIRONMENTAL CHANGE

Humans have long had an impact on their biological and physical environments, exhausting local forests, overhunting nearby animals, depleting regional supplies of minerals, destroying the productivity of plots of soil. They have also sometimes drained swamps (for better or worse), planted trees, and improved soil quality. It is only more recently, however, that we have begun to broaden the scope of our impact from particular watersheds, valleys, and coastal plains to the entire globe.

It is almost impossible to touch on all of the environmental concerns that have emerged in the last two decades, and this discussion will therefore single out three issues of wide-scale, potentially global importance: the release of greenhouse gases into the atmosphere, the buildup of ozone-depleting gases in the upper atmosphere, and the destruction of tropical forests. It is very difficult to simply present environmental trends without some comment on issues of causal linkage (such as the impact of changes in the scope of human activity); we have encountered that difficulty in our earlier discussions as well. In the case of our environmental discussion, however, we will more consistently cross the line between extrapolation and causal analysis.

Figure 2.9 shows atmospheric measurements of the primary greenhouse gas, carbon dioxide ($CO_2$), over the past 30 years. Note the clear exponential trend surrounded by annual cycles. The cycles correspond to seasons and the ability of vegetation to take some carbon dioxide from the atmosphere. The basic reason for the underlying trend is the increased burning of fossil fuels; the oxidization (burning) of carbon-based fuels generates carbon dioxide. The reason we need to be concerned about increased carbon dioxide is that the gas allows sunlight to pass through relatively easily but reflects a substantial amount of heat radiation back toward the earth. It thus acts much like the glass in a greenhouse.

We have noted before the danger of using too short a baseline for forecasting. Figure 2.10 extends Figure 2.9 dramatically. It draws upon data

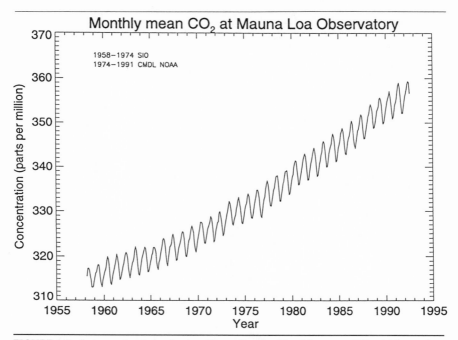

FIGURE 2.9    Increase in atmospheric carbon dioxide: Monthly mean $CO_2$ at Mauna Loa Observatory. *Source:* Carbon Cycle Group, Climate Monitoring and Diagnostics Laboratory, National Oceanic and Atmospheric Administration, Boulder, Colorado.

from ice cores to construct a record of atmospheric carbon dioxide over a period of 160,000 years. Note that there are clearly cycles in the concentration of carbon dioxide (and perturbations within cycles). Note also that the levels of contemporary carbon dioxide in Figure 2.9 exceed considerably even the highest levels in that entire 160,000-year period.

Figure 2.10 provides more information than simply carbon dioxide levels. It also reconstructs global temperatures over the long term. Note the very close relationship between movements in levels of carbon dioxide and those of temperature. As the authors of the *World Resources* volume point out, "Showing clear links between carbon dioxide levels and temperature, the Vostok ice core has been recognized as irrefutable evidence for a fundamental link betweeen global climate system and the carbon cycle. However, it is still not clear whether rising carbon dioxide levels caused or followed rising temperatures" (World Resources Institute, 1988: 197). As that analysis suggests, parallel behavior does not prove causality. These two graphs make it easy to understand, however, why many scientists are forecasting a 1.5 to 2.5-degree-centigrade increase in global surface temperatures over the next 50 years.

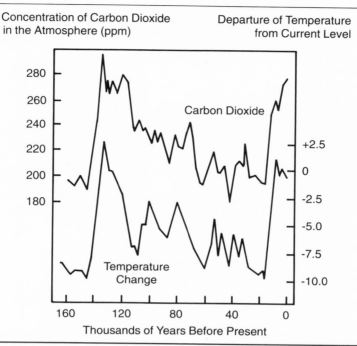

FIGURE 2.10   Long-term variations of global temperature and atmospheric carbon dioxide. *Source:* J. M. Barnola et al., "Vostok Ice Core Provides 160,000-year record of Atmospheric $CO_2$." Reprinted with permission from *Nature* 329, no. 6138 (October 1–7, 1987):410. Copyright 1987 Macmillan Magazines Limited.

A set of chemicals called chlorofluorocarbons (CFCs) serve as aerosol propellants, refrigerant fluids, foam blowing agents (hence they appear in Styrofoam), and solvents. Like $CO_2$, CFCs act as greenhouse gases, but scientists identify another principal concern with their increase in the atmosphere. The chemicals interact with ozone in the upper stratosphere and reduce its prevalence. Because atmospheric ozone protects life on the surface from ultraviolet (UV-B) radiation, the entire process threatens humans through an increase in skin cancer and also indirectly through damage to the plants and animals on which we depend.

Figure 2.11 shows the annual releases of two CFCs since they were first used in the 1930s. Measurements at Cape Meares, Oregon, indicate that their presence in the atmosphere roughly doubled between 1975 and 1985 (World Resources Institute, 1988: 170). A substantial hole in the ozone layer now appears annually over Antarctica, and measurements in both hemispheres indicate an ongoing decrease in ozone levels.

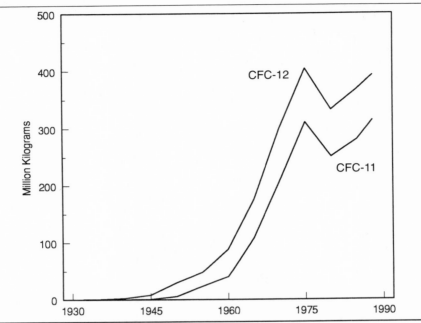

FIGURE 2.11  Global annual releases of chlorofluorocarbons. *Source:* Council on Environmental Quality, *21st Annual Report* (Washington, D.C.: Council on Environmental Quality, 1991), 319.

Loggers, farmers, and ranchers clear approximately 0.9 percent of the world's tropical rain forests annually (World Resources Institute, 1992: 118). Table 2.5 shows some of the countries in which the rate of deforestation is greater than that average or which are important because of the extent of forest in the country (such as Brazil and Zaire). At current rates Nigeria, Costa Rica, Sri Lanka, and El Salvador are at risk of losing all of their forests by early in the twenty-first century.

The condition of rain forests is less obviously a global problem than are emissions of $CO_2$ and CFCs. Scientists do worry, however, that substantial reductions in the extent of those forests can also contribute to global warming (by releasing the carbon that forests "bank") and will reduce the capacity of the earth to tolerate other changes. The forests also serve as habitat for large numbers of species that exist nowhere else and whose loss would be a cost borne by the entire world. By one estimate, 4–8 percent of species in rain forests will become extinct by 2015, and 17–35 percent will disappear by 2040 (World Resources Institute, 1992: 128).

TABLE 2.5 Deforestation: Worst Cases of the 1980s

| Regions and Countries | Natural Forest Area (thousand hectares) | Annual Deforestation 1981–1985 (thousand hectares) | Percent Deforestation per Year |
|---|---|---|---|
| Africa | | | |
| Algeria | 1,767 | 40 | 2.3 |
| Cote d'Ivoire | 9,834 | 510 | 5.2 |
| Guinea-Bissau | 2,105 | 57 | 2.7 |
| Liberia | 2,040 | 46 | 2.3 |
| Malawi | 4,271 | 150 | 3.5 |
| Mauritania | 554 | 13 | 2.4 |
| Niger | 2,550 | 67 | 2.6 |
| Nigeria | 14,750 | 400 | 2.7 |
| Zaire | 177,590 | 347 | 0.2 |
| Latin America | | | |
| Costa Rica | 1,798 | 65 | 3.6 |
| Guatemala | 4,452 | 90 | 2.0 |
| Honduras | 3,997 | 90 | 2.3 |
| Mexico | 48,350 | 615 | 1.3 |
| Nicaragua | 4,496 | 121 | 2.7 |
| Argentina | 44,500 | 1,550 | 3.5 |
| Brazil | 514,480 | 2,323 | 0.5 |
| Colombia | 51,700 | 890 | 1.7 |
| Ecuador | 14,730 | 340 | 2.3 |
| Paraguay | 19,710 | 212 | 1.1 |
| Peru | 70,640 | 270 | 0.4 |
| Venezuela | 33,870 | 245 | 0.7 |
| Asia | | | |
| Indonesia | 116,895 | 620 | 0.5 |
| Malaysia | 20,996 | 255 | 1.2 |
| Nepal | 2,121 | 84 | 4.0 |
| Sri Lanka | 1,659 | 58 | 3.5 |
| Thailand | 15,675 | 379 | 2.4 |

*Source:* World Resources Institute, *World Resources 1992–93* (New York: Basic Books, 1992), 286–287.

Forecasts of the global environmental condition are subject to the same types of debates as other forecasts. Although it is relatively easy to forecast the increase in atmospheric $CO_2$ (based on forecasts of energy use), there remains much debate over the impact of that increase and the degree to which unknowns, such as increased cloud cover, might ameliorate or intensify a greenhouse effect.

There is also uncertainty concerning the degree to which effects will be gradual and the degree to which they might "tip" the equilibrium state of the global physical and biological systems quite dramatically into another state. Our earlier discussion of forecasting mentioned threshold changes—sudden changes in the level of one or more variables. It is possible that the earth's living systems have a capacity to absorb and dampen much insult to them but that at some point the damage could become too great, causing fundamental patterns of temperature and living matter interaction to change.

One additional and very important uncertainty is the speed and extent to which human behavior may change in the face of growing evidence of damage to the environment. Already, global conventions are in place that will rapidly phase out production and use of CFCs. We will return to some of these causal issues subsequently.

## TECHNOLOGICAL CHANGE

Technological change often exhibits exponential patterns. Most of us are familiar with this phenomenon in the area of computing power. Figure 2.12 traces the growth in functions per chip, beginning with the invention of the transistor. It indicates also the growth in the storage capacity of those chips over time. That figure uses a semilogarithmic scale; that is, each unit on the scale at the left is actually a multiple of 10 relative to the unit below it. Were that graph to use traditional arithmetic scaling, the curve would appear as an exponential one with an exceptionally steep rate of increase.

You may also have seen graphs that show the exponential drop in the cost of computing. It is obvious that there must be some limits on such drops (and on the increases in computing power). Therefore, the curves will eventually flatten. We do not know when such leveling will begin; the turning points are not yet apparent.

Consider also the growth of transportation speeds. Figure 2.13 traces the speeds of human conveyances historically, from fast horses through chemical-fueled rockets, and projects them into the future. It uses a device called an **envelope curve** (the primary exponential curve envelops or incorporates a number of subsidiary curves). The particular envelope curve of Figure 2.13 is an exponential line that traces the upper boundaries of the speeds attained by various individual transportation technologies, including trains and autos.

As we have seen with other issues, the historical record of transportation speeds does not provide a clear basis for forecasts. Some might be tempted to extrapolate transportation speeds ever upward in continued exponential growth; those familiar with Star Trek episodes know that the "warp speeds" of the Enterprise are vastly greater than the "impulse speeds" that it obtains from more traditional rocket engines. In a note of caution, however, one author argues that exponential extrapolation of earlier trends would have led to the following technological forecasts (Ayres, 1969: 20):

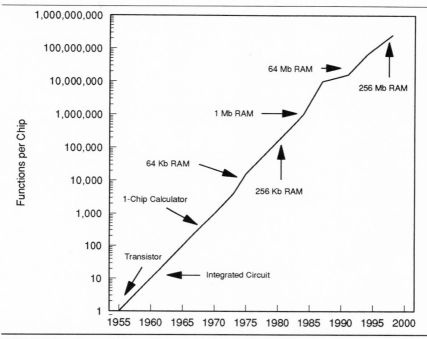

FIGURE 2.12   The evolution of integrated circuits. *Sources:* James A. Cuningham, "Using the Learning Curve as a Management Tool," *IEEE Spectrum* 17 (June 1980):48; *Economist,* February 23, 1991:66; *Business Week,* December 10, 1990:185; *Business Week,* June 8, 1992:110.

□  Vehicles will attain the speed of light by 1982
□  Humans will achieve immortality by the year 2000
□  A single person will control the power of the sun by 1981

Others therefore look to Einstein's theory for an argument that speed has an upper limit—as a body approaches the speed of light, the body gains mass and it therefore becomes ever harder to accelerate the object to still higher velocity. We may have already reached a turning point, such that future gains in the speed of human conveyance will come ever more slowly.

Unlike our uncertainty about turning points with respect to gains in transportation speed and computing power, in other processes there exist definite technological limits and we increasingly approach them. For instance, clear limits bound the efficiency of energy conversion from the burning of fossil fuel (only 100 percent of the energy in the fire is potentially available for transfer to electricity generation or other use). Figure 2.14 shows the record of capturing the energy in fossil fuels; it strongly

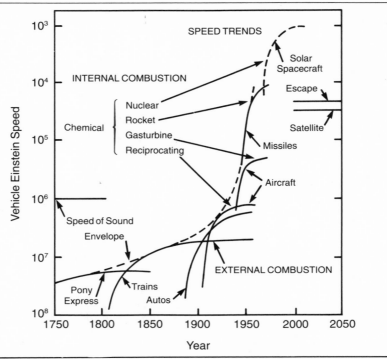

FIGURE 2.13   Trends in transportation speed. *Source:* Robert U. Ayres, Hudson Institute, Indianapolis, Indiana. Reprinted by permission of Hudson Institute.

suggests that we have reached the turning point and will achieve lesser gains in the future.

Even such limits, however, may be deceiving. As we approach them, we are discovering other ways of getting energy from matter, including the splitting and fusion of atoms. We may wish to avoid the pessimism with respect to future breakthroughs of Robert A. Millikan, a Nobel Prize winner and founder of the California Institute of Technology. In response to concerns expressed by science writer Frederick Soddy about the potential of nuclear power, Millikan writes (prior to 1945): "Since Mr. Soddy raised the hobgoblin of dangerous quantities of available subatomic energy, [science] has brought to light good evidence that this particular hobgoblin—like most of the hobgoblins that crowd in on the mind of ignorance—was a myth. ... The new evidence born of further scientific study is to the effect that it is highly improbable that there is any appreciable amount of available subatomic energy to tap" (Sinsheimer, 1980: 148).

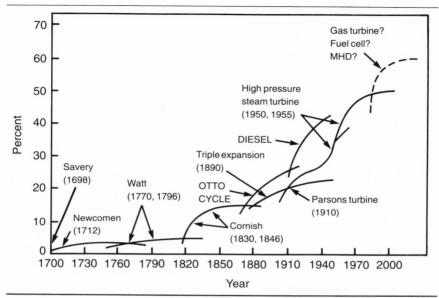

FIGURE 2.14   Trends in energy conversion efficiency. *Source:* Hans Thirring, *Energy for Man* (Bloomington: Indiana University Press, 1958). Reprinted with permission.

Technology obviously brings tremendous benefits to humanity. In addition to the provision of computing power, transportation and communication capabilities, and energy for the satisfaction of a wide range of needs and wants, technology has allowed increases in the length of human lives, has helped food producers keep pace with the growth in our numbers, and has assisted in the protection of our environment (for instance, through recycling). Technology does, however, also have a dark side that can be seen in human development of advanced military technology at the pace of other breakthroughs. Table 2.6 traces the development of explosive power over time and also indicates the years in which countries have openly or most probably become nuclear powers. There has been exponential growth in destructive capability.

More generally, technology has contributed to the massive increase in human impact on the environment. That impact is not just the control of disease and the production of food; it is also destroyed forests and threats to the global oceans and atmosphere. Often the secondary effects of new technologies are largely unpredictable, even though organizations like the U.S. Office of Technology Assessment try to foresee them.

This discussion should have made clear the difficulties in extrapolating technological advance (or its implications). It sometimes appears exponential and at other times appears very much bounded. In addition, there

TABLE 2.6  Milestones in Military Potential

| Year | Explosive Power (tons of TNT equivalent) | Weapon |
|------|------|------|
| 1500 | .001 | Gunpowder "bombs" |
| 1914 | 1.000 | Large cannon |
| 1940 | 10.000 | Blockbuster bomb |
| 1946 | 20,000.000 | Hiroshima atomic bomb |
| 1961 | 50,000,000.000 | Largest hydrogen bomb |

| Year of Test or Probable Acquisition | Approximate Number of Current Warheads | Declared* and Probable Nuclear States |
|------|------|------|
| 1945 | 12,100 | United States* |
| 1949 | 11,320 | Soviet Union* |
| 1952 | 96 | United Kingdom* |
| 1960 | 372 | France* |
| 1964 | 284 | China* |
| 1974 | Unknown | India |
| Early 1980s | Unknown | Israel |
| Early 1980s | Unknown | South Africa |
| Early 1990s | Unknown | Pakistan |

Sources: Robert U. Ayres, Technological Forecasting and Long-Range Planning (New York: McGraw-Hill, 1969), 22; The Columbia Desk Encyclopedia, 3d ed. (New York: Columbia University Press, 1963); Harold Sprout and Margaret Sprout, Toward a Politics of the Planet Earth (New York: Van Nostrand Reinhold, 1971), 403; Stockholm International Peace Research Institute, SIPRI Yearbook 1990 (Stockholm: SIPRI, 1990), 23; Leonard S. Spector with Jacqueline R. Smith, Nuclear Ambitions (Boulder: Westview Press, 1990).

is no clear understanding of the degree to which technology advances regularly over time. In fact, a common argument is that such advance occurs in long cycles. We return later to some of these uncertainties.

## ECONOMIC CHANGE

In spite of periodic economic downturns (recessions and depressions), global economic growth has characterized almost all of the past two hundred years. Figure 2.15 traces the growth of gross world product, the total production of goods and services, over the last three decades of those two centuries. After removing the effects of inflation, the global economy has tripled in 30 years. During that same period, population grew by about two-thirds, suggesting that the global per capita GNP nearly doubled.

Although the 1980s were a decade of relatively slow increase, global economic growth generally exhibits an exponential pattern and has done so since the beginning of the industrial revolution in the late 1700s. In fact, although we do not have data on gross national or world product before

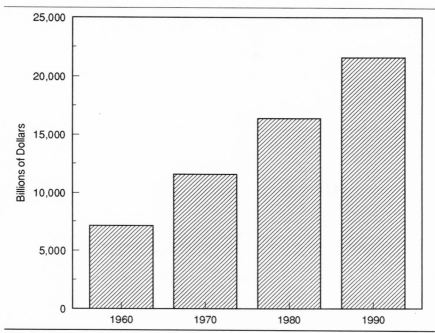

FIGURE 2.15   Gross world product. *Source:* Central Intelligence Agency, *Handbook of Economic Statistics 1991* (Washington, D.C.: Central Intelligence Agency, 1991), 26.

the twentieth century (the concept was not developed until the 1930s), data on industrial production trace that long-term growth curve. Figure 2.16 shows industrial production over the past two hundred years on a semilogarithmic scale. There is a slightly superexponential pattern to that curve—the twentieth century claims higher rates of growth than the nineteenth, in part because a greater and greater portion of the world has exhibited the phenomenon of industrialization.

We should supplement such an aggregated view of the global economy with two types of disaggregation: by geographic region and by economic sector. The industrial revolution began in England, spread to France, Germany, and elsewhere in Europe, and then moved around the world to the United States, Japan, and, more recently, to a considerable number of economies in Latin America and Asia. In the process, the world became generally divided into rich industrial countries and poor preindustrial countries. The industrial economies developed primarily in the northern half of the globe, whereas most of the preindustrial countries populate the southern half. Figure 2.17 sketches the ratio of per capita GNP in the two sets of countries (industrialized versus preindustrialized) and shows the

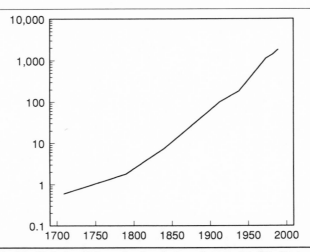

FIGURE 2.16 World industrial production index. *Sources:* W. W. Rostow, *The World Economy: History and Prospect* (Austin: University of Texas Press, 1978), 49, 662; UNCTAD, *Handbook of International Trade and Development Statistics* (New York: United Nations, 1991), 472.

fairly steady increase in that gap until recent decades. The data for that graph are, at best, skimpy, but it is useful to have even a crude image of the long-term pattern. There is an active debate as to whether the gap has now stabilized and may even be poised for decline. Again we see how difficult it is to recognize turning points (or the tops of bell-shaped curves).

The second disaggregation we need to consider is one that a focus on industrialization already suggests, namely, the division of the global economy into sectors. Prior to industrialization, the agricultural sector of an economy dominates it. At the time of the American Revolution, about 80 percent of the U.S. population was engaged in producing food. Over time the industrial sector became dominant, and the agricultural sector experienced a very long relative decline (relative because it generally continued to increase its overall production but used less labor and became less important in the total economy). The third large portion of an economy is the service sector. Figure 2.18 shows the relative sizes of these three sectors in four different groupings of countries.

Note in Figure 2.18 that even in what the World Bank calls "low-income countries," the industrial sector is large, whereas the agricultural sector is shrinking quite rapidly. In fact, within what the Bank calls "high-income countries," the industrial sector is actually smaller than it is in the low-income group. The high-income countries, which the World Bank

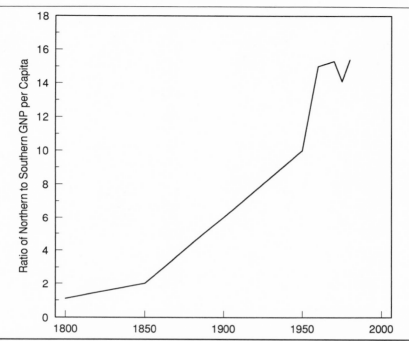

FIGURE 2.17    Ratio of GNP per capita in global North and South. *Source:* Constructed from estimates collected by Barry B. Hughes for *Continuity and Change in World Politics,* 2d ed. (Englewood Cliffs, N.J.: Prentice-Hall, forthcoming).

called "industrial economies" until 1990, are clearly becoming predominantly service economies.

Even more important, the nature of the service economies is changing. For example, between 1945 and 1991, service workers in the United States increased overall by 271 percent; workers in finance, insurance, and real estate increased by 347 percent (Information Please Almanac, 1992: 59). We should explicitly identify a fourth sector of the economy and category of workers, much of which most data sources now misleadingly lump with the service sector. That fourth category is the information sector, and in the most economically advanced countries of the world it may now be the largest sector. Figure 2.19 supports that claim for the United States. Readers should be aware, however, that in spite of the importance of the information economy, statisticians have not yet begun confidently to evaluate its size. Although the activities of teachers, scientists, and librarians obviously belong to the information sector, those of many other individuals prove harder to classify. Thus the size of that sector shown in Figure 2.19 is a crude estimate.

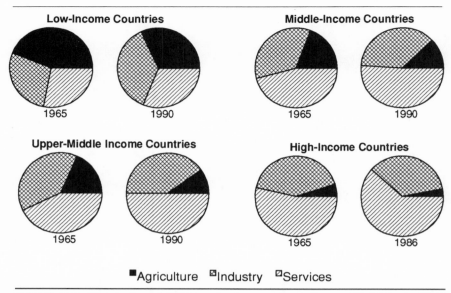

FIGURE 2.18 Distribution of GNP by development level. *Sources:* World Bank, *World Development Report 1992* (New York: Oxford University Press, 1992), 222–223; also *World Development Report 1988.*

There are many uncertainties in forecasting the global economy. To what degree has the transformation of many countries that industrialized early into service and information economies made the character of their growth so different that we can no longer adequately measure economic size, rate of growth, or productivity of workers? Will the less-industrialized countries of the world automatically follow in the path of the first to industrialize, or has the widespread industrialization of the globe and the steady march of technology created new patterns for growth? Such questions will later move us into causal analysis and beyond the initial extrapolative exploration of this discussion.

## SOCIAL-POLITICAL CHANGE

Social and political change is tightly interwoven with the other changes that this chapter has reviewed. It both gives rise to many of those other changes and is in turn shaped by them. Summarizing quickly the major trends in the social and political spheres is difficult. To simplify the task somewhat, we will divide the changes into two categories: changes that affect the lives of individuals and changes in social organization. In reality, of course, this division is artificial and the two sets of changes interact strongly.

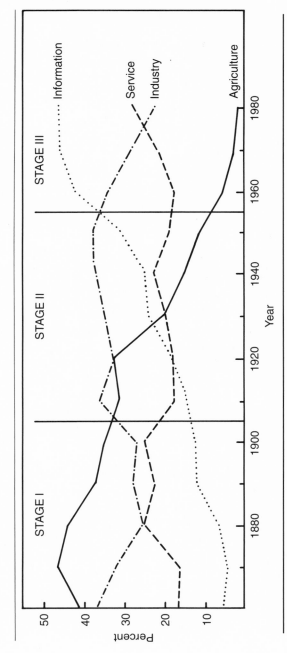

FIGURE 2.19   Four-sector breakdown of the U.S. work force, 1860–1980 (in percentages). Note: Median estimates of information workers are used. *Source:* Marc Porat, *The Information Economy: Definition and Measurement* (Washington, D.C.: U.S. Department of Commerce, Office of Telecommunications, 1977).

The lives of individuals have changed and continue to change in several important respects. Most fundamentally, perhaps, people live longer. The pace of that change has been dramatic. In 1900 a very astute observer of change, John Elfreth Watkins, wrote an article in the *Ladies' Home Journal* in which he predicted that by the year 2000 the average American would "live fifty years instead of thirty-five as at present" (Shane and Sojka, 1990: 150). He thereby forecast a 15-year increase in life expectancy; the reality was a 40-year increase by 1991. In fact, the average human (across the globe) had a life expectancy of 65 in 1991, only 10 years less than Americans at that time and 30 years more than Americans at the beginning of the century.[3]

Second, as we have already seen, in spite of continued widespread poverty in many parts of the globe, the average human is also much richer than in any previous era. Global GNP per capita advanced from $2,331 in 1960 to $4,053 in 1990 (constant 1990 dollars) (CIA, 1991b: 216).

Third, the average human is increasingly well educated. Statistics on the education of primary school–aged children in the poorest countries of the world suggest that the portion of those children actually in school climbed from 37 percent in 1950 to 99 percent in 1990 (Hughes, 1991: 27). Figure 2.20 shows the increase in adult literacy since 1960. It has been estimated that a majority of the world's adult population was literate in 1955 for the first time in history.[4] Now even a majority of adults in the world's poorest countries are literate.

Fourth, the extent of interhuman contact has increased sharply. Rapid urbanization provides one reason for this. Whereas 28 percent of the world's population lived in urban areas in 1950 (Council on Environmental Quality, 1981b: 300), 43 percent of humanity was urban in 1991 (Population Reference Bureau, 1991). This suggests an increase in the urbanization level of about 4 percent per decade; a majority of humanity may live in cities by 2010.

Other avenues for increased contact also exist. The written word obviously reaches a much higher percentage of people as literacy increases. Televisions and radios supply more people with outside contact each year. In 1989 there were 155 televisions and 375 radios for every thousand people in the world. Similarly, the option of "reaching out and touching someone" by telephone is spreading with incredible speed. Figure 2.21 traces the number of telephones per thousand people since 1930. Note the exponential rate of increase.

All of these trends, and arguably the increase in human contact in particular, have an impact on social organization. People now have the time, the money, the ability, and the instruments by which to become involved in social structures beyond their immediate families and villages. Alvin

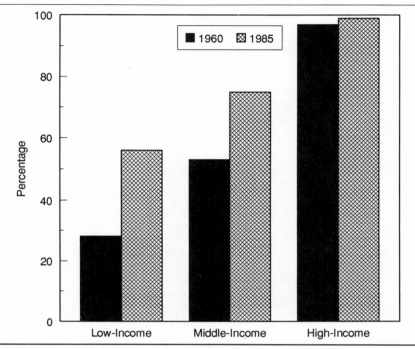

FIGURE 2.20  Adult literacy rate by development level. *Sources:* World Bank, *World Development Report 1982* (Washington, D.C.: World Bank, 1982), 110–111; World Bank, *World Development Report 1991* (New York: Oxford University Press, 1991), 204–205.

Toffler writes therefore of the "global village." Moreover, there is much evidence that large numbers wish to further extend their social contacts.

We can see the effect of these individual-level changes on the types and structures of social organization. With respect to the types of organization, one of the most dramatic trends has been the spread of European-style states (like England, France, and Spain) around the globe. Figure 2.22 indicates the rapid growth in the numbers of those types of organizational units throughout the twentieth century. In the contemporary era, the entire world is characterized by such states, and almost all of the multiethnic empires that ushered in the century, including the former Soviet Union, have given way to states built more closely around ethnic-cultural units.

Figure 2.22 also indicates the even more rapid growth of two other forms of social organization: intergovernmental organizations (IGOs), based on state membership, and international nongovernmental organizations (INGOs), based on individual membership. Intergovernmental organizations like the United Nations, the North Atlantic Treaty

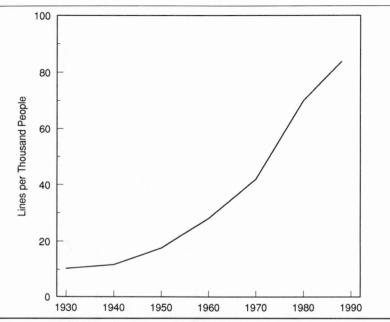

FIGURE 2.21   Global telephone lines. *Sources: The World's Telephones* (Morris Plains, N.J.: AT&T, 1982), 14; *The World's Telephones* (Whippany, N.J.: AT&T, 1989), 11.

Organization, and the European Community have proliferated considerably more rapidly than states. Nongovernmental organizations, like Greenpeace or Amnesty International, have grown even more quickly than either IGOs or states. They now number about 4,500. The existence of these social institutions across state borders reflects the growing interdependence of the world's peoples and their desire for governance responsive to that interdependence.

The pressures for democracy provide another indication of that desire for governmental responsiveness. Democracy in the modern era is about as old as the industrial revolution and, although subject to more setbacks and less regular growth, has spread at a generally similar pace. Figure 2.23 traces the percentage of countries in Latin America and Europe with what Gurr, Jaggers, and Moore (1990) call a "coherent democratic polity." Theirs is a somewhat more demanding test of democracy than that of many other observers.

There are, of course, many uncertainties with respect to all of these social and political trends. For instance, a flowering of democracy characterized the period immediately after World War I (with which some compare the contemporary post–cold war era). By the late 1930s many of the flow-

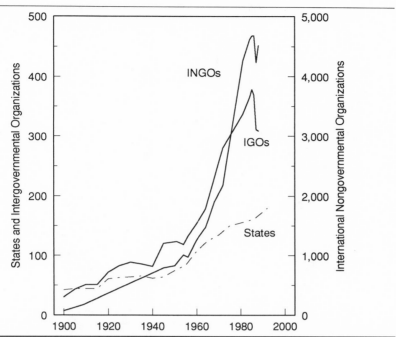

FIGURE 2.22    Global actors. *Sources:* J. David Singer and the Correlates of War Project; Union of International Organizations (UAI), *Yearbook of International Organizations* (Brussels: UAI, various years).

ers had wilted and died. Once again we must be wary of simple extrapolation.

## CONCLUSION

Throughout this chapter we have simultaneously utilized trend extrapolation and inveighed against the uncritical extension of trends into the future. It is impossible to know whether a trend will continue or whether it will soon reach a sudden limit, pass an important turning point, or even end abruptly with a threshold change in the underlying process. Nonetheless, trends are of great use in helping us understand the present and anticipate the future. Many patterns will continue to evolve much as they have in the past. In addition, critical examination of trends moves us quickly to a consideration of the causal dynamics that might underlie changes in the patterns. This chapter has already suggested many causal linkages that we will wish to investigate further in subsequent chapters.

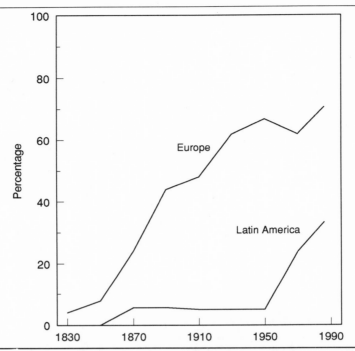

FIGURE 2.23   Coherent democratic polities as portion of regional polities. *Source:* Based on data in Ted Robert Gurr, Keith Jaggers, and Will H. Moore, "The Transformation of the Western State," *Studies in Comparative International Development* 25, no. 1 (Spring 1990):94.

In addition to the complexity of choosing an appropriate form for extrapolation of trends, many readers will have noted a second difficulty with the use of trends that also pushes us toward causal analysis. Many of the patterns we have seen interact with one another. Although we have attempted to look at trends in isolation, there has been recurrent pressure to consider that interaction. Again, we must turn to causal analysis to do so.

In spite of the limitations of trend analysis, we must keep in mind the problem that we face: We are under pressure to act (including foregoing action alternatives) even though we are unable to know the future. Our examination of trends has given us a better idea of where change is taking us. That will assist us in moving to a consideration of the kind of future we want and the leverage we have in bringing it about.

# THREE

□ □ □

# Using a Model
# to Investigate Change

A careful examination of global trends, like the one we undertook in Chapter 2, contributes considerably to helping us understand where change is taking us. We saw in that chapter, however, that it is not a trivial matter to extrapolate trends into the future. For instance, it is often far from clear whether a trend will follow an exponential growth path, will trace an S-shaped curve, or will peak and decline. Our examination of trends often forced us to make some additional assumptions about the world. In short, the difference between trend extrapolation and causal analysis may not be as great as we initially suggested. In reality, trend extrapolation inevitably takes place within the context of a broader understanding of the world around us. We bring an understanding of that world, a mental map or model of it, to any investigation of trends.

One difficulty with such mental maps or models is that they often remain largely implicit. A second is that they are frequently very simple. Consider again the issue of forecasting the weather. You ask a friend what the weather will be tomorrow, and she says, "Warm and sunny." You know that it is warm and sunny today. Yet how do you judge the reasonableness of her forecast for tomorrow? Is she simply extrapolating the weather from today? Or did she look at the weather map in this morning's paper and see that no new weather front is moving in this direction? Or did she hear a forecast on the radio that was based on a complex computer model?

If the weather tomorrow is important to you, perhaps because you are planning a long hike, you may ask your friend how she knows. That is, you may begin to explore her mental model and to compare that with your own. You may have more trust in her forecast if it is based on the weather map and even more if it is based on computer-generated forecasts that have in the past proven quite accurate. Presumably our understanding of the future adequacy of global food supplies and the quality of the earth's environment requires asking the same question: How do you know?

This chapter introduces the use of computer modeling as a tool for investigating such futures and also introduces a specific computer model called International Futures (IFs). Computer models formalize mental models mathematically. Computer models are *not* automatically superior to mental models simply because of that formalization. In fact, many computer models are less sophisticated than a good mental model and produce unreliable forecasts.

Nonetheless, the careful use of computer models has some significant advantages. The first is that a computer model is highly explicit. One can examine the model very carefully. In contrast, we often have difficulty explaining our own mental models and may find that we haven't the least idea about the mental models of others. Even if we reject a computer model, careful examination of it might well add considerable sophistication to our own mental model in the end. In fact, that is probably the single most important reason for using computer models—because they represent the mental models of others, sometimes the cumulative understandings of many others, they help us learn.

Second, a computer model sometimes can attain a level of complexity that surpasses our mental models. That might allow the computer program to probe the secondary consequences of change and action in ways that we cannot. For instance, computer models of chess probe the implications of moves far more fully than the typical human player (on the other hand, complexity can also introduce error). Third, we can often use a computer model to investigate a variety of different assumptions. For instance, we might examine the possible consequences of several courses of action. Again, chess programs typically investigate far more possible moves than the average human player. Or we might investigate the consequences of a single plan under differing assumptions about the workings of some key element in the environment of our action.

Those readers who do not intend to use the computer model that accompanies this book might wish to proceed directly to Chapter 4. We invite those who do continue with this chapter to sit down with it next to their computer. Like riding a bicycle, the best way to learn how to use a computer model is to do it.

## SOME BACKGROUND ON IFs

There are many models of issues such as world population, the world economy, and the world climate. There are even more models of specific issues with limited geographic scope (a country or region). The first model to devote attention to both the environment and the economy, and to do it on a global scale, was the one used to produce the book *Limits to Growth* (Meadows et al., 1972). That volume received worldwide attention for its pessimistic forecasts of the global future. Many models followed that one in the 1970s and 1980s.[1]

IFs draws on many of the features of other world models (Hughes, 1985b, 1988). It represents a greater range of elements from what we earlier called the human development system than do most other world models. Specifically, it represents human demographics, food production, energy supply, the economy, and some aspects of political structure. It allows us to look at these elements individually and in interaction.

In fact, our use of IFs will proceed in two stages. First, in this chapter we will look in turn and individually at the same global trends that we considered in Chapter 2. This will allow us to learn how to use IFs and also to learn something about how it operates—about the mental model that underlies it. Second, in subsequent chapters you will have the opportunity to begin investigating the complex interaction of various elements in the model as you do substantial causal analysis of the future.

## EXAMINING FORECASTS

Chapter 2 traced trends that are reshaping the world in seven issue areas. This section will assist you in using International Futures 1990 (IFs90 or simply IFs) to examine those same trends or forces. The use of IFs to examine the trends is, however, significantly different from the simple extrapolation of them in the last chapter. The most basic difference is that IFs is a fully integrated computer model so that changes in any part of it affect the rest of it. Thus demographic, energy, environmental, and economic trends in IFs are very much interactive, even when we focus on each individually. Although the results IFs produces may be very similar to the figures and tables of the last chapter, they will never be identical. And even quite minor changes in any of the assumptions of IFs will affect all forecasts. Thus it will be necessary that we not only learn how to produce forecasts with IFs but that we begin to understand the mental model that lies behind the computer model.

▶ **Starting IFs and Using the Main Menu.** Before you can examine the workings of the seven forces, you need to know how to use IFs. Assuming that the model is installed on your computer (see Appendix 3 for installation instructions and re-quirements), you need only be located in the directory named IFs90 to initiate in-teraction with the model. At the DOS (operating system) prompt, type IFs90 (up-percase and lowercase letters are always interchangeable) and then touch the <Enter> key.

As IFs begins to run, you will see an Introductory Screen that identifies the model, its developers, and the version of IFs you have. When IFs has completed the loading of its data files, it will instruct you to press any key in order to pro-ceed. Doing so will display the Main Menu. You will see that one of the options on the Main Menu is always shaded (initially the RUN option). That means that it is selected; you need only touch the <Enter> key to implement the selected, shaded option. Before doing that, however, let us explore the use of the Main Menu (if you accidently implement an option, you can touch the escape <Esc> key to return to the Main Menu). To select another option (for instance, DIS-PLAY, next to RUN), you can use the left and right arrow keys on your keyboard. Touch those arrow keys and see how the shading (selection) moves across the Main Menu. Notice also how the Status Line in the box at the bottom of the screen changes as you move from one menu option to another; it gives you a brief description of what the selected menu option does. It is also possible to se-lect and simultaneously implement a menu option by typing the first letter of the option name. For instance, type C to enter the variable or parameter change pro-cedure; then touch the <Esc> key to return to the Main Menu.

IFs also has a help system to assist you in learning about its use. At almost any point in the use of IFs, you can press the <F1> key, and a help screen will appear. Try that now and follow the directions for getting additional screens of help in-formation about the Main Menu. When you wish to return from the help system to the point at which you accessed it, simply touch the escape <Esc> key. In gen-eral, <Esc> allows you to return from subsidiary activities (like the help system) to higher-level ones.

You are now physically ready to use IFs but perhaps not mentally ready. How does one use a computer simulation? Model use normally has seven steps:

▶ 1. *Load data files.* Data files contain the initial conditions for the model (1990 values in this case). They also contain the "parameters" of the model, the numer-ical values of the equations. Many of these parameters are numbers that you will change as you work further with the model in order to represent either different assumptions about the way the world works or different policy options avail-able to society.

2. *Run the model to create a "base case."* The model uses the 1990 or base year data, its equations, and the base case parameter values to calculate values for a large number of indicators in 1991, 1992, and so on, to the end year of the forecast period. The base case is not a prediction of the future. It is a statement of how the future might look *if* the initial conditions, equations, and base case parameter values were all correct.

3. *Evaluate the forecast of the base case.* Compare it with your own expectations or with forecasts from other sources (like those in Chapter 2). Simultaneously evaluate the initial conditions, equations, and parameters of the model. Consider where there may be uncertainty or disagreement with respect to these model specifications or where policy changes might suggest the possibility of other parameter values.

4. *Change assumptions of the base case.* IFs makes it easy to change initial conditions or parameters. IFs even allows you to make some equation changes by using parameters as switches. More sophisticated users can also change equations by altering the computer program.

5. *Run the model again.* After you have introduced new parameters or initial conditions, run the model again. Your changes will often create what you consider to be a more accurate (or more desirable) representation of the world.

6. *Compare the forecast generated by the new assumptions (what we call a **scenario**)* with the base case. Make sure that you understand why the new scenario has produced different results. Your search for understanding may require still more changes of assumptions and runs of the model.

7. *Evaluate what you have learned about the model and about the world it represents.* To what degree are the results you have obtained artifacts of a model that you either do not understand or with which you disagree? To what extent have you stretched your own understanding of the world and therefore improved your own mental model of it? Your work with a computer model can productively continue until you feel that your mental model is superior to the computer model (and can continue still further, if you are then willing to extend the computer model itself).

These seven steps are somewhat idealized, but you should periodically refer back to them. They will help you make the most efficient use of IFs.

In this chapter we will initially restrict our efforts primarily to the first three steps and explore steps 4 through 7 briefly in anticipation of subsequent chapters. In fact, we will focus overwhelmingly on Step 3, examining and evaluating the base case. If you have reached the Main Menu of IFs, you have already loaded the initial conditions and parameters and could run the model to produce the base case. In order to save you time, however, a copy of the base case forecast is included with the IFs model and was loaded into computer memory when you initiated interaction with IFs. We therefore can proceed to examine the base case in detail.

### Demographic Change

**Research Questions.** How large is the world's population? How fast is it growing? Is the rate of growth increasing or decreasing? Is that true everywhere or only in some parts of the world? Where is it growing fastest? Are there any parts of the world in which it has stopped growing? Is it decreasing anywhere? Is global population growing because birthrates have increased or because death rates have decreased (or both)? What might be the population of the world and its growth rate in 2035? You will be able to use IFs to answer these and similar questions by the time you finish this section.

A massive demographic change is taking place globally—so massive and important that it affects essentially all other processes of global change. One manifestation of this change is steady and substantial growth in the global population. Let us look at that growth in the forecast of the base case.

▶ **Examining Results: The Basics.** To examine any variable (a **variable** is a measure like global population that changes over time) in IFs, we need to activate the DISPLAY feature of the model. To do so, use the arrow keys to select (shade) the DISPLAY option on the Main Menu and then press <Enter> to implement it. You will now see the Display Menu with several ways of presenting output from the model. The primary display forms are tables of numerical values (either shown on the screen or printed), graphs of variables over time, and pie charts. We can usefully show global population in both tabular and graphical form.

To produce a table on the screen, select the TABLE option from the Display Menu and implement it by touching <Enter>. Doing so drops you to the "dialog" level of interaction with the model. Specifically, the model asks you for the name of the variable you want to display. At this point you must know the variable name. The name for world population is WPOP. To find the names of all the variables that you can display, look in the glossary of Appendix 1 at the end of this book (or use the help feature of the model). The glossary also indicates the units for all variables; world population is in millions. You may want to mark those pages, because the variable names are your key to the model. Type WPOP (uppercase or lowercase) in response to the question and touch <Enter>. The Status Line will show the variable(s) you have selected (ignore the zero in brackets; we will explain that later). The model asks you to select another variable for printing. Because you want no other variable, you can simply type GO over the top of the variable name you last selected (followed, as always, by pressing <Enter>). Your table appears on the screen.

The table shows the rapid growth of global population, from over 5 billion in 1990 to well over 8 billion in 2035. It is useful, however, to also see that in graphical form. When you are finished viewing the table, touch <Esc> twice to move back up to the Display Menu. Now select the GRAPH option and touch <Enter> for dialog mode. Again provide the variable name (WPOP) and close off variable selection with GO. Now you will see a plot of world population over time.

If you have a printer attached, you could select the HARDCOPY option from the Display Menu to get a table on the printer. The rest of the procedure would be identical to that for TABLE or GRAPH, except that the dialog will also ask additional questions, including whether you want a title for the table (you might, for example, label it Base Case and put the date on it).

Note that the graph of global population suggests that although population is continuing to grow, it may begin to approach a level value sometime in the next century. That implies that the growth rate of global population is slowing. To verify that, graph (or display in tabular form) the rate of growth of global population WPOPR.

Population growth is far from identical in countries around the world. IFs calculates population (and most other variables) for each of ten geographic regions of the world (four of these "regions" are individual countries and a fifth, the European Community, is becoming increasingly integrated economically). The glossary in Appendix 1 at the end of the book shows you the regional names and the abbreviations used in the model. You can look at the population of these regions individually, in either tables or graphs.

▶ **Examining Results: By Region.** Select TABLE from the Display Menu and type the variable name POP for regional population. The model will provide a list of the 10 geographic options and ask you to select a specific region. You type the *number* of the country or region you want. You can then select the variable population (POP) again simply by pressing <Enter>. Choose another geographic unit by number. Note that the variable and region names of your selections appear in the Status Line at the bottom of the screen. You can continue selecting different countries or regions until you have chosen seven of them. Only seven fit on the screen, so the model then provides a table, whether or not you type GO to close off variable selection.

After examining the table, select GRAPH from the Display Menu and look at selected populations in graphical form. You are allowed to put up to seven variables on the same graph.

Another, and perhaps superior, way of examining the development of regional population is to compare a pie chart of global population in 1990 with one of the population in 2035. To produce a pie chart, select PIE from the Display Menu and respond to the questions of the dialog; initially choose 1990 when asked to provide a year. Note that the pie chart shows the percentage of the world's population in each of the ten geographic regions as well as providing the numbers for each region. When you have examined the pie chart for 1990, and perhaps made notes about the global distribution, you can create another one for 2035.

The world is now in the middle of a global demographic transition from high birth and death rates to low birth and death rates. During that transition, death rates initially declined faster than birthrates, especially in economically less-developed countries (LDCs), and that has caused population to grow rapidly. To see this phenomenon more clearly, look at the crude birth rate (CBR), or number of births per thousand population, the crude death rate (CDR), and the net population growth rate (POPR) for a single developing region like Latin America. Compare the pattern you see (in table or graph form) with that for a country like the United

States or Russia (you could put all three variables for two regions on the same table).

Explore the population model on your own by looking at population (POP), population growth rate (POPR), crude birth rates (CBR), crude death rates (CDR), total births (BIRTHS), total deaths (DEATHS), life expectancy at birth (LIFEXP), and infant mortality (INFMOR) for a variety of countries and regions.

*You may now be asking how the model generates these numbers.* The model keeps track of the number of people in each of 17 age categories or cohorts. The first 16 cohorts are five-year groupings—people from 1–5 years of age, 6–10, 11–15, and so on (infants are counted separately). The last cohort combines all those over 70 years of age. The model also represents a fertility distribution by cohort. That is, it has recent data (by region) on the number of births per thousand for people in the 16- to 20-year-old cohort, the 21- to 25-year-old cohort, and so on. By multiplying the fertility distribution by the age distribution, the model calculates the number of births, and after one year those infants are added to the bottom cohort. Finally, the model maintains a mortality distribution. That records recent data on the portion of each cohort that dies in an average year (obviously that portion is greater for older cohorts). Multiplying the mortality distribution by the age distribution provides the number of deaths in each cohort, and those diminish the cohort each year. In addition, one-fifth of each cohort passes to the next age group in every year.

One obvious weakness of such a population module, as described so far, is that it seems to assume that fertility and mortality patterns do not change with time. In fact, the model recognizes that they do change and computes that change internally—that is, fertility and mortality change as a result of the change in other variables within the model. For instance, fertility responds to changes in assumptions about family planning programs (assumptions you will be able to alter); mortality changes in response to availability of adequate food supply (you cannot directly alter food availability, but you can affect it by modifying other assumptions). Both fertility and mortality change with income level and income distribution. We will return to these determinants later.

### Food Availability

**Research Questions.** Is food production in the world as a whole growing as rapidly as population? Where might it be growing more rapidly and where less rapidly? Do some parts of the world rely on food imports to maintain adequate calorie levels? In which regions of the world is starvation a danger?

Two other critically important forces that are reshaping our world are growth in food production and the "race" between it and population growth. You can display WAPRO (world agricultural production) in a table or plot it in a graph. It is in million metric tons. At the dialog level you will need to specify whether you want to look at crop or meat production (build a table or graph with both). You can also look at AGP (agricultural production) by region. Or you can examine AGM (agricultural imports) or AGX (agricultural exports).

Information on food availability may be more meaningful when it is converted to calories available for consumption, whether produced locally or imported. Look at WCLPC (world calories per capita). The units are thousand calories per day. On a region-by-region basis you can look at CLPC (regional calories per capita). The model also calculates millions of potential starvation deaths each year in each region (SDEATH) and the accumulated starvation deaths (since 1990) for the world (WSDACC). Explore for more food and agricultural variables of interest in the glossary at the end of the book (Appendix 1).

*How does the model make these forecasts?* The model calculates crop production (AGP) by multiplying the number of millions of hectares of land devoted to crops (LD) times the number of tons of food yielded by each hectare (YL). Land under cultivation depends on the capital investment made in improving land (KAG) and the cost of clearing additional land (CLD). Yield levels depend on the use of inputs such as fertilizer. Both investment in land and the use of yield-boosting inputs depend in turn on the price of food. Meat production depends on the livestock herd size and the slaughter rate.

The model determines human food demand (FDEM) as a function of population, income levels, and prices; the more you earn, the more food you buy (but this represents a decreasing portion of your total income), whereas the higher prices are, the less food you buy. The coefficients that represent the responsiveness of food consumption to income and price are called the income and price elasticities of food demand. The model calculates the demand upon crop production for livestock feed (FEDDEM) as a function of herd size and grazing land availability. It further calculates an industrial demand for agricultural production (INDEM) (for instance, demand for cotton) as a function of economic size. These components sum to total agricultural demand.

The model maintains buffer stocks (inventories) of agricultural products so that a surplus of supply relative to demand in one year will increase those stocks, whereas a surplus of demand relative to production will decrease them. Because food price (FPRI) affects both food demand and food supply, it is a critical variable in the model. It is calculated by the model **endogenously** (internally) rather than being given **exogenously** (externally) to the model by the user. When the buffer stocks rise, they depress food prices; when they fall, they increase prices. Prices then affect both demand and supply in the next year. Thus changes in buffer stocks and prices act to bring supply and demand into balance over time (in reality, there are always some imbalances, and the process chases balance or equilibrium rather than reaching it).

**Energy Transition**

**Research Questions.** What primary energy form supplies most of the world's energy? How much does it provide? Which countries or regions consume the most energy? Which produce the most? Which import and export the most? How big are the world's known reserves of oil and gas? How do those compare to the reserves of coal? How large might unknown (undiscovered) oil and gas resources be?

The world's relative dependence on oil and gas is declining steadily, even as the production and consumption of oil and gas continue to increase. In fact, the world is fairly steadily making a transition from an energy system predominantly dependent on oil and gas to one that will eventually rely much more heavily on some combination of coal, nuclear, and solar (renewable) energy inputs.

To explore this phenomenon in the base case, we can begin by looking at world energy production (WENP). IFs calculates production of four primary energy forms: oil and gas together as one (they face comparable production futures); coal; renewable (which aggregates biomatter, photovoltaic, hydroelectric, and other renewable forms); and nuclear (which fusion as well as fission plants could eventually supply). When you select WENP to display, print, or plot, you will be asked to select one of these forms. Pie charts of WENP in 1990 and later years provide a good picture of how the energy supply pattern may change over time. Look also at energy production on a regional basis (ENP).

OILGPR (oil and gas production as a portion of total energy production) most clearly shows the energy transition. Look at it in either tabular or graphical form. It declines in the long run because the world does have limited supplies of oil and gas. The variable RESER contains estimates by region of known and producible oil and gas in 1990 and thereafter (WRESER carries the world total). Production decrements that variable over time, whereas new discoveries augment it. The total regional resource base of oil and gas, RESOR, ultimately bounds new discoveries (WRESOR shows the world total). Note how much greater global resources are for coal.

One of the key characteristics of the world energy system is the concentration of oil and gas production in OPEC countries, whereas the economically more-developed countries account for most energy demand (ENDEM). You can see this by comparing a pie chart of ENDEM with one of ENP for oil and gas.

▶ **Displaying Results: More on Pie Charts.** When you select ENP as the variable for a pie chart, you choose between looking at ENP across all regions (the pie slices) for a single energy type or looking at ENP across all energy types (the pie slices) for a single region. To do the former, supply a zero when asked for the region number and then select the energy type you want to see.

A more direct way of examining the gap between production and consumption is to look at energy exports (ENX) or energy imports (ENM). Note that it is possible for a country or a region to be both an energy exporter and importer; even the United States exports some refined products, for instance.

*How does the energy submodel of IFs work?* It has much in common with the agricultural submodel described earlier. Specifically, it calculates demand, supply, and buffer stocks to balance demand and supply in the short run. Changes in buffer stocks lead to changes in prices, which in turn affect demand and supply in the longer run, so that the model always chases equilibrium (balance).

Energy demand (ENDEM, nonspecific with respect to energy type) is a function largely of economic size, as measured by gross national product, and of energy prices (see ENPRI for regional prices and WEP for a world average). Because of the resource constraints on oil and gas and because of base case assumptions about the capital costs of alternatives (QE), the model forecasts a long-term increase in energy prices. This leads to slower growth in energy demand than in GNP, or gross national product (ENRGNP is the ratio of energy demand to GNP and is an interesting indicator of energy efficiency).

Energy is a highly capital-intensive industry. Thus the major determinant of energy production in any energy type is the capital investment that has been made over time in its production. That investment increases or decreases with the price of energy relative to the cost of energy production. For instance, if the price of energy increases less rapidly than the cost of oil and gas production increases (due to ongoing resource depletion), capital investment in oil and gas will decline. If the price of energy increases, however, while the capital cost of renewable energy declines (due to technological progress), capital investment in renewable energy will increase substantially. Thus the supply side of the energy submodel determines not just how much energy each geographic region will produce but the balance among production levels of various energy forms.

You have probably realized already the importance of the assumptions in the base case about current capital costs of various energy types and about the future changes in those costs (and about the responsiveness of energy demand to price changes). The uncertainty of such assumptions is the reason we earlier said that any single forecast of a model should be examined very skeptically. We will learn later how we can identify and change these and many other assumptions.

### Environmental Impact

**Research Questions.** How much damage are humans doing to the environment? What is the rate of global deforestation? How does the progress of deforestation vary by region? How fast is the amount of atmospheric $CO_2$ increasing?

As populations grow, food production increases, and energy production rises, environmental damage is inevitable. For instance, we noted earlier that increases in agricultural production depend on either additions in land under cultivation or improvements in yield per hectare of cropland. Thus forest area (including rain forests) declines as a result of conversion to cropland.

Two of the potential environmental problems of greatest concern to scientists and environmentalists today are the greenhouse effect and global deforestation. Fossil fuels contain carbon, and their burning (oxidization) inevitably adds carbon dioxide ($CO_2$) to the atmosphere. Carbon dioxide allows sunlight to pass through easily, but it retards the radiation of heat back into space (like the glass in a greenhouse). $CO_2$ is the primary "greenhouse gas," the set of which may ultimately cause earth's climate to become warmer.

You can display or plot the increase in atmospheric carbon dioxide over time. The model tracks that phenomenon in terms of the percentage increase in carbon dioxide (PERCO2) relative to the amount in the atmosphere early in the industrial era (about the year 1800). This measure has interest because some scientists have estimated that a doubling in carbon dioxide might raise average global temperatures by about 2 degrees centigrade (a variety of other estimates of temperature change compete with that one). The impact of increasing $CO_2$ is not, however, a threshold phenomenon; that is, temperature rise will not suddenly occur when $CO_2$ doubles but will instead happen gradually throughout the process.

To examine the impact of human activity on forest area, look at the amount of land (LD) in various categories and regions, measured in million hectares. In many countries and regions you will see increases in cropland and land used for urban areas (and other human activities such as roads) and decreases in forest area. You can also look at the decline in total world forest area (WFORST).

*How does the model calculate these environmental indicators, and how do changes in them affect the model's assessment of human well-being?* Deforestation is a side effect of agricultural activity in both the world and the model. As described earlier, investment in agriculture flows in part into bringing new land under cultivation (the model determines the relative economic efficiency of investing in new land and investing in increased inputs such as fertilizer and machinery on existing land). Although there are important ramifications of forest destruction for humanity, including the extinction of plant and animal species with important pharmacological potential, the costs of the process are essentially incalculable. The model therefore does no more than indicate the extent of the process.

Similarly, the generation of carbon dioxide is an inevitable side effect of energy consumption. There are some uncertainties, however, including debate concerning how much of the annual increase in carbon dioxide the oceans absorb. The model therefore represents that absorption rate as a parameter (CO2ABR). As important, scientists have begun to speculate about the implications of increased global temperatures on agricultural productivity. The model therefore includes a linkage between rising $CO_2$ levels and diminished or increased agricultural yields (the parameter is ELASAC).

## Technological Change

**Research Questions.** How much contribution does technological advance contribute to economic change? What portion of increase in agricultural production is a result of technological improvement? How rapidly is the technology of global destruction progressing?

Technological change is pervasive in the world around us. It affects medical treatment and thus life expectancy. It alters our agricultural system and thus food availability. It changes the costs of extracting or producing energy and therefore the price and availability of that energy. It is often very difficult to draw out measures of technological advance from the broader processes of change.

One way of looking at such deeply imbedded technological advance is to compare over time the resources that go into a production process and the output of that process. For instance, you can obtain a table or graph over time comparing the amount of land used for crop production (LD) with the amount of crop production (AGP). Similarly, you can examine the amount of total production by any sector of the economy (ZS) relative to the amount of labor (LABS) used in that sector.

Chapter 2 suggested, however, that technological advance brings not just economic efficiency gains but also improvements in the destructive power of humanity. Since the American Civil War, sometimes considered the first modern war, humanity has added machine guns, torpedoes, exploding shells, a variety of chemical and biological agents, and both atomic and hydrogen warheads to its armory. It has added submarines, metal ships, aircraft, tanks, and a wide variety of missiles to its list of delivery vehicles. Most of these implements of destruction originated in

Europe or North America. All of them have now proliferated around the world. Additional countries continue to adopt them annually, and the world total of each rises steadily.

IFs has no individual measures of this weaponry. Instead you can examine their spread only in the aggregate, by looking at conventional and nuclear power (CPOW and NPOW). For instance, look at the growth of conventional power of various less-developed regions of the world in comparison with the power of Russia (or even the United States).

Forecasts of conventional power are uncertain, but forecasts of nuclear power are little more than wild guesses. We have little idea how rapidly nuclear weaponry might proliferate in the South. Nor do we know whether contemporary arms control agreements in the North really will substantially reduce inventories of both bombs and rockets in the long run. Such uncertainty in no way diminishes the importance of our identifying the underlying trends of weaponry improvement and spread.

*How does IFs forecast technological change?* IFs does not contain a separate model of technological change. Instead, as the above discussion suggests, such change is represented in various ways throughout the model. In the agricultural sector, improvements in agricultural yield (YL), the metric tons of crops produced on every hectare of land, reflect various other changes. Simple increases in the intensity of agriculture (the amount of capital and labor provided to the land) account for some improvements in yield. IFs also contains, however, a parameter that specifies the annual rate of increase in the efficiency of capital use (RKEF). A similar parameter (RLEF) strongly influences the rate of increase in the efficiency of labor use, but expenditures on education influence that as well. In short, the improvements in agricultural productivity are partly specified from outside the model (exogenously) and partly from within (endogenously). Similarly, parameters and internal linkages determine the rate of technological advance throughout the economy.

## Economic Restructuring

**Research Questions.** What are the major changes taking place in the world's economy? Which region has the largest economy, and how fast is it growing? Which region will have the largest economy in 2035? Which economic sectors are growing most rapidly?

There are at least two important and highly interrelated structural changes reshaping the world economy. First, the economically less-developed countries of the world were at one time overwhelmingly producers of raw materials such as minerals and agricultural products. They are now increasingly industrialized economies, supplying larger portions of their manufactures to the economically more-developed countries. Second, the service sector (including advanced information and communication activities) of the more-developed countries is increasingly their dominant sector. In short, manufacturing is shifting to the poor countries, while the rich countries concentrate more on services, including high-tech ones.

The basic measure of economic activity in all countries and regions is the GNP, or gross national product (total final production of goods and services). You should begin exploring the economic submodel by looking at the variable GNP across geographic units; consider pie charts as well as line graphs. Explore also the rate of GNP growth (GNPR) and the GNP per capita (GNPPC). You can also look at world GNP (WGNP) and world GNP per capita (WGNPPC).

How much of the world's manufacturing is located in what we call the South of the world (the less-developed countries are often physically south of the more developed)? How fast is that portion increasing? The percentage share is summarized in the variable SMAN. Its values suggest that although manufacturing is growing in the South, the South is by no means taking global manufacturing away from the North.

To see more clearly how the manufacturing sector is becoming an increasingly large part of the economies in southern regions, however, we must look at those regions individually. The economic submodel calculates production for each country or region in five sectors: agriculture, primary energy, other raw materials, manufactures, and services. For instance, gross production by sector (ZS) in Africa shows that manufacturing will become an increasingly important portion of the economy. Look also at how manufacturing in Africa compares with manufacturing in other regions.

Even more substantial changes are occurring in global services. The service sector is already the largest of the five in the United States, and the dominance of that sector appears likely to increase (see again ZS). Relatively faster growth in service production and consumption is true both in other richer, "northern" countries and in the South.

How is the increase in manufacturing in the South and the continued rise of services in the North affecting the aggregate world economy? The percentage of the world's production in each sector (WPROD) will give you the answer. Note especially what is happening to the share of agriculture.

The economic submodel is in many respects the core of IFs, because nearly all other portions of the model provide input to it or utilize calculations from it. *How does it work?* Like the agricultural and energy submodels, it has demand and supply sides, balanced by changing buffer stocks and prices.

On the supply side, production in each sector depends on the availability of labor (LAB) and capital (KS). The production function that combines those factors of production is called a Cobb-Douglas function. Assumptions about the annual rate of improvements in the quality of labor (RLEF) and the technological sophistication of capital (RKEF) also influence production. Over time the labor force grows with the population (depending also on how much of the population participates in the commercial economy) and the capital stock in each sector grows with investment (in new buildings and machinery). Much of gross production (ZS) goes to satisfy the production requirements of other sectors (for instance, steel production goes into the production of screws and bolts, which in turn go into the production of cars). These intersectoral flows are subtracted from gross supply to calculate how much of gross production is actually available to meet what we call final demand (PFD). We use something called a technological coefficient matrix (or input-output matrix) to calculate those intersectoral flows (A).

The (final) demand side begins with total income (dependent on production levels) and allocates part of that to government (G) through taxes. It then splits the remaining portion between investment (I) and household consumption (C). Government, investment, and consumption all make demands upon the supply side of the economy by sector. The government (GS) primarily buys services. Investment (INVS) largely requires manufactures and construction. Private or household consumption by sector (CS) demands largely food, manufactures, and services (the model uses something called a linear expenditure system, which shifts the allocation of household spending as income rises).

Exports by sector (XS) and imports by sector (MS) among countries depend on the past pattern of trade (there is a strong inertial element in trade flows) and on the relative prices of products in the various geographic regions modified by exchange rates (EXRATE). You can also look at total exports (X) and imports (M).

Local demand (from government, investors, and households) and foreign demand (from exports) reduce inventories or buffer stocks in a sector. Local and foreign supply (from imports) increase buffer stocks. Change in the level of stocks (and the rate of their change) determines the rise or fall of prices (PRI). Rising prices increase investment in sectors and depress consumption. Thus the entire economic model chases balance between demand and supply, using the buffer stocks to absorb temporary imbalance. This is the same process in the economy as a whole that we saw earlier in the agriculture and energy submodels. In fact, the demand and supply calculations from those two single-sector submodels, because they are based on more detailed representation of the sectors than that in the economic submodel, override the calculations in the economic submodel (unless the user wishes to turn off those linkages).

Many key assumptions obviously influence the behavior of the regional and world economies in the base case. These include the relative importance of labor and capital in the production process; the rate of increases in labor efficiency and capital sophistication; and the portion of income taken by the government. We will see subsequently how to change these and other assumptions.

## Social-Political Change

**Research Questions.** Are citizens around the world becoming more involved in politics and in more general forms of collective social action? If so, why?

It now appears that democracy as we know it in North America, Western Europe, Japan, Australia, and New Zealand is spreading around the world. Multiple changes of government in Latin America, Central and Eastern Europe, and Asia provide support for such a hypothesis. It also seems possible that the level of public involvement in political and social interest groups (including international ones such as Greenpeace and Amnesty International) and in street protests (such as those that toppled governments in Czechoslovakia, East Germany, and Rumania) may be rising. In short, the mobilization of people behind social purposes of various kinds seems to be increasing (some manifestations, like terrorism, will be violent).

Why might that be? One part of the explanation is that people are now more able to participate. They are more literate, and they have much greater access to electronic communication media than ever before. A greater portion also live in cities where they can more easily have face-to-face interaction. A second part of the explanation may be that larger numbers have satisfied the basic needs of existence and therefore can direct their attention to other human objectives.

Some of the indicators in IFs verify that the changes that might facilitate social mobilization are indeed underway. Look, for instance, at the numbers for literacy by region (LIT) and globally (WLIT). Consider also the trends in GNP per capita (GNPPC and WGNPPC) and those in life expectancy (LIFEXP and WLIFE). Consider again regional and global calorie availability (CLPC and WCLPC). Improvement in the physical quality of life (PQLI and WPQLI) summarizes much of what happens regionally and globally. That measure often serves as a noneconomic summary of the human condition; it combines literacy rate, infant mortality, and life expectancy with equal weighting.

*How does IFs capture and handle the important phenomenon of social mobilization?* There are three elements in the answer to that question. First, we have seen that the model makes available to us a handful of measures of the factors underlying mobilization: literacy, life expectancy, GNP per capita, and physical quality of life. Second, the model incorporates some important mechanisms that drive the levels of such variables as life expectancy and literacy. For instance, government spending flows to both health and education and increases life expectancy and literacy. Third, the progress on those measures should influence other variables in the model in turn. In IFs the level of spending on education (and thus by implication the literacy rate) does affect the efficiency of labor in the production process, and medical spending does improve health. Otherwise, however, there are no "forward" linkages of social mobilization to other variables in the model. One can imagine linkages of social mobilization to democratization and then to the propensity for warfare. Or of social mobilization to the nature and distribution of government expenditures. These are just examples of many potentially important linkages that IFs does not contain. No computer model can ever be as rich as our imagination (although they can often be more consistent than our memories and more coherent than our understandings).

### Examination of Trends as a Beginning

You now have a basic understanding of the structure of IFs and have seen how the model allows you to consider more carefully seven important forces that are reshaping the world. There is, however, a great deal more that one can do with the model; it has several additional levels of complexity. The glossary of variables in Appendix 1 gives you some help in going further on your own.

To this point, although we have examined only the base case of the model, we have already emphasized several times the importance of various assumptions. We thus need to learn how to change the assumptions of the base case and to construct scenarios (alternative futures based on alternative assumptions) that we can compare with the base case.

## CHANGING FORECASTS

Up to now our use of IFs has been relatively passive. We examined the base case and saw one possible way in which the world might evolve. In this section we become more active. Through the procedure of scenario development, we investigate how we may collectively alter the directions of development in the base case. In the last section we learned how to examine the output of the model through tables and graphs. In this section we learn how to manipulate parametric assumptions of the model, in some cases even changing model structure.

Changing parameters requires that you understand more than you now do about model structure and about how the parameters control the working of the model. Subsequent chapters will help you gain that under-

---

**Important Note 1**

Appendix 2 to this volume lists the major parameters of IFs and describes how to use them. It also contains an introductory discussion that will help you better understand parameters. It is a very good idea to use that aid heavily while developing your own scenarios of the world; otherwise you may find yourself making changes that are quite different from those you intend.

---

standing. This section will simply introduce you to the mechanics of parameter change and model use for examining alternative understandings of the world or the impact of alternative human behavior (refer to Important Note 1).

China, like most countries, presumably has a desire to increase its power over time (or at the very least to avoid decreases in it). In this section we want to explore how China might pursue that aim. To do so, we need to learn how to (1) change the parameters of IFs, (2) run the model with new parameters, (3) compare results from the new run (scenario) with those of the base case, and (optionally) (4) save a result set or scenario file based on the new parameters.

▶ **1. Changing parameters.** A **parameter** is an exogenously specified number (or series of numbers over time) that influences the relationship between variables in the model. To change a parameter, it is necessary to know its name. The parameter that controls the allocation of government spending among categories is GK (governmental coefficient). Appendix 2 provides more detail on GK and other parameters. Look at its value in the base case for China across all types of spending (military, health, and so on). Note that the values for China are fixed, indicating that (in the model) China always allocates a constant percentage of government spending to the military and other categories. One approach China might take in an attempt to increase its power in the world is to boost its military spending.

To change the value of Chinese military spending, select CHANGE from the Main Menu and provide the variable/parameter name (GK), region number (10 for China), and spending category (1 for military). There are some variables, such as population (POP), for which one can provide only the initial (1990) conditions; the model limits your changes to those initial conditions and computes subsequent values itself. For most parameters, including GK, however, one can provide different values for each year, and in these cases the model will give you three different ways in which you can specify values. The first is to select a single value that will remain constant over time. The second is to indicate first and last values and to let the model compute intermediate values itself (it **interpolates** linearly—that is, it gradually and steadily changes the values for the years between first and last). The third is to proceed year-by-year and to specify unique values for each year.

Using this third option, we can create arms spending patterns of considerable complexity for China. In this case, let us begin by keeping the level unchanged for five years (1990 through 1994), then increasing it steadily between 1995 and 2000, and thereafter holding it at the higher level; we thus select the option of unique values every year (use the arrow keys). Although we could specify this pattern by typing in a value for each year, there are some tricks that make the introduction of this scenario easier:

a. *Repeating values.* To repeat the initial value from the base case for the first five years, type the initial value, followed by a colon, followed by 5 (e.g., .28:5). The model will then fill in five years (1990–1994) and request the value for 1995. Do this.

b. *Ramping values up or down.* We can increase the value from its level in 1994 to a higher level in 2000 by specifying that higher level, followed by an "@" sign, followed by the number of years over which we wish to climb to the higher or lower level. For instance, now specify .4@6.

c. *Stabilizing the value.* To hold the new value for the remaining years, simply specify the new value, colon, and a number equal to or greater than the remaining years (e.g., .4:40). The model will fill in the remaining years. <Enter> or <Esc> accepts the change and will give you the chance to change another parameter.

**2. Running the model.** You are now ready to run the model. From the Main Menu select the RUN option. You will be asked how many years you wish to forecast with the model. The maximum period is 46 years (1990 through 2035), but unless you have a fast computer, that would take a long time. For this analysis, it is quite adequate to look 16 years into the future (until 2005), so specify 16 and let the model run by touching <Enter>. IFs is a large and complicated model (as you have begun to see already) and therefore takes a long time to compute. The table in Appendix 3 will give you some idea how long. Unless you have an advanced microcomputer, you may wish to schedule some other activities (like reading ahead in this volume) for the periods in which the model is running.

**3. Comparing results from one model run (such as the base case) to others.** You may have noticed that whenever you display a variable from IFs it always appears in the Status Line at the bottom of the page (and in the table or graph header) with the number 0 in brackets. The zero refers to the active result set. Now that you have changed a model parameter, your working scenario (high Chinese military expenditures) is the active result set. Display both GK and GDS (government expenditures by destination sector) for Chinese military expenditures and see the results of your scenario.

You can compare these results with those from previous model runs (such as the base case). To understand how one does this, first go to the Main Menu and select FILES. Accept the default disk designation by touching <Enter>. Note the list of files under the heading "Files to Manage." The first of those files is automatically file number 1, the second is file number 2, and so on. That file number allows you to retrieve variables from individual result files or scenarios.

To put a variable from any file into a graph or table, simply call for it by name, followed by its number in brackets (no spaces). For instance, to compare military expenditures of China in the active "working" scenario you have just created (it is "working" because you have given it no name) with that in the base case (always file number 1 among those to manage), just ask for a table or graph showing two versions of GDS: GDS[0] and GDS[1]. It is unnecessary, but permitted, to use [0] to specify the active file because whenever you specify a variable name without brackets and a file number, the model provides [0] and references the active file. Note that, as we intended, Chinese military expenditures are higher after 1995 in the new scenario (GDS[0]) than they were in the base case (GDS[1]).

4. **Saving result files.** The working file you have created with changed Chinese military expenditures (which is also now the active file) is a temporary file and will be erased if you QUIT the model or reactivate the base case. To save the results from this or other working files, select SAVE from the Main Menu. Specify a default disk drive, such as A:, B:, or C:. Then give the working file a name (it must begin with a letter and can have up to eight letters or numbers in it). Try saving the new scenario you have created under a name such as HIGHEXP. Then return to the Files Management screen and you will see the new file in place and active (as indicated by an asterisk). When you create a complex scenario (this one is, of course, quite simple) you will often want to SAVE it before you QUIT the model.

You could subsequently save another version of the "working" file into the same "permanent" file (HIGHEXP) if you want; doing so will erase the earlier version. At no time are you allowed to save new results into the base case (file IFSBASE), which is protected from alteration.

5. **Managing result files.** Once you begin saving files, you must understand file management. You are allowed by the model to SAVE a maximum of eight result files. Since each result file takes nearly 0.5 megabytes of storage space on your disk, however, it is possible that you will have inadequate room to SAVE that many. If your disk fills up, a message will inform you that you can save no additional files. Even if your disk has room for the eight result files that IFs allows, you will eventually need to delete files to make room for others. To delete a file, select FILES from the Main Menu, use the arrow keys to point to the file (shade its name), and touch the <Del> key.

6. **Activating a result file.** At any time you can activate any of the files you have saved from earlier scenario analyses or can reactivate the base case. Reactivating the base case is especially useful if you have created a working scenario that you do not like and want to abandon. Simply select FILES, point to the file you want to (re)activate, and touch <Enter>. This will activate the file you have selected, and an asterisk will appear next to its name. The revised working file will disappear.

Explore further the high-Chinese-military-expenditure scenario you have created. For instance, compare the conventional and nuclear power (CPOW and NPOW) of China with that in the base case. Although you have increased the military power of China, you probably suspect that this was not without cost. Compare the physical quality of life (PQLI) or some of its components, such as literacy (LIT) or life expectancy (LIFEXP), with the base case.

There is a substantial debate concerning the implications of military spending for economic growth. Specifically, does military spending put people to work and increase the GNP, or does it divert resources from other uses (including education and health spending) that make a greater contribution to economic performance. Look at the GNP or GNP per capita (GNPPC) for China relative to the base case and determine the answer to that question that IFs provides. You should be aware that IFs does not give the definitive answer—the results of IFs depend totally on the structure and parameters of the model.

That dependency of results on parameters raises another issue. How does the model translate increased military spending into a measure of overall relative power (POWER)? It does so by weighting four elements of power (population, GNP, conventional military power, and nuclear power). The weights it uses are in the parameters PF1, PF2, PF3, and PF4, respectively. Those weights are arbitrary, and you can imagine different decisionmakers applying different weights (since World War II, those in Japan seem to have weighted GNP more heavily than conventional or nuclear military power). You may wish to look at, and perhaps alter, the power weights within IFs before you feel content with the scenario you have created.

When you are satisfied with development of the high-Chinese-military-expenditure scenario, it would be useful for the analysis in Chapter 4 to SAVE your working file into one called HIGHEXP (you may have already done this). Should you exit IFs now after saving HIGHEXP, you could start IFs again later, go to FILES, activate the HIGHEXP scenario, and proceed with further analysis.

## CONCLUSION

You now have all the basic tools you need to use IFs fully. Although you may not yet be fully comfortable in working with a computer simulation, what you primarily need at this point is experience. In addition, Chapters 2 and 3 have fairly fully explored the first of the three questions that we identified initially: Where do current changes appear to be taking us?

The next three chapters continue our exploration of the future in two ways. First, each addresses the second and third of our questions: How do we want the future to look? What leverage do we have? Second, each provides us with additional opportunity to match our mental models against the computer model of IFs and to use the simulation to explore possible alternative futures.

# FOUR

□   □   □

# The Pursuit of Security
# and Peace

What values do you bring to your thinking about the future, and how do you rank them? For instance, do you value maintenance of national security against external threat? Do you also value the development of cooperative and peaceful interaction among countries? If you value both, might there be some tension between the two values? For instance, might not actions intended to enhance national security, such as developing a new weapons system, actually threaten global peace?

Similarly, do you value economic well-being? How about equality of opportunity for individuals at birth? Is there any tension in this instance? For example, might an emphasis on efficient economic growth lead to a concentration of income in fewer hands and therefore the birth of more children into homes characterized by relative poverty? Do you value harmony with the environment? Do you also value human progress? Might progress ever disrupt the environment?

If your eyes begin to glaze over in reaction to such a barrage of questions, you are not alone. Nonetheless, stop to think for a moment about those questions (you may need to go back and read them again). None of them is unimportant. In fact, they are all central to choices about the human future. You do not need to answer them to your satisfaction now, and the fact is that you may never be able fully to resolve the trade-offs and hard choices they demand of you. It is, however, required of citizens in democracies that they regularly grapple with these questions.

The central question of this volume remains How do we act in the face of an uncertain future? Chapter 1 suggested, however, that we could proceed more efficiently by decomposing that question into three others:

69

1. Where do current changes appear to be taking us?
2. What kind of future do we value?
3. What leverage do we have in bringing about the future we value?

Chapters 2 and 3 explored where current changes appear to be taking us. This chapter initiates a set of three that turn our attention to preferred futures and to leverage. The three chapters provide six ways of looking at the world:

1. States (countries) struggling with the eternal need to provide their own security in the face of potentially hostile power from other states.
2. Communities of people, both local and global, seeking stability and peace.
3. Increasingly integrated and powerful markets providing an abundance of goods.
4. Rich and poor interacting in structures that maintain their relative position.
5. Knowledge and technology conferring benefits on humanity.
6. An ecosystem in which humanity is only one species, but one whose growth strains many elements of its physical and biological environment.

Each of these images gives rise to some preferences and understandings with respect to the world and thus can help us address questions concerning the kind of world we want and how we might bring it about. In essence, exploration of the understandings mapped by these alternative worldviews makes our very general problem more specific—that is, it helps us define some more specific choices we must make.

This chapter focuses our attention on the first two images of the world: competing states and evolving communities. Before we consider those two worldviews, however, we should return briefly to the issue of how we study change.

## CAUSAL UNDERSTANDINGS OF CHANGE

As we looked at trends and attempted extrapolations in the last two chapters, we quickly found that simple linear and exponential extrapolations were very often inadequate. Some growth processes are clearly limited. For instance, literacy cannot surpass 100 percent of the population, and oil production cannot grow indefinitely in the face of a fixed resource base. We therefore began to introduce alternative forms of extrapolation, such as S-shaped and bell-shaped curves, that *implicitly* recognized those limits.

Causal analysis helps us *explicitly* recognize such limits and more generally assists in understanding how complex processes might evolve in the future. At the root of causal analysis is the distinction between independent and dependent variables, or between cause and effect, respectively. Up until this point, we have discussed population growth as if it were a phenomenon independent of any other. We all know, however, that a large number of factors affect population growth. For instance, the availability of contraception changes birthrates. So too does the availability of opportunities for employment of prospective mothers. Similarly, the quality of medical care affects death rates, as does the prevalence of diseases such as AIDS and cancer. Thus changes in availability of contraceptives, employment of women, medical technology, and existence of disease are all causes (independent variables) of changed birthrates and death rates (the dependent variables).

We generally divide causal relationships into two categories. **Positive relationships** exist when an increase in the independent variable (such as AIDS) leads to an increase in the dependent variable (such as death rate). In such instances, of course, decreases in the independent variable lead also to decreases in the dependent variable. In contrast, **negative relationships** exist when an increase in the independent variable (such as contraception availability) causes a decrease in the dependent variable (such as birthrate). In those cases, decreases in the independent variable will lead to increases in the dependent variable.

It is, however, sometimes difficult to distinguish independent and dependent variables that clearly. For instance, a high rate of population growth in an Asian country might lead (cause) the government to institute a family planning program and increase the availability of contraceptives, which we have already suggested might cause the population growth rate to decline. In such a situtation we have a system of variables that *feed back* on each other in complex cause and effect relationships.

If population growth gives rise to family planning programs that control that same population growth, the process is reminiscent of a home thermostat that controls temperature by turning heat on and off as necessary (when temperature increases, the thermostat assures that heating ceases, which in turn leads temperature to decline). Figure 4.1 portrays the causal linkages in both the family planning and home heating examples. Note that one linkage in each case is positive and one is negative and that changes in a variable like population eventually feed back in a loop of linkages to that same variable. We call such a combination of linkages a **negative feedback loop**, and as these two examples suggest, such loops tend to produce relative stability in the processes they represent. A feed-

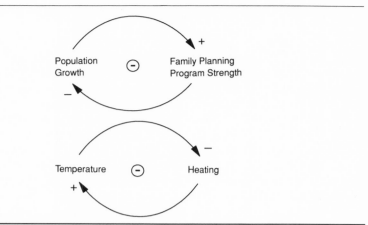

FIGURE 4.1    Negative feedback loops

back loop becomes a negative loop whenever it includes an odd number of individual negative linkages (for instance, three negative linkages out of six or seven relationships).

In contrast, consider what might happen if the death rate from AIDS in an African country overwhelmed the medical establishment in that country, which in turn made it impossible to cope with AIDS and led the death rate from AIDS to rise. This would be similar to the situation of a thermostat with its "wires crossed"—sensing too high a temperature, this rogue thermostat turns up the heat. Figure 4.2 portrays the two causal linkages in each of these examples. Note in the heating example that both linkages are positive, and we call this a **positive feedback loop**. The feedback loop will be positive, or self-reinforcing, whenever there is an even number of negative linkages (such as zero, two, or four). Thus the AIDS example is also a positive feedback loop. Processes in positive feedback loops tend to either collapse precipitously (like population in the AIDS-ridden country) or grow without bound (like the temperature in the afflicted home).

Many growth processes are combinations of positive and negative feedback loops. Consider, for instance, the growth of world oil production. On the one hand, increases in production facilitate further increases in production (for example, by leading to improved technology or by fueling deeper drilling). On the other hand, increases in production begin to deplete resources, which leads to restraints on production. If the first and positive loop is dominant, as it was globally for most of this century, oil production grows exponentially. When the second and negative loop becomes dominant, as it has in the United States and may soon be globally,

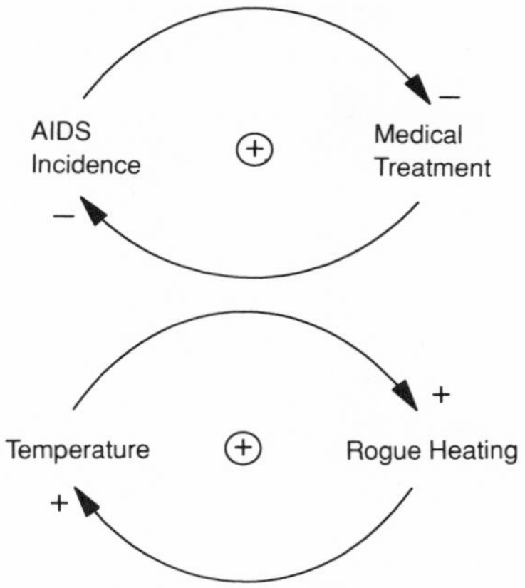

FIGURE 4.2    Positive feedback loops

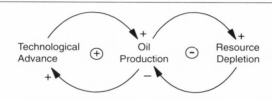

FIGURE 4.3    Interaction of feedback loops

oil production stabilizes and eventually declines. Figure 4.3 represents this interacting pair of feedback loops.

Causal analysis of human systems can quickly become very complex because the number of interacting variables and feedback loops to which they give rise grows rapidly. One strength of computer models is that they represent that complexity explicitly and can rapidly compute its consequences. The complexity can easily overwhelm the ability of creators of such models, however, and we will always be uncertain if all important causal linkages are present and specified correctly.

Looking at human systems through the perspectives of the six worldviews will allow us to build the complexity of our own mental models incrementally. By the time we finish considering the six worldviews, we may have a mental model with a quite large number of explicit linkages. We begin by considering the world of those who emphasize linkages built around states.

## STATES AND THEIR
## INTERACTION: REALISM

The state is a universal modern variant of what we can call "security groups"—that is, organizations devoted in significant part to assuring the physical security of their members. Other examples include tribes, empires, clans, criminal associations, and street gangs. Every state (or street gang) has a territory with reasonably well-established borders, a defined population, a functioning government, and recognition by other states as a legal equal. We more commonly designate states as countries (although Taiwan is a country that many states do not recognize as an equal and therefore do not treat as a state).

States have functions other than the provision of security for their citizens. The security function is so central to their existence, however, that we frequently define their pursuit of it as "high politics" and designate struggles over economic, environmental, or other benefits they might provide as "low politics."

The world has no organizational units that can dictate to states or maintain order in conflicts among them. In fact, the global environment for states is fundamentally anarchic. Thus states act to provide their own security, although they may enter into alliances of convenience with other states. Again, one can see the analogies with a society that has powerful clans or street gangs but lacks effective central police authority. Alliances of convenience also form in such societies but seldom persist. It is often said that states have permanent interests but no permanent friends or enemies.

According to the worldview we call realism, the world is a self-help system. States that want to protect or enhance their own security must rely on their own efforts and skills to do so. Frequently this requires the development of substantial military capabilities. Power is a central concept or variable in the realist worldview. Power is such an important means to an end (enhanced security) that it practically becomes an end in itself. Central to the purposes of states must be the protection and enhancement of power.

The pursuit of power may set in motion positive feedback loops. Those states that have power may be able to use that power to obtain still more. In the colonial era, for instance, Spain used its naval power to conquer most of Latin America and to extract gold and silver from its new territories. It could then use that plunder to build more ships and motivate more soldiers. Figure 4.4 represents that positive loop.

Similarly, an economically powerful country like Britain during the eighteenth century could use its high productivity to conquer foreign markets and exchange its products for raw materials that it could bring

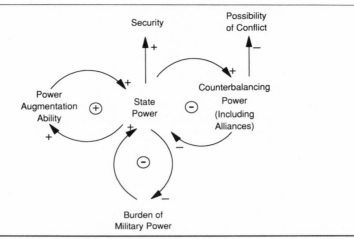

FIGURE 4.4    A simplified model of realism

home and use to further enhance its productivity. Moreover, it could use those economic strengths to hire nationals in its colonies to create overseas military capabilities with limited drain on its domestic resources. The overseas military forces could then, in turn, assist traders in opening up further markets for the British. For instance, the British shipped opium produced in India to China. When the Chinese banned the import in 1839, the British responded with military action. A series of opium wars and treaties following British victories opened an increasingly large number of ports in China to British trade. History abounds with examples of power begetting power that are perhaps less odious but little less clear-cut.

As these examples suggest, power includes but is not limited to military capabilities. Power also benefits from economic and demographic strength. The most powerful countries of the world today are, in general, the economically and demographically largest: the United States, Russia, China, India, Japan, and Germany.

Whereas a country's own power may enhance its security, that power will threaten others. Those others will normally react by establishing counterbalancing capabilities, thereby bringing under control the power of any state that threatens to become dominant and potentially aggressive. In so doing they will not only increase their own security but lessen the probability of conflict. Conflict among relative equals will inevitably be expensive, and the outcome will be uncertain. Therefore a balance of power makes conflict an irrational enterprise (see Fig. 4.4). Realists argue that military conflict is inevitable in relations among countries because there will always be conflicts of interest among them and there is no central arbitrator. Nonetheless, pursuit of power balance can produce peace most of the time by making conflict irrational.

It is, however, not always possible to offset the power of others by building one's own. Turkey could hardly have been expected to cope alone with the buildup of the Soviet Union during the cold war. Thus alliances become necessary because they augment the negative, counterbalancing feedback loop on power. Most of Europe joined an alliance against Napoleon's France when that country's power was growing without clear limits. Similarly, Turkey joined with much of Europe in the North Atlantic Treaty Organization (NATO) to counteract the growing power of the Soviet Union after World War II. One might argue that most of Europe has now also joined an economic alliance called the European Community, or Common Market, to balance the overwhelming economic power of the United States and, more recently, Japan.

Realists also often argue that the growth of potentially overwhelming state power (through the positive loop of power breeding power) is further controlled by the economic burden it begins to place upon the country. Historically, empires have not always ceased to grow simply because they met opposing power. They sometimes have overreached their ability to sustain a military buildup and thereby weakened the economic base of that military. Paul Kennedy (1987: xvii) argues that the Hapsburg monarchs "overextended themselves in the course of repeated conflicts and became militarily top-heavy for their weakening economic base."[1] The United Kingdom did the same in the nineteenth and early twentieth centuries, and both the Soviet Union and the United States reached critical points more recently. Figure 4.4 represents this additional negative feedback loop as well.

The prescriptions of the realist view are quite obvious from its causal portrait of the world. Each state, in the absence of any protective central authority, must fend for itself in the anarchic global system. It can do so in two ways. First, it can build its own power and wisely use its existing power to attain still more. Second, it can join in temporary alliance with other countries to oppose any state that threatens to achieve a dominant position.

There are, as with any recipe, difficulties in the implementation. Consider modern Germany, faced with the very proximate power of Russia. To what degree should Germany rely upon building its own counterpower? There are dangers there, including overburdening the economy and eliciting attempts by other states to balance the power of Germany in turn. And to what degree should Germany trust other countries to be faithful in their NATO alliance commitments to Germany should Russia once again become a significant military threat? There are dangers there as well.

In the modern world economy, the United States faces a significant economic challenge from both Japan and the European Community. Should it react primarily by strengthening its domestic economy, or should it enter into economic alliance, perhaps with Canada and Mexico? Realists see international politics as much more an art than a science. Great diplomats and leaders have historically been able to strike the critical balances among strategies, whereas lesser souls have failed.

There is another prescription, however, that competes with the realist set. It rejects the premise of inherently antagonistic relations between polities such as Germany and Russia or between economies such as the United States and Japan. It argues instead that extensive and ongoing cooperation is possible on a broad scale internationally. It views the world not solely through the lens of state system anarchy, state interest, and power but in considerable part through the lens of growing global community.

## THE GROWTH OF GLOBAL COMMUNITY: GLOBALISM

The globalist perspective generally begins with an attack on realism. First, it criticizes the assumption that states will behave as rational, unitary actors. Misperception of power balances and the intentions of other actors are so common that those balances do not sufficiently dampen conflict. Internal forces within a state (from intense nationalism to religious or ideological dogmatism) may drive even experienced and otherwise cautious leaders into unwise foreign adventures. Thus, say globalists, the realist is too sanguine with respect to the ability of power seeking and power balancing to produce security and relative peace. Remember that Iraq attacked Iran in 1980 and invaded Kuwait in 1990. Neither war secured the gains that Iraq anticipated but both cost very large numbers of lives (casualties in the Iran-Iraq war approached 400,000). Efforts at power balancing in the Middle East by Iran, Saudi Arabia, the United States, and even Iraq itself did not succeed in avoiding catastrophe.

The critique goes further. The attempt to balance power with power, say the globalists, often sets up a destructive positive feedback loop. What one state views as a defensive buildup in reaction to the overly great power of another, the second will likely view as a potentially offensive threat. Thus it will, in turn, undertake a buildup. Both realists and globalists know this logic as that of the **security dilemma.** Globalists argue that the logic sets up arms races that increase the probability of war. They

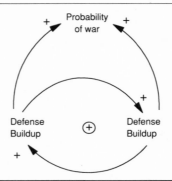

FIGURE 4.5   The security dilemma

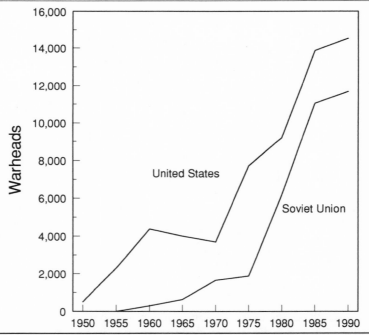

FIGURE 4.6   Strategic nuclear warhead balance. *Sources:* John P. Holdren, "The Dynamics of the Nuclear Arms Race," in *Nuclear Weapons and the Future of the Arms Race*, ed. Avner Cohen and Steven Lee (Totowa, N.J.: Rowman and Allanheld, 1986), 41–84; International Institute for Strategic Studies, *The Military Balance* (London: IISS, 1989), 212.

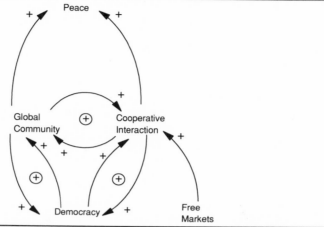

FIGURE 4.7   A simplified model of globalism

point to the arms race before World War I as one example. Perhaps increasing levels of arms will by themselves raise the probability of their use. Perhaps one state will finally achieve an advantage or recognize an imminent disadvantage and therefore initiate conflict.[2] Figure 4.5 represents such a destructive pattern of interaction, and Figure 4.6 shows one possible real-world result of that dilemma, the arms race between the United States and the USSR during the cold war.

If it is too dangerous to rely on the rational judgment of states in power balances and the competitive logic of the security dilemma constantly works to initiate and fuel dangerous arms races, what can globalists offer in place of the realist vision? Fundamentally, they put forward a competing vision of growing global community, accompanied by increasing levels of cooperative interaction (see Fig. 4.7). The mutual strengthening of community and cooperative interaction creates a positive feedback loop that makes war increasingly expensive (by disrupting valuable interchange), unproductive, and difficult to initiate, thereby encouraging peace.

Globalists point to the increased integration of world economies through trade and financial flows. They draw our attention to steadily increasing levels of interpersonal contact across borders through tourism, business travel, and governmental linkage. They argue that rising demand for international approaches to transboundary environmental problems underlies additional cooperative initiatives. They claim that the sharp rise in numbers of intergovernmental and international nongovernmental organizations that we saw in Chapter 2 verifies the growth of global community and cooperative interaction.

Realists are quick to point out that increased interaction does not always lead to cooperation. The United States had a lower level of interaction with Europe during the nineteenth century than during the twentieth and managed in the former century to avoid involvement in most European disputes. Britain had closer interaction with much of Asia prior to 1950 than subsequently, and its relationships with Asian countries have been better in the postcolonial period.

Globalists acknowledge this issue and emphasize that it is the combination of growth in global community and increased interaction that is beginning to dampen international conflict. Moreover, to the extent that the global community is becoming increasingly unified around the principles of Western liberalism (individual freedoms, market economies, and political democracy), that community promises to be even more peaceful. Whereas democracies have frequently fought with nondemocracies, it is remarkably difficult to cite examples of democracies going to war with other democracies. Some have suggested that the War of 1812 and the American Civil War are such examples.[3] Yet the War of 1812 between the United States and Great Britain preceded the British Reform Bills of 1832, 1867, and 1884 that granted voting rights to the middle and working classes. The Confederacy that fought the Union not only protected slave holding but never existed prior to the Civil War. In the case of essentially all exceptions, the commitment of one or both countries to democracy appears shallow.

## THE CONTEMPORARY DILEMMA

Our summary of two competing understandings of the world suggests two primary conclusions. First, there is literally almost no one who does not value peace in global affairs and who does not, in fact, rank it exceptionally high on their list of values. Both realists and globalists do so. Second, the real problem we face is in deciding how to pursue peace, in gauging what leverage we have in bringing about our desired futures. Is it best, as the realists argue, to pursue primarily security, both as a value in itself and as a way of establishing a balance of power and therefore relative peace? Or is it best, as the globalists claim, to emphasize the development of global community, again because we value that community, but also because we believe it will further peaceful interaction? The problem is not simply abstract. It frames our answer to the question concerning the leverage we have in shaping the future.

Consider the contemporary position of the United States. The cold war is over. The armed forces of the former Soviet Union have left Czechoslovakia and Hungary and are scheduled to exit the former East Germany by 1994. The republics of the former USSR have declared their indepen-

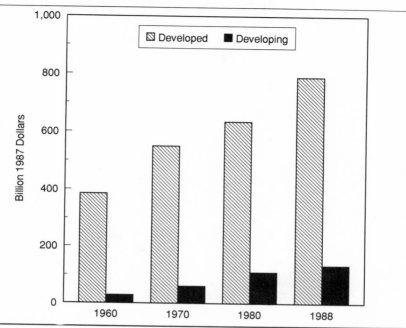

FIGURE 4.8  Military expenditures. *Source:* Based on data in Ruth Leger Sivard, *World Military and Social Expenditures 1991* (Washington, D.C.: World Priorities, 1991), 50.

dence, and it appears that most, if not all, will gradually become sovereign states in reality and not just in name. Moreover, nearly all political units of the former "Soviet empire" have denounced communism and officially instituted liberal democracy and opted for market economies. Obviously, the reality will lag behind the official commitments to political and economic reforms, and some regression is inevitable, but the old bipolar world order, centered on the conflict between East and West, has collapsed.

There is now much discussion of a new world order. What might be the character of that new world order? How should we bring it into being? In general terms, this chapter suggests two competing visions of that order. The first emphasizes the enduring nature of security concerns and the importance of giving them primary and active attention. The second stresses the opportunity for significantly advancing an emerging global community.

The breadth of support by Americans in 1991 of President Bush's call for action against Iraq after its invasion of Kuwait owed much to his creative fusing of these two disparate visions of the new world order. On the one hand, the United States took strong military action in the name of pre-

TABLE 4.1    Satellite Launch Capabilities

|  | Date of First Launch | Launches in 1990 |
|---|---|---|
| USSR | October 1957 | 96 |
| United States | February 1958 | 31 |
| France | November 1965 | NA |
| Japan | February 1970 | 7 |
| China | April 1970 | 5 |
| Britain | October 1971 | NA |
| India | July 1980 | 1 |
| Israel | September 1988 | 1 |

NA = not available.

Sources: *Christian Science Monitor*, May 15, 1990, 13; World Almanac, *The World Almanac and Book of Facts 1992* (New York: World Almanac, 1991), 667; Leonard S. Spector with Jacqueline R. Smith, *Nuclear Ambitions* (Boulder: Westview Press, 1990).

serving the balance of power in the Middle East and of preventing one country from securing territory, oil resources, and nuclear weapons in an effort to upset that balance. On the other hand, a global coalition came together under the auspices of the United Nations to give military action the blessing of what appeared to be a newly unified global community.

The first vision stresses that important security threats remain. The former Soviet Union poses the most obvious and near-term threats. There are myriad difficulties associated with the breakdown of the country, including the control by several republics of nuclear weapons, the possiblity that some weapons will fall into the hands of other countries or even terrorist forces, and the danger of conflicts among and within the republics. In the somewhat longer run, a Russia liberated of costly external burdens could undergo still another political change and emerge as a revitalized threat. It will remain the only country able to threaten the basic existence of the United States for at least a decade and possibly much longer.

In addition, there is the growing military strength of many countries in the less-developed world. As Figure 4.8 shows, military expenditures in the South (the developing countries) have risen faster than those in the North (the developed countries) for many years (the ratio has narrowed from 14-to-1 in 1960 to 6-to-1 in 1988). Also an increasing number of countries have one or both of two important elements of nuclear capacity: an atomic bomb and missiles capable of launching satellites into orbit and therefore delivering bombs. Table 4.1 documents the proliferation of the missile capabilities (Table 2.6 presents information on the proliferation of nuclear capabilities). Many other countries, including Iraq, North Korea, and Pakistan, seek or have sought both capabilities.

Finally, there is always the possibility that one or more of the countries that the United States now considers allies could become a military adversary. Realists emphasize that the era of goodwill among countries in the early 1920s succumbed very quickly to intense rivalries as the economic pressures of the Depression pitted countries against each other in economic competition, and the rise of fascist and militaristic governments quickly squelched perceptions that World War I had made the world safe for democracy and therefore peaceful coexistence. In the post–cold war era some foresee similar economic desperation and comparable political changes.

The second contemporary vision emphasizes that global community is developing. We traced with the trend analysis of Chapter 2 the global spread of democracy and the historical growth of intergovernmental and international nongovernmental organization. Both have advanced quite steadily during this century, and the cumulative growth of both is remarkable.

Globalists recognize that the existence of any major cleavage line greatly weakens global community. In the post–World War II period there were two such cleavages. The first pitted the communist world, or East, against the more market-oriented economies of the West. The second divided the relatively wealthy and economically developed global North from the poorer global South. With exceptions such as China, Cuba, Vietnam, and North Korea, the communist world has evaporated and the old East-West cleavage has healed. The primary global cleavage now is between the global rich and poor (Chapter 2 showed the evolution of the income gap), reinforced to some degree by secondary cleavages such as that between some within the Moslem world and the North. It is easy to predict that the primary attention of globalists in the next decade will be to narrowing the North-South gap, economically, politically, and socially.

## SPECIFIC CONTEMPORARY ISSUES AND CHOICES

Given competing visions for the new world order, citizens and leaders in countries around the world face many key decisions. For instance, what should be the balance of attention devoted to domestic versus international issues? Both globalists and realists tend to provide the same answer to that question: attention to international issues remains critical, even after the cold war.

There are, however, many citizens in all countries, and especially in the wearied superpowers, who now call for a return to domestic issues. Variations of nationalism underlie many of those calls (consider the growth of nationalist movements in Germany, France, Russia, and elsewhere). Some such voices come also from a realism that emphasizes the need for attention to rebuilding the domestic bases of power after a prolonged period of spending that power abroad. Most contemporary realists, however, argue that the proponents of inward attention ignore the necessity of constant attention to potential external threats. The argument from former President Richard Nixon in 1992 grew from such sentiments: By not giving substantial aid, he asserted, the United States was missing a historic opportunity to shape events in Russia and consolidate improvements in its own security position. Most globalists similarly believe that the potential for solidifying the worldwide forces for democracy in the last decade of the second millennium constitutes a truly unique opportunity.

One decision that all the proponents of active international involvement now face is primary issue focus. Should most attention be on military-strategic issues (high politics) or on economic and environmental issues (low politics)? Involvement with all issues requires resources, both financial commitment and the commitment of time by busy top decisionmakers. Here realists and globalists begin to diverge. Most of the former continue to emphasize military-strategic issues, including the building of entirely new security structures. Globalists participate in the discussion of those issues but also see increased cooperation on economic and environmental issues as a key to strengthening community.

### Security Structures and Issues

Important general choices face us with respect to security structures. Should the approach to them emphasize individual-country or small-group action, or should it stress broad collective action? Memos leaked from the U.S. Department of Defense in 1992 suggested that the United States could and should actively pursue unilateralism, that it had the option of strengthening its position as the only viable superpower. That argument seems to flow from a naive realism (perhaps even nationalism), one that fails to recognize realism's own arguments about the inevitable growth of power to balance power. Would the rest of the world really accede to such a dominant position of the United States?

An alternative to unilateralism for the United States and other developed countries (and one that a revision of the Defense Department report subsequently supported) is military cooperation. One aspect of such cooperation would be to maintain an active NATO, even though the cold war mission for which it was created has vanished.

A globalist might build upon such a prescription but give it a different twist. The United States could potentially propose that NATO become an alliance of democracies in collective defense of democracies against internal or external threats and be open to all other stable democracies. Many globalists would, moreover, shift considerable attention to the much broader and nonmilitary Conference on Security and Cooperation in

Europe (CSCE), an organization that now includes the Central and Eastern European states of the former Soviet bloc and Soviet Union, even those in which democracy is far from consolidated. Still others would argue that it is most important now to build a real security capability within the United Nations. Realists remain wary of strengthening any organization that has the potential of restricting state sovereignty. Even they will, however, sometimes look to the UN or to other international organizations for instruments with which to address key problems such as nuclear proliferation.

It is likely that competing visions of the best route to peace will lead to some interim compromise attachment to each of these options. That is, it is quite possible that NATO, the CSCE, and the UN will all become at least temporarily stronger after the cold war.

Moreover, there are some actions on which nearly all analysts can agree. For instance, there is steadily increasing international support for conscious adoption of nonprovocative defense. That is, whatever the appropriate level of arms, they should be as clearly defensive as possible in order not to provoke reaction by potential adversaries, bound to us by the logic of the security dilemma. For example, anti-tank weaponry is generally preferable to tanks because the latter can quickly capture territory while the former is most useful in defending it. This consensus underlay the quick acceptance in 1991–1992 by large numbers of countries (including Russia) of the U.S. proposal for open skies, that is, for allowing aircraft overflights of each other's territory to verify compliance with arms control agreements and the adoption of generally defensive postures.

Beyond the issue of structure for a new security system, more specific security concerns face states in the post–cold war order. One involves identification of potential threats. Where will the major threats to global peace arise in the next decade or two? One answer is that most will probably arise from escalation of South-South conflicts. In the past such conflicts, like those in the Balkans before World War I, often became the kindling for larger conflagrations. Today the existence of extremely well-armed states in the less-developed world creates substantial dangers. Some of those became evident as the UN experts in Iraq disclosed the extent and achievements of the military buildup in that country before its invasion of Kuwait. Another example is that many of the new states arising in the area of the former Soviet Union, including Russia itself, face major economic problems while simultaneously possessing great military strength. It is not difficult to imagine old wounds, such as the treaties imposed by imperial Russia on China, giving rise to new conflicts of considerable magnitude.

A second type of future security threat comes from the substantial dependence of large numbers of countries on the energy resources of a relatively small number of exporters. States have long sought to guarantee access to energy sources and preferably to gain long-term control of them. That impulse led, for instance, to the rivalries between Britain, France, and Germany over concessions for oil in the Middle East between the two world wars. The United States temporarily ended that rivalry after World War II by moving firmly into a dominant position within the region. Counterbalancing actions of the Soviet Union, coupled with nationalistic and religious forces within the region itself, gradually eroded U.S. dominance. Today the countries of OPEC, especially those of the Middle East, potentially have great control over energy resources that have become essential to the economies of the Western developed world. The OPEC countries demonstrated the disruption that such control can cause when they reduced oil exports for political-economic reasons in 1973–1974 and drove the world price of oil up by a factor of four. Oil-importing states face continuing choices with respect to minimizing threats of supply disruption and dramatic price increases. How disruptive to their economies might another oil shock like that of 1973–1974 be?

Globalists see opportunities for peace as well as security challenges in the contemporary environment. One of the opportunities is for dramatic arms reductions in light of the new relationship between the former superpowers. Arms control gained considerable momentum in the late 1980s and early 1990s, starting with the Intermediate-range Nuclear Force (INF) Treaty in 1987 that committed the United States and the USSR to eliminate all missiles with ranges between 500 and 5,500 kilometers. In late 1990 the leaders of NATO and the former Warsaw Pact signed another key treaty defining and greatly reducing Conventional Forces in Europe (CFE). In mid-1991 the United States and the USSR signed the Strategic Arms Reduction Treaty (START), concluding a negotiation initiated in 1982 to reduce nuclear arms. They followed the signing with a series of unilateral actions to reduce various conventional and nuclear forces, to end long-standing alert status for some nuclear systems, and to postpone or cancel assorted weapons-development plans. In mid-1992 the United States, Russia, Belarus, the Ukraine, and Kazakhstan signed a treaty that extended the START agreement to those newly independent states of the former Soviet Union and committed all but Russia to eliminate nuclear weapons completely by the end of the decade. Pursuit of such cooperative opportunities (and similar ones with respect to energy) is a choice in quite stark opposition to the proposal of some that the United States unilaterally pursue security through maintenance of military pre-eminence. What economic and security benefits might arms control bring?

### Economic Structures and Issues

Specific and difficult choices also face countries with respect to economic structures in the new world order. Again, there is the option of economic nationalism, based either on purely nationalistic sentiment or on a realism that wishes to focus on internal economic power building. Especially in a world of prolonged and deep economic travail, like that of the 1930s, such individualistic options attract much support. Moreover, there is a long global history of mercantilist (economically nationalistic) policy choices—of putting up protectionist barriers to foreign imports and of simultaneously promoting one's own goods abroad. One important variation on such economic nationalism in the modern environment is the formation of trade blocs. It can be argued that in response to a United States that is seeking with Canada and Mexico to cobble together a North American Free Trade Agreement (NAFTA) and to a European Community that may become a Fortress Europe discouraging goods from outside, it is natural that Japan should create an Asian trading zone to guarantee itself access to raw materials and markets.

Naturally, most citizens of Europe and the United States believe that the causality, or action-reaction, based on trade issues is the reverse of that just suggested—that Japan initiated the closure of markets. As with security issues, however, even many economic realists (mercantilists) recognize that economic hostility often begets further closure of markets abroad (like the upward spiral of arms in the security dilemma) and therefore a downward spiral in trade.

Whereas nationalists may not care (and may favor a return to economic independence even at some cost in lost economic options), many realists and most globalists argue instead for the choice of pursuing open international trading systems. They often differ, however, on means. Globalists frequently propose aggressive strengthening of the post–World War II Bretton Woods economic order, including use of the multilateral General Agreement on Tariffs and Trade (GATT) to reduce barriers against imported goods. Realists frequently propose selective use of unilateral pressure and negotiations to break through barriers in specific trading relationships. For instance, realists in the United States have advocated a get-tough stance with respect to access to Japanese markets. In fact, some supporters of NAFTA see it not as an end in itself but as a way of putting leverage on recalcitrant trading partners. What balance should countries strike between regional and global trading arrangements?

Additional choices face us with respect to the use of foreign aid in efforts to narrow the wide economic gap between the world's rich and poor. Globalists generally support increased assistance, frequently arguing that some of the "peace dividend" from the ending of the cold war should flow to the global South. Realists are again less certain. They are much less likely than globalists to support aid as a mechanism for economic development of states that ultimately may become adversaries. Should the rich countries really support the advance in relative power of China, India, or

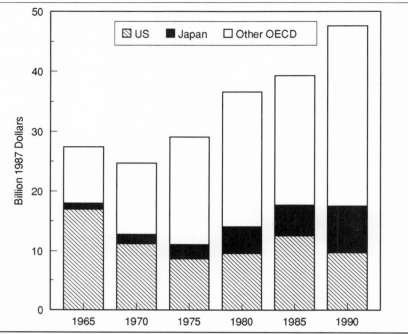

FIGURE 4.9  Net flows of development assistance by donor. *Source:* Based on data in World Bank, *World Development Report* (New York: Oxford University Press, 1992), 254–255.

Brazil? Especially when there is a real need for the resources at home? Realists are more likely to support such aid if it maintains political stability in recipient countries and thus reduces a source of larger state system friction or if it actually provides some leverage for the donor, such as securing favorable votes in the United Nations. Figure 4.9 traces the historical flows of aid from the OECD, or Organization for Economic Cooperation and Development (which includes almost all of the economically developed, market economies).

An important new foreign aid issue has arisen, that to which former U.S. President Nixon and many others helped draw attention in 1992. Should aid now flow to Russia and the other independent states of the old USSR? If so, how much and under what conditions? For instance, should aid depend on particular changes in economic, political, and security structures?

What future do we want and what leverage do we have? Answers to those two questions depend not on extrapolation but on causal analysis and soul-searching value clarification. And it is clear that there are no easy answers. Scholars and politicians are divided. You may be uncertain.

Nonetheless, you will be asked to make decisions, minimally in the voting booth and often in your own career and personal life. That is the quandary you face. Inaction is, of course, simply acceptance of the choices that others make on your behalf.

## THE PURSUIT OF SECURITY AND COMMUNITY: EXPLORATION OF IFs

In this section we turn to the computer simulation, IFs, for help in extending our understandings of the issues surrounding security and peace. Use of that model will by no means resolve the problem of choice in the face of uncertain futures. In fact, no computer model can fully capture the complexity of the choices we have discussed. The model can, however, help us better grasp the complex causal dynamics of state interaction. Moreover, interaction with it will involve you actively in the process of choice.

You may need to return to Chapter 3 and review the use of the model. This discussion assumes that you know not only how to examine results from the base case of the model but also how to change parameters, run the model, and compare results with the base case (as discussed in the last section of Chapter 3).

We begin our analysis with IFs by looking at the long-term relative power decline of the United States and Russia (that will also allow you to refresh your memory on the display of the base case before plunging into scenario analysis). We then move into a consideration of the action-reaction dynamics that might characterize the Chinese-Russian pair in response to the kind of buildup of arms spending by China that we explored at the end of Chapter 3. We also consider the possibility that such an arms race might lead to war. In addition, we look at the possibility of embargoes by OPEC on the export of oil and the threat they might pose to importing states.

After this exploration of IFs through largely realist eyes, we turn to a globalist perspective. In particular, we consider the leverage that developed countries might have to reduce the wide income gaps between the rich and poor countries of the world. Throughout all of this guided analysis, you should feel free to explore your own avenues of thought, which is, of course, the principal purpose of a model like IFs.

### The Relative Decline of the United States and Russia

The distribution of power among the largest countries of the world influences the way in which those countries interact with each other and the manner in which they interact with less-powerful countries. After World

War II the United States and the former Soviet Union emerged as the most powerful states in the interstate system. They engaged in an intense rivalry that several times came near to erupting into war. They used their power to bind less-powerful countries to themselves in military and economic relationships.

In recent years the relative power of the two superpowers has declined (especially that of the former USSR). Although both have grown demographically and economically and both have added to their military capabilities, their rates of growth in all of these areas have lagged behind those of other countries. As other actors such as Japan and the European Community have emerged with comparable demographic and economic size, and with growing military capability, the rapt attention the superpowers long devoted to each other has been increasingly diverted to those other actors. And the ability of the United States and Russia to lead groupings of states in conflict with each other has declined. These consequences of shifting power balances became especially obvious in the last half of the 1980s, but the probability is that the global political structure will continue to change dramatically throughout the 1990s.

How large are the populations, economies, and military capabilities of the United States and Russia relative to other countries? What are the trends over time? How fast is Japan surpassing Russia economically? How fast is the European Community overtaking the United States? To begin answering such questions, call up from the base case tables, graphs, and pie charts of population (POP) and gross national product (GNP).

IFs also contains some indicators of absolute military power. It breaks that power into two types, conventional (CPOW) and strategic, or nuclear (NPOW). In addition, you can look at an overall index of relative power (POWER) that summarizes the demographic, economic, and conventional/nuclear military positions of countries and regional groupings.

*How does IFs compute these power measures?* We discussed in Chapter 3 the computation of GNP and population size and thus will explain here only the military and aggregate power measures. Government spending is directed into five categories: military, education, health, foreign aid, and other. Military spending is split between conventional and nuclear spending (for most countries it is entirely conventional). Conventional military spending is converted to conventional military force units that augment existing strength (but gradually depreciate in value). Nuclear military spending is converted to megatons (million tons) of nuclear explosive capability (these, again, gradually depreciate). The measure of relative aggregate power (POWER) computes a country's (or region's) portion of total world population, of total world GNP, of total world conventional power, and of total world nuclear power. It then weights those four portions (by PF1, PF2, PF3, and PF4), providing a crude guess at the country's share of world power. Where does the measure suggest aggregate power is rising and falling? Why?

## The Action-Reaction Dynamic: China and Russia

In a system characterized by the necessity of self-help with respect to security, one common pattern is that actors like China arm themselves in efforts to enhance their security. Since most arms can be used either defensively or offensively, however, even honestly defensive actions can lessen the security of other states. Re-create the scenario for increased Chinese power that we created at the end of Chapter 3 (or reactivate it, if you saved it). The increase in power that China managed in that scenario came at the expense of other countries and regions (to see this you could compare the power [POWER] of other actors in the high-Chinese-military-expenditure scenario with that in the base case).

Under the conditions of the security dilemma, when defensive action is viewed as potentially threatening to other states by reducing their relative power, it leads them to attempt similarly to improve their own defenses, setting in motion the action-reaction dynamic of arms races. The nature of the dynamic will vary over time and across groupings of states. For instance, significant increases in arms spending by Argentina would be unlikely to cause any reaction in Pakistan, because leaders in the latter state would see no conflict of interests between the states and would doubt that Argentina could pose a credible threat, even after a major buildup. The leadership of Britain would take more notice; when Argentina used its military strength in 1982 temporarily to occupy the Falkland Islands (claimed by the Argentines as the Malvinas), Britain sent a naval task force to recapture them. Nonetheless, Britain's military strength is so much greater than that of Argentina that it might respond with a very marginal increase in its own arms spending.

In Brazil the reaction could be proportionally much greater, especially if the buildup in Argentina were to ignore the agreements with Brazil that restrict spending on nuclear weapons programs. One can imagine circumstances under which Brazil would match every 1 percent of additional spending by Argentina with increases of 2 percent.

We can use IFs to examine such arms races and to investigate their consequences. Let us focus on the relationship between China and Russia. There have been a few small military clashes between the two states since World War II. China has never fully accepted the loss of lands to Russia in "unequal treaties" during the late 1800s. A China that declared its antipathy to Russia, while initiating a program of substantially increased military spending (as in the earlier scenario), might elicit a substantial reaction in Russia.

► Let us explore the implications of a response in kind by Russia to the military buildup we have created in China. That is, let us build on the scenario of increased Chinese defense spending developed in Chapter 3 (either activate the file you saved as HIGHEXP or create such a file with the procedures described in Chapter 3). We will build on that earlier scenario by changing some parameters in addition to the government spending coefficient (GK) for the military of China. You can change as many parameters as you want when building a scenario. Unless you reactivate the base case or stop the model and begin again, all of your changes remain cumulatively in effect. It is a good idea, however, to change only one parameter at a time and to examine the results of your changes before making others; otherwise you will be uncertain as to which parameter change is responsible for the results you obtain.

In order to set up and look at an action-reaction dynamic, we need to specify the members of the acting alliance (in this case only China) and the reacting alliance (in this case only the Soviet Union). The parameter name is ALLY. Set a constant value for all years for China equal to 1 (actor) and for Russia equal to 2 (reactor). As discussed above, the reactivity of Russia (REACM) might also vary. Although you could change that, for now leave it at the default value of 1.0 (Russia will increase its military expenditures at the same annual percentage rate that China does). (Refer to Important Note 2.)

► Before running the model again, it is a good idea to display GK (the military expenditures of China), ALLY, and other initial conditions/parameters you have changed (such as the power-weighting factors) and to make certain that they now have the values you want them to have.

After you have run the model (from 1990 to 2005), explore some of the results. In particular you might want to compare military expenditures of Russia with those of the base case. And look also at the loss in quality of life (PQLI) and economic performance (GNPPC) that Russia must bear in order to react proportionately to the Chinese buildup.[4]

---

**Important Note 2**

If you have just now created and run the HIGHEXP scenario (rather than reactivating the file you saved under that name) and you attempt to change the value of ALLY, you will find that you have been moved forward in time to the end of your run horizon. You can reset your position in time to 1990 by typing RESET instead of a variable name within the dialog section of CHANGE or by selecting the option to reset the current file to 1990 within the dialog portion of RUN. If you do not reset time before making changes in parameters, your changes will affect only the years beyond your current position in time.

The basic action-reaction dynamic that we see in this arms race cannot go on without limit. When increases in military expenditure on either or both sides are sufficiently large, they will have a negative influence on economic growth. In this particular scenario, you have forced the Russians to increase military spending at the expense of other governmental spending (when they increased the allocation to the military, the model automatically decreased the spending on health and education [it uses a procedure called normalization to assure that total expenditures are unchanged]). You can see that this scenario has a considerable cost to both parties to the arms race in terms of slower growth in some aspects of quality of life that depend on other governmental expenditures. That has a secondary effect on economic growth, because in IFs quality of the work force affects its productivity. Were you to increase the tax rate (TAXRA) in order to augment total Russian governmental spending and protect spending on health and education in the face of higher military spending, the economic cost might be still greater, however, because you would begin to cut into the investment potential of the private economy.

The model monitors the cost of higher military spending to economic growth in a variable called burden (BURDM), which is computed as the ratio of economic growth in the reacting state(s) (given higher military spending) to the rate of economic growth. It is called a multiplier variable because it modifies a preliminary calculation of defense spending by multiplication. Thus as the economic burden *grows,* the values of BURDM *shrink* and begin to constrain military spending. Because the model computes BURDM internally, it is called an endogenous *variable;* it is not a *parameter* that you can change.

The analysis in the next section will build upon what we have done so far. If you wish, you can SAVE the arms race scenario you have created under the name ARMSRACE. That will allow you any time later to pick up the analysis that follows by reactivating that file. If you QUIT IFs without saving your results, you will lose the working file and will have to reintroduce the parameter changes we have discussed (GK and ALLY) before proceeding with the next section.

## The Possibility of War

The preceding discussion of economic and noneconomic consequences of an arms race assumes that it does not end in a military conflict. If it does, the implications for other variables could be much greater.

▶ Normally, the conventional war factor (CWARF), the parameter switch that controls the computation of a probability of war, is deactivated (set to 0). Change it to 1 (on) and rerun the model using the arms race you created above as the active scenario (refer to Important Note 3).

---

**Important Note 3**

If you enter CHANGE after running and exploring the arms race scenario, it will indicate that you are now positioned in a year other than 1990. Before making changes in CWARF, type RESET in order to reset time to 1990.

---

Run the model. IFs computes a probability of conventional war (CWARPB) every year. That probability is based on the intensity of the arms race—on the difference between the level of military spending in the base case and the level in the scenario. During every year of an arms race, that probability determines the likelihood of outbreak of conventional war. When a war breaks out, the model simultaneously calculates the length of the war.

Casualties and economic damage depend on the conventional power of the two sides and the length of the war. Whenever either or both parties to a conventional conflict have nuclear weapons (as both China and the Soviet Union do), there is the constant danger of an escalation to nuclear war (the nuclear war probability during a conventional war is NWARPB; setting NWARF to 100 during a conventional war would guarantee escalation to nuclear war). Should that happen, both casualties and economic damage can increase dramatically.

After rerunning the model, look at the conventional war probability (CWARPB). Even when that probability is high, a war may not begin (the model uses a random number generator to determine war outbreak; the higher the probability, the greater the likelihood that the random number generator will begin a war). You can see whether or not conventional or nuclear wars occurred in your scenario by looking at CWAR and NWAR. Their values are 0 normally and 1 during war. (A graph of both shows clearly whether and when a war has occurred.)

This is the only portion of the model that has a random (or stochastic) element, and it makes the occurrence and length of conventional and nuclear wars unpredictable (although an intense arms race will almost always generate warfare eventually).[5] The sad reality is that we are incapable of foreseeing when potential conflicts will lead to war and when they will not. International politics is much less a science than is demographics.

There are many other dimensions of cleavage in the global system that could give rise to arms races. For instance, substantial militarization in Latin America could cause a reaction in the United States. So could a major buildup in some of the OPEC countries (like Iraq). If some of that increased spending were directed toward nuclear weaponry (the parameter that directs a portion of military spending into nuclear arms is NMILF), it might cause an especially large reaction. Another basis for an arms race would be increased military spending by Japan and reaction by China. Still another would be increased military spending by Russia and collective reaction by the United States, the European Community, and Japan. The model will not forecast alliance combinations for you; you must specify them with the ALLY parameter.

Spend some time exploring possible arms races and the conflicts that might result from them. At the end of this volume, Appendix 2 contains more detailed description of the major parameters in the model and some guidelines with respect to their use. Explore that listing to better understand the kinds of scenarios you might develop. Never be afraid to change parameters and see what happens. Although extreme or nonsensical parameter changes can lead to nonsensical results (garbage in, garbage out), the model is not supposed to "blow up," regardless of what you do. If you do something that does cause the model to abort, please send the author a description of what you did. Then simply start again; the model, base case, and any scenarios you have saved will always be unchanged.

### Energy and Security

Although realists focus heavily on military power, states mobilize other forms of power to achieve objectives. For example, in 1973 a number of OPEC countries used their control over a significant portion of global oil resources to drive up oil prices by limiting exports. You can introduce such limitations on energy exports by invoking the energy trade limit parameter (ENTL). That parameter is a switch. A value of 0 means that there is no trade limit. Positive values turn on a limit and simultaneously specify the limit to annual energy exports in billion barrels of oil equivalent. Negative values switch on and set a limit to imports. In addition to using this parameter for scenarios involving conscious and planned limitations to energy trade, one can also use it to represent the unplanned consequences of political or social instability.

▶ Reactivate the base case (in FILES). Try a five-year reduction of OPEC oil exports (ENX) by approximately one-half in the years 1995–2000. To do so, first investigate the level of ENX in the base case. Second, change ENTL for OPEC to 3 for that period; if you leave its value at 0 for other years, the parameter will constrain OPEC exports (to 3 billion barrels per year) only between 1995 and 2000. Run the model for 16 years again.

Look at the results with special attention to the impact on major importers like the European Community or Japan. What does the OPEC restriction do to their GNPs? How does it affect energy prices (ENPRI) in those countries? Does the restriction help or hurt OPEC? What does it do to the European Community? In each case, compare the working file with the base case.

Realists also recognize the possibility that states will use general economic power to secure advantage relative to other states. For instance, some states limit all imports or exports either to punish other states or to protect their home markets. We will return to these possibilities later.

**Research Suggestions.** Explore further the consequences of the scenario built around higher Chinese military expenditures and Soviet reaction. For instance, compare Soviet military expenditures with those of the base case. Compare also the implications of the higher military spending for Chinese and Soviet education and health expenditures. And for economic growth. Does the scenario even affect population growth in the two countries? How about life expectancy or literacy rates? What about implications for other countries? For instance, does it change imports or exports of the two Asian powers enough to influence developments in Western Europe?

For most effective research use of the model, it is best to begin with a specific question. What might be the U.S. reaction to renewed Russian military spending increases? How big would the economic growth penalty be were Japan to double military spending relative to the base case? How much damage would a war involving OPEC do to the economies of the oil-importing countries? How substantial would be the population losses in a war involving the European Community and the Soviet Union? But your questions might not be geographically specific: Do more- or less-powerful countries suffer most in wars? How often do arms races (of specified intensity) lead to war?

After you clearly identify a question, consider how to implement the scenario(s) needed to answer it. Always review your results carefully to be certain that the scenario you intended to implement is the one you actually generate. And perhaps most important, do not simply accept the results of the model as the answer to your question. Examine them carefully and try to explain why the model produced them. Do they make sense? Why or why not? Use the model as a thinking tool, not as a crystal ball. Where might the model be inadequate?

### The Growth of Global Community

States seek more power and security in a global competition that sometimes ends in war. Exploration of security and community with IFs in this chapter has so far introduced you to the dynamics of that process, emphasizing the action-reaction character of it. That discussion has taken a largely realist perspective and ignored possible growth in global community.

Yet we know that there is a great deal of cooperation in the world as well. Countries work to control arms races. They give foreign aid to countries in need. Often the basis for that cooperation is very obvious self-interest. Even foreign aid donations, like the money that the United States gives to Egypt, sometimes have clear ties to security rather than to humanitarian purposes. Nonetheless, the basis for some of this activity is a commitment to the global community. Idealists, or globalists (we use the labels interchangeably here), direct our attention to that community.

Since World War II two primary cleavages have retarded the development of global community: the first is between the countries tied to the former Soviet Union (the global East) and the countries allied with the United States (the global West); the second is between the rich, or industrialized, countries of the world (the global North) and the poorer countries (the global South). Globalists have sometimes proposed two sets of policies that they have felt could help close these two cleavages: arms control and increased foreign aid, respectively. In the next two sections, we explore the potential of these two packages of proposals.[6]

### The Promise of Arms Control

In the late 1980s the Soviet Union attempted to defuse or even reverse its arms race with the United States by unilaterally announcing some measures of restraint (including a ban on nuclear testing). How did the United States and its NATO allies in Europe respond? Initially with distrust and inaction. The reactivity parameter of the real world remained high with respect to conflict but low with respect to cooperation. Eventually, however, the NATO members began to perceive the efforts to be sincere, even while they interpreted them as self-interested attempts to reduce strain on a weakening Soviet economy. Gradually NATO began to respond in kind, and a certain amount of trust emerged. The Soviet Union announced that it wanted to rejoin the global community, and its actions gained it some access.

▶ Although there is much uncertainty with respect to the future of relations between Russia, as the principal successor state of the former Soviet Union, and the rest of the world, there is at least some reason to hope that, in spite of inevitable setbacks, the process it set in motion in the late 1980s will ultimately lead to a more peaceful world. Develop a scenario in which actions of Russia lead to a broad-scale, even global, process of arms reduction.

You can do this by reversing the action-reaction process with which we worked in the last section. Return to the base case (either by starting the model again or by reactivating the base case in FILES). Identify Russia as the acting alliance (set the ALLY parameter to 1) and all other countries and regions as the reacting alliance (ALLY value of 2). Then introduce a substantial reduction of military spending in the Soviet Union, reducing GK to .05 (5 percent of total government expenditures) gradually between 1990 and 2005 (you can use the interpolation feature of the CHANGE option to do that: specify .05@16).

Before you run the model again (for 16 years) with this pattern of arms reduction, consider what changes you think such reductions would make in the world. What variables do you want to look at? How much change do you think there might be? At the very least, you probably want to (1) compare the military spending of the United States, the European Community, and other countries and regions with that in the base case and (2) look at the GNPs and physical quality of life indicators (PQLI) for a variety of regions and for the world. Are the changes comparable to those you expected? Why or why not? One thing we are always doing with scenarios involving policy changes is asking how much leverage we really might have in the world.

The world you forecast with this arms reduction scenario is quite different from that of the base case and dramatically different from that you created with the arms race between China and the Soviet Union. This world of arms control presumably would also be a great deal more peaceful, although there is no single indicator in the model that can assess the extent of cooperation.

### North-South Transfers and the North-South Gap

Although this new world may have considerably narrowed the long-standing gap between East and West, it has not directly tackled the cleavage between North and South. Look at the ratio of GNPs per capita in North and South, that is, at the relative North-South Gap (NSGAPR) and also at the absolute difference in GNPs per capita in the two global regions (NSGAPA). The persistence of these gaps has led many globalists to propose a substantial aid program from northern to southern countries. Either in a new scenario that builds on the base case or through changes that extend the world you have begun to create with arms control (if you build on arms control, be sure to reset to 1990 before making changes), implement such a massive aid program.

▶ The aid mode (AIDM) parameter determines whether a given region is a donor (value of 1) or recipient (value of 2); you do not need to change this from the base case. The amount of aid given by countries or regions is determined by an aid value parameter (AIDV). That coefficient specifies the percentage of their GNP that donor countries give as aid (that percentage is unlikely to much exceed 1.0 in even a very substantial North-South aid program; values like 0.3 are now common). In this scenario you will presumably want to change the value of AIDV for all aid donors (the first five regions plus OPEC), perhaps ramping it up to 1 percent from the 1990 value over a 5- or 10-year period. (CAUTION: If you were to alter the values of AIDV for 1990, the model would compensate to preserve initial conditions; instead, gradually increase aid levels, leaving the 1990 values unchanged.)

Note: Remember that if you ran the model for 16 years until 2005, it is positioned for future analysis beginning in 2006. To return to 1990, type RESET in the dialog portion of CHANGE before proceeding to change AIDV.

All of the aid given by donor countries goes into a pool that the model then splits among recipients. The same aid value parameter (AIDV) determines the percentage of the pool received by a given recipient; you need not change this. AID is the amount of interstate aid calculated by IFs; it is positive for recipients and negative for donors.

Once again, before you run the model with increased North-South aid transfers, consider how much impact you expect the scenario to have on the quality of life or GNP per capita in both donor and recipient regions. How much might the increased aid narrow the absolute and relative North-South gaps? How much impact will the aid have on different recipient regions? Overall, how much leverage does the model suggest we have with this policy "handle," and how does that compare with your expectations?

Especially if the model results differ from your expectations, you will want to know more about the basis for the model calculation: *How does foreign aid affect the economies of donors and recipients in IFs?* In three primary ways. First, aid affects governmental revenues and expenditures. For recipients it is an addition to government revenues; for donors it competes with other governmental expenditures. In both cases, it therefore has secondary implications for other categories of government spending and thereby for the economy. Second, aid affects investment. Those who study aid debate how much an increment in foreign aid adds to the investment (capital formation) within the economy of the recipient. In IFs the parameter AIDI specifies the portion of the aid that augments investment (or reduces it for donors), and you may wish to examine the impact of aid under alternative assumptions. Third, aid is either a credit or a debit to the external capital account balance (CAPACT). As such, it will affect the exchange rate (EXRATE) and the availability of imports (which in turn affects economic performance).

**Research Suggestions.** Experiment with different arms control and foreign aid scenarios. Overall, do these policies prove more or less important than you expected? How do you explain the results? To help understand the results, you might want to look at the relative magnitudes of arms spending, foreign aid, investment, and trade. And you may want to run the model 20 years or more for some analyses. How substantially and how rapidly could a large-scale "globalist" program reasonably be expected to narrow the two cleavages of the post-1945 world?

## CONCLUSION

In this chapter we initiated the exploration of competing worldviews, which carry both different emphases on values and different causal understandings of the world. Specifically, we considered what realism and globalism have to say about the prospects for security and peace.

To facilitate our discussion of causal analyses of change, we introduced the concepts of positive and negative relationships and feedback loops. Using those elements in causal diagrams, we saw that the understandings of the world that realism and globalism offer us contrast very sharply. Whereas realists emphasize the constraints of the security dilemma and its zero-sum, action-reaction logic, globalists provide a nonzero-sum image of growing global community, reinforced by commerce and democracy. It is therefore hardly surprising that their prescriptions also differ.

In part, of course, the differences between realism and globalism express themselves in attention to very different contemporary issues. The realist asks us to consider the importance of the relative decline in power of the United States and Russia, the possibility of new conflicts elsewhere (for instance, between Russia and China), and additional concerns such as trade wars or competition over energy supplies and prices. The globalist directs us to the promise of new global institutions, of arms control, and of development assistance to the poor from the rich.

Once again, however, this book declines to make predictions about the future. You must make your own judgments about the kind of world you want and believe to be possible.

# FIVE

□ □ □

# The Pursuit of Economic Well-Being and Equality

In the last chapter we explored the dilemma of those who value both security and peace (thereby making our general problem of choices about the new world order in the face of uncertainty more specific and hopefully more manageable). We saw that realist and globalist perspectives provide quite different understandings of global politics and that their prescriptions often lead us in very different policy directions.

What about those of us who value a global future with both economic well-being and some measure of equality? This chapter suggests that we once again face competing understandings of how best to achieve that which we value. Classical liberals draw our attention to the benefits of freely functioning markets and emphasize the economic well-being they produce. Although they relegate equality to a secondary concern, classical liberals argue that over time attention to growth and well-being will provide the foundations for increased equality. Structuralists point us directly to existing and substantial disparities in economic condition and argue that growth often exacerbates those disparities.

This chapter will first elaborate the causal arguments and value preferences of classical liberalism and structuralism. It will then consider the contemporary dilemma as we struggle to create a new world order. As in the previous chapter, the overall objective of this chapter is to help us to specify the kind of global future we want and to investigate the leverage we have in bringing it about.

## MARKETS AND THEIR
## BENEFITS: LIBERALISM

Although Europeans will recognize classical liberals as those who support free-market-oriented liberal parties in Britain, France, and elsewhere, citizens of the United States will identify *classical* liberals as *modern* economic conservatives. The U.S. political system has quite thoroughly adopted classical liberalism and its emphasis on free markets, and thus modern economic conservatives want to preserve (conserve) that orientation. In much of the rest of the world, however, restrictions on free markets are more common, so classical liberals in liberal parties often seek to change the system by freeing the market, while democratic socialist parties often become the "conservatives" (in Russia after the breakdown of the USSR, the communists ironically became the conservatives and the free-market, or classical, liberals became "radicals"). This volume adopts a more universal terminology because it wishes to clearly and directly associate liberalism (by which it means classical liberalism) with liberal or free markets, both domestically and internationally. It is very useful to have concepts that are less place- and time-bound than contemporary political labels in the United States or elsewhere.

At the core of classical liberalism stands the proposition that freely functioning markets produce benefits for all participants in them. Economic exchanges must reward both buyers and sellers, whether they trade goods, labor, or capital; otherwise the transactions would not occur. Free domestic and international markets lead to an expansion of economic product because participants can specialize in the production of whatever they make with relatively greatest efficiency, that in which they have a **comparative advantage.**

On regional and even global bases, free exchange will therefore lead to increasing specialization of production in a division of labor. In much of the eighteenth and nineteenth centuries, the United States and the countries of Central Europe (such as Poland) provided grain and other agricultural and mineral products to England, France, and Germany. Those more industrialized countries (especially England) provided the capital and equipment to build the railroads that brought such products from the American heartland to the coastal ports. The expansion of output facilitates reinvestment by producers into the capital (buildings and machinery) with which they can produce still more goods or services for the open markets. More output and trade leads to even more capital investment, setting up a strong growth cycle.

Figure 5.1 portrays in simplified form these positive feedback loops at the heart of liberal thought. Economic output both benefits from and contributes to capital formation and increased market exchange. Because of

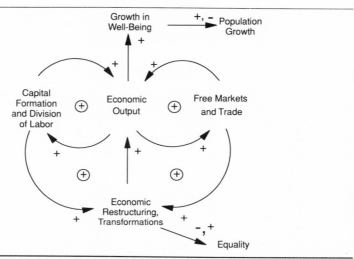

FIGURE 5.1   A simplified model of liberalism

these positive feedback loops (or virtuous cycles) the liberal perspective incorporates an inherent sense of progress. In that respect, it is much more like the globalist perspective than like the realist one. In fact, as we saw in Chapter 4, many globalists look to the progressive expansion of world markets as one of the driving forces behind the growth of global community.

The emphasis by liberals on positive feedback loops does not, however, stop with these two. Figure 5.1 indicates also that the processes of capital formation and participation in free markets will lead to ongoing economic restructuring. Economic structures and divisions of labor, once established, do not remain fixed. Changing technology and the steady march of capital accumulation continue to alter the most efficient divisions of labor. In general, liberals feel that economies will progress through stages, although the progression will be far from uniform across countries or time.

Whereas economies may initially specialize in agricultural products and minerals (the primary economy), they will eventually begin to produce manufactured goods (the secondary economy). In fact, the relative poverty of many food producers in largely agricultural economies will attract industrial capital because it will mean low wages and low costs of production. Hence, we can understand the rush of British capital to the United States late in the nineteenth century, the movement of American capital to Latin America in much of the twentieth century, and the surge of Japanese investment throughout Asia in the late twentieth century.

Eventually, however, increased investment and production lead to sufficiently high labor demand that wages rise. Moreover, the satisfaction of many material demands by industrial production begins to shift the attention of consumers to other issues, including education, health care, and leisure time. Thus economies increasingly become more mature and service-oriented (the tertiary economy). Canada, the United States, most of the countries in Europe, Australia, New Zealand, and Japan are all increasingly at this advanced stage of development. Other countries around the world, liberals generally argue, will follow similar paths of economic development.

These constantly ongoing economic restructurings, driven by the steady advance in capital formation (and by technological progress) and faciliated by open domestic and international markets, contribute to steady advance in economic output. They thereby set up additional positive feedback loops in the simplified liberal model (see again Fig. 5.1) and further improvement in average well-being.

Most classical liberals recognize, however, that even while *average* well-being improves, the condition of some may stagnate or even deteriorate. Early in the industrialization process of any country, only a few really benefit. For the large mass of farmers, conditions of life may not change at all. For those in the sweatshops of new industry, conditions may actually deteriorate.

Both the specialization within international divisions of labor and the transformations in those divisions obviously have costs for some in society. English farmers in the 1800s found it difficult to compete with food imported from countries richer in land and inexpensive labor. Those who wanted to begin manufacturing businesses in Central Europe or the United States found it difficult to compete with producers in countries possessing well-established industrial sectors that boasted advanced capital and skilled laborers. When the U.S. economy industrialized rapidly in the late nineteenth and early twentieth centuries and dramatically improved efficiency in agriculture, its less-productive agricultural producers suffered. As it transforms itself into a predominantly service-oriented economy in the late twentieth century, many manufacturing workers suffer.

Although classical liberals recognize the burdens borne by those working within sectors in relative decline, they understand those burdens to be generally temporary and to be offset by increased opportunities elsewhere. Thus after a transition period, the manufacturing jobs of mid-twentieth century America provided greatly improved living standards for the farmers who initially struggled to survive in a declining sector and then abandoned their farms for the cities. Presumably, the "Okies" who lost their land and migrated to California, often surviving only as seasonal farm laborers, frequently doubted that the new industry of California would ever offer much to them or their children, but it eventually did so.

Similarly, it is argued, service-sector jobs will eventually improve the conditions of those forced from manufacturing in the United States during the contemporary era, and new manufacturing jobs in Mexico and Taiwan will similarly improve the conditions over time of those leaving the farms in those countries.

Thus the effects of economic growth and restructuring on equality are complex in the liberal model. Any restructuring, but perhaps particularly the early stages of industrialization, condemns some to relatively and even absolutely worse conditions, thus lessening equality. In the later stages of the restructuring, however, large numbers of workers enter the newly dynamic economic activities, and equality improves. The Kuznets curve (Fig. 5.2) shows the pattern of equality that this process should generate across countries at different levels of GNP per capita (as a proxy for different stages of economic development). In reality, however, the empirical evidence for the relationship is very mixed, and the debate remains quite intense. Moreover, the Kuznets curve focuses on the process of restructuring associated with industrialization. It does not represent that associated with the transformation to service-oriented economies.

Liberals do not, however, restrict their attention only to overall economic performance. The logic of individuals rationally pursuing improvement in their economic conditions through exchanges in the market has more general implications. For instance, individuals may also make rational decisions with respect to family size in order to improve their economic conditions. In poor societies it may be rational to have large families. The costs of raising children may be low when they do not expect expensive brand name clothing and college educations. The benefits of raising them may be high when they go to work on the land or on the street at a very young age and later care for their aged parents. In rich societies, the cost-and-benefit calculus changes dramatically.

Liberals thus provide a causal basis for the model of population growth that demographers characterize as the demographic transition (Chapter 6 will discuss it in more detail). As economic well-being begins to improve, individuals quickly (and rationally) improve their diet, sanitation, and health care and thereby lower their death rates. This raises population growth rates. Over time the increased income begins to lower birthrates through the logic just described, and the population growth rate falls.

The same assumptions of individually rational economic behavior help liberals to elaborate many more specific causal understandings of the world that Figure 5.1 does not show but that many models, including IFs, capture. For instance, liberals emphasize how higher prices lead to deci-

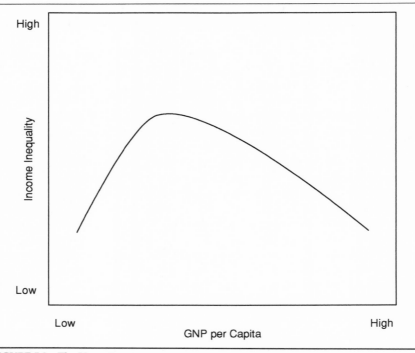

FIGURE 5.2    The Kuznets curve

sions by consumers to reduce consumption of a product. Empirical studies allow liberals to estimate the percentage reduction in consumption of a
specific good, such as natural gas, for every percent increase in its price.
They express the ratio of the percentage reduction in consumption to the
percentage change in price as a **price elasticity of demand.** Similarly, they
can express the ratio of the percentage increase in demand for cars to the
percentage increase in income of consumers as an **income elasticity of demand.** The IFs model takes advantage of such elasticities in many of its
calculations.

The prescriptions of the liberal model follow quite clearly from its elaboration. Most important, we should not interfere in any significant manner with the workings of free markets or capital accumulation, because
these are the mainsprings of an efficient economic system. In fact, we
should work to increase the extent of both.

Although there will be costs associated with economic restructurings
and they will be borne unequally, these changes are important processes
generating higher economic output and well-being. Therefore, we should
resist the obvious temptation to interfere with these changes. Many mod-

ern liberals, sometimes called "compensatory liberals," do argue, however, that society should ease the pain of transition for those who suffer it most.

## THE PERSISTENCE OF INEQUALITY: STRUCTURALISM

The structuralist perspective moves equality from the peripheral position it holds in liberalism to the center of consideration. Structuralists see inequality to be a direct result of the concentration of economic power in relatively few hands. Unlike liberals, structuralists do not make a strong distinction between politics and economics. On the contrary, they argue that concentrations of political and economic power strongly reinforce each other in a positive feedback loop. Figure 5.3 portrays that loop and its implications for equality (namely, an increase in inequality).

Much like realists, structuralists claim that power begets power. Those who have economic power are able significantly to affect the terms of exchanges. Whereas liberals focus on the fact that no two parties will freely enter into an agreement unless both benefit, structuralists draw our attention to the fact that they may benefit very unequally. In a society with much unemployment, for instance, an employer may be able to hire the labor of a worker for little more than survival wages, while selling the fruits of that labor for a very considerable price. Similarly, a rich country with the capability of producing most of what it needs itself will find itself in an enviable bargaining position relative to a country with little to sell other than bananas or coffee and no ability to produce cars or computers.

In such unequal relationships, the economically more powerful country may be able largely to dictate the **terms of trade**, that is, the prices of the goods it sells relative to the prices of the goods it buys. Similarly, the richer individual or society may be able to shape the terms (interest rate and repayment period) at which it lends money to the poorer, as long as the desire to lend money is less pressing than the need to borrow. The desperation of many Latin American and African debtors in the 1980s, a decade many label the "lost decade" for those countries, suggests the power that comes with lending money.

On the political side, we have already discussed (with respect to realism) how political-military power may be self-reinforcing. We can extend that to a discussion of political-economic power. When rich countries set up the formal institutions that give guidance for international trade and capital flows (such as the General Agreement on Tariffs and Trade, the World Bank, and the International Monetary Fund) and in addition reserve for themselves an overwhelming majority of the votes within those institutions, it is likely that those institutions will seldom challenge the in-

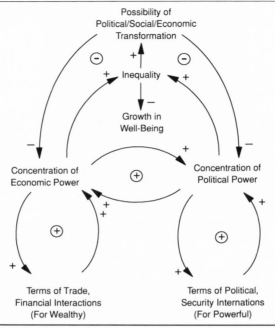

FIGURE 5.3    A simplified model of structuralism

terests of their founders. Thus Figure 5.3 shows two loops that reinforce
the concentration of political and economic power through the terms of
interaction that the rich and powerful set in dealings with the poor and
weak. Together with the loop linking political and economic power, the
system suggests a very powerful self-reinforcing dynamic that works
against any relative advance of those at the bottom of it.

Structuralists disagree among themselves, however, with respect to the
degree to which this cluster of three positive feedback loops works to increasingly intensify the divisions among global classes or simply works to
maintain them. Some structuralists argue that the developed world
emerged only in the process of "underdeveloping" the rest of the world
and that the process of impoverishment continues with little-diminished
intensity. Others see some advance in the absolute position of the global
poor and weak, even though the relative gap between them and the rich
and powerful has not been reduced. In light of the empirical evidence we
saw in Chapter 2 with respect to the absolute advances made around the
world in life expectancy, literacy, and even income, it is difficult to accept
the former and stronger structuralist position.

One source of the dispute about the degree to which these positive feedback loops continue to work against the poor and weak is some uncertainty with respect to the negative loops at the top of Figure 5.3. Traditional Marxist perspectives foresaw increased inequality leading to increased pressure for political, social, and economic transformations that would redress the balances by elimininating the concentrations of economic and political power (the transformations would transfer that power to the masses). Marx and others believed, however, that the inequality would intensify to the point of a social explosion and that the transformations would be revolutionary. That is, they saw the negative feedback loops as having a threshold character—they either functioned or did not.

It is possible that the processes of transformation may be more continuous, at least in some societies. Thus some ongoing transformations may occur that redress at least partly and intermittently the concentrations of wealth and power, therefore restricting the growth of inequality. One could argue that the New Deal policies of the Roosevelt era and, more generally, the welfare states established by all developed Western states illustrate the possibility of such partial transformations. One could also argue, however, that these examples simply illustrate the ability of rich states to buy off their own relative poor, whereas the global system provides no such option to the Nicaraguas or Philippines of the world. Table 5.1 shows some data on the internal income distributions of countries in the global North and global South. It supports the proposition that the poor in less-developed countries receive proportionately less income than the poor in more-developed countries. The data buttress, however, *both* the structuralist assertion that the global economic system especially exploits the poorest and weakest and the liberal argument of increased inequality during the early phases of structural change (see again the Kuznets curve).

Structuralists do not ignore economic growth. In fact, they commonly argue that reducing inequality will facilitate that growth. Illiterate, underfed workers are not highly productive ones. Studies have investigated the relationship between economic growth and the emphasis by a less-developed country on basic human needs such as food, housing, and medical care. For many years, for instance, structuralists pointed to Sri Lanka as a success story of a country that achieved growth by satisfying basic needs. Like those studies that look at the liberals' Kuznets curve, those linking attention to basic needs with growth have not been definitive.

Although the model of structuralist thought in Figure 5.3 oversimplifies the complexity of understanding within that perspective, it

TABLE 5.1 Income Distribution: Most Recent Year

| | Percent of Income Received | | | Percent of Income Received | |
|---|---|---|---|---|---|
| | Lowest 20 Percent | Highest 10 Percent | | Lowest 20 Percent | Highest 10 Percent |
| Latin America | | | Africa | | |
| El Salvador | 5.5 | 29.5 | Kenya | 2.6 | 45.8 |
| Peru | 4.4 | 35.8 | Zambia | 3.4 | 46.4 |
| Costa Rica | 3.3 | 38.8 | Côte d'Ivoire | 5.0 | 36.3 |
| Brazil | 2.4 | 46.2 | Ghana | 7.1 | 28.5 |
| Mexico | 2.9 | 40.6 | Botswana | 2.5 | 42.8 |
| Panama | 2.0 | 44.2 | Average | 4.1 | 40.0 |
| Argentina | 4.4 | 35.2 | | | |
| Venezuela | 4.7 | 34.2 | | | |
| Guatemala | 9.8 | 25.4 | | | |
| Colombia | 4.0 | 37.1 | | | |
| Average | 4.3 | 36.7 | | | |
| | | | Selected developed countries | | |
| Asia | | | Spain | 6.9 | 23.5 |
| Bangladesh | 10.0 | 23.2 | New Zealand | 5.1 | 28.7 |
| India | 8.1 | 26.7 | Italy | 6.8 | 25.3 |
| Sri Lanka | 4.8 | 43.0 | Great Britain | 5.8 | 23.3 |
| Indonesia | 8.8 | 26.5 | France | 6.3 | 25.5 |
| Philippines | 9.9 | 32.1 | Germany | 6.8 | 21.2 |
| Thailand | 5.6 | 34.1 | Japan | 8.7 | 22.4 |
| Malaysia | 4.6 | 34.8 | Sweden | 8.0 | 20.8 |
| South Korea | 5.7 | 27.5 | Canada | 5.7 | 24.1 |
| Hong Kong | 5.4 | 31.3 | United States | 4.7 | 25.0 |
| Pakistan | 7.8 | 31.3 | Switzerland | 5.2 | 29.8 |
| Average | 7.1 | 31.1 | Average | 6.4 | 24.5 |

Sources: World Bank, World Development Report 1989 (New York: Oxford University Press, 1989), 222–223; World Bank, World Development Report 1992 (New York: Oxford University Press, 1992), 276–277.

does suggest some of the key leverage points for improvement that structuralists identify. For instance, some reforming structuralists look for ways to weaken the positive feedback loop linking concentration of economic power to the terms of trade and financial interaction. Examples include global agreements that would purposefully alter the terms of trade or forgive indebtedness. Similarly, other suggestions target the second lower feedback loop of that figure, including substantial revisions in the voting and operating structure of international financial institutions (IFIs) like the World Bank. Proposals in the 1970s for a new international economic order (NIEO) included many such elements.

Structuralists also look to strengthening the negative feedback loops at the top of Figure 5.3. More moderate structuralists differ little from compensatory liberals in their calls for transfers from rich to poor as a way of reducing economic concentration. More radical structuralists see such measures, as well as most proposals in the NIEO, as mere palliatives. The only real solution, they argue, is thorough system transformation through revolution, breaking once and for all the control by the rich and powerful over economic and political power.

## THE CONTEMPORARY DILEMMA

Our discussion of liberals and structuralists suggests that almost everyone does value both well-being and some measure of equality. The real difficulty is in deciding which to emphasize most heavily and what the relationship between them might be. Is it best, as the liberals argue, to pursue economic growth and increase in average well-being, letting natural economic processes (perhaps with limited governmental assistance) compensate those who suffer from or in spite of that growth? Or does better public policy lie, as structuralists insist, in focusing primary attention on correcting inequalities, letting growth take care of itself?

Once again, the problem is not an abstract one. In the last two decades, global economic performance has faltered. During the 1960s, the world economy grew at an average of 4.9 percent annually. In the 1970s, that fell to 3.4 percent, and in the 1980s it dropped further to 2.7 percent (CIA, 1991b: 26).[1] Over that same period, as we saw in Chapter 2, the ratio of GNP per capita in the global North to that in the global South largely stagnated. The gap between the richest 20 percent of countries and the poorest 20 percent has increased, however, from 30-to-1 in 1960 to 59-to-1 in 1989 (United Nations Development Program, 1992).[2] We now know that we must substantially discount the economic claims of the former Soviet bloc and classify most countries within it as southern rather than northern. That means that a handful of new, politically unstable, and quite poor countries control much of the military power (including nuclear capacity) of the world.

Figure 5.4 suggests how overwhelming the inequality and poverty of the world appears: In 1990 a large majority of the world's population lived in countries with a gross domestic product (GDP) per capita of less than $1,000 (World Bank, 1991: 204–205). At the same time, countries with a GDP per capita of more than $15,000 controlled most of the world's economic output.

Whereas the obvious necessity of reformulating the world order in security arose only with the collapse of the former Soviet Union, various states have issued calls for a new world order in economics for many years. In a summit meeting during 1973, leaders of southern states called explicitly for a new international economic order, a call they subsequently

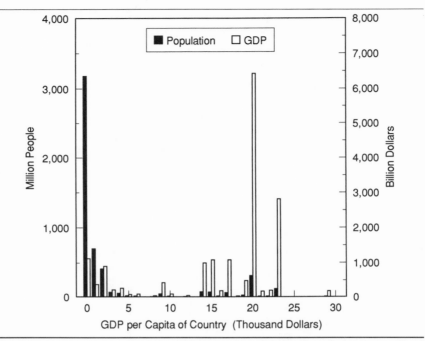

FIGURE 5.4   Distribution of global population and gross domestic product. *Source:* Based on data in World Bank, *World Development Report 1991* (New York: Oxford University Press, 1991), 204–205, 208–209.

took to the United Nations and passed in resolution form. In particular, poorer countries have long expressed great dissatisfaction with respect to their positions on trade and finance in the old world economic order. The shift of the old East to something approximating global southern status has now given added impetus to calls for change in the order.

We have seen that there are two competing visions with respect to the clearly interrelated issues of growth and equality. They provide us with strikingly different prescriptions for general approaches to the future we face and to the world order that we must build. The liberal vision foresees the development of a truly global free-trade system, made up of countries that also pursue generally free-market domestic policies. Most of the institutions for this order exist by virtue of the Bretton Woods Conference of 1944 and the general consensus behind liberal policies under U.S. leadership in the succeeding years. Classical liberals look to negotiations within the framework of the General Agreement on Tariffs and Trade to consolidate and extend free trade. Although they often fear that more localized free-trade areas, like the European Community and the North American

Free Trade Agreement, could become protectionist, they hope that they will become building blocks for ever more comprehensive agreements. Liberals look to the International Monetary Fund (IMF) for guidance to countries in the pursuit of free-market domestic policies. The IMF imposes "conditionality" on countries that want to draw upon its resources, as do very large numbers of countries in the South, including the former Soviet empire. Those conditions include reducing the intervention of the government in the economy through subsidies and state ownership and reducing barriers to trade.

The fall of communism and the rise of liberal policies have greatly weakened the appeal of the structuralist vision. In particular, the radical version calling for revolution in the center (the rich countries) has lost adherents. The more reformist versions, however, in concert with the reformist or compensatory versions of liberalism, continue to pose strong counterarguments to the pure liberal vision. The reformists point to recent widening of income gaps within many developed countries, including the United States, as evidence of the continuing and even growing viability of their concerns.[3]

Structuralists remain unconvinced that the large global North-South gap will close within any reasonable time without substantial efforts to narrow it. Calls for economic assistance to both the old South and the new South (the old East) continue to emerge. The South uses every occasion to push its claims for help. For instance, the global conference on the environment, held in 1992 on the twentieth anniversary of the first conference in Stockholm, quickly became the UN Conference on Environment *and Development*.

## SPECIFIC CONTEMPORARY
## ISSUES AND CHOICES

Given the positive feedback loops of Figure 5.1, it is not surprising that the issues that lead the agendas of liberals include strengthing free trade and increasing investment. In contrast, structuralists direct our attention especially to the terms of the trade between North and South and to the debt burden carried by many less-developed countries. We look briefly in turn at the contemporary aspects of each issue.

Trade issues are now near the top of the agenda for almost all states. Liberals push for freer trade. Although structuralists skeptically view free trade as a potential tool of the rich in their efforts to penetrate and dominate the poor, it is increasingly realism that serves as the basis for most contemporary attacks on liberalism. Many realists distrust, often as much as do structuralists, the interdependence and lack of state control over the economy that free trade can bring.

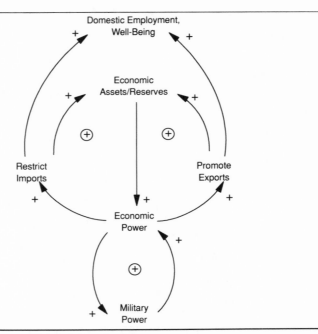

FIGURE 5.5   The mercantilist variation of realism

A school of economic realists called **mercantilists** has argued for centuries that economic and political power reinforce each other and that the state must act to protect and enhance both. With respect to economic power, mercantilists desire a strong economy capable of producing all that the state needs, including the instruments of war and the goods necessary to survive economic isolation during war (thereby increasing military power). In addition, mercantilists desire the accumulation of wealth in the hands of the state, either in the form of gold and silver reserves or in the form of claims upon the resources of other states (in holdings of their currency). And mercantilists favor putting their own citizens to work within their own country rather than seeing potential jobs lost to other countries. Figure 5.5 represents the simple mercantilist view.

Many of the desires of mercantilists obviously put their states in direct conflict with other states. Not all states can simultaneously export more than they import, thereby providing jobs for their own citizens and increasing their treasury's holdings of gold and foreign currencies. Figure 5.5, like much state-centric mercantilist thought, ignores these obvious systemic problems with the argument. Because mercantilism suffers from such obvious contradictions at a systemic level, few elaborate it explicitly

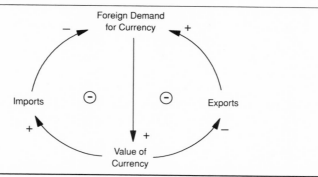

FIGURE 5.6   The liberal view of self-correcting trade and financial markets

as a creed; nonetheless, it remains the implicit basis for many urgings to restrict market access by other countries and simultaneously to increase market penetration of those countries.

Mercantilist proposals directly contradict those of liberals for letting markets work, even at the expense of periods in which imports exceed exports. Liberals argue that such periods are inevitable and self-correcting; when exports of a country become large relative to imports, attempts by other countries to obtain currency of the exporting country in order to pay for those exports will drive up the value of the exporter's currency. When the value of a country's currency rises, this automatically raises the prices of its exports, decreasing demand for them, and also encourages the mercantilistic country's citizens to import relatively inexpensive foreign goods (see Fig. 5.6). Thus mercantilist policies may work for a while but inevitably prove fruitless.

Nevertheless, decisionmakers around the world, especially in countries and periods in which imports exceed exports, face mercantilist pressure from their citizens to "do something" in order to protect jobs and boost the local economy. From the early 1970s into the 1990s, the United States found itself in this position, especially relative to Japan, a country that ran trade surpluses often easily linked (for instance, through automobile exports) to the trade deficits of the United States and whose surpluses did not seem to diminish over time as liberal theory predicted. Although the traditionally liberal trade orientation of the United States and the strongly classical liberal orientation of its leadership during the period prevented a rapid shift toward mercantilist policies (fighting fire with fire), some elements of mercantilism emerged.

Specifically, the United States pressured a number of countries, especially Japan, to restrict their U.S. sales of goods such as textiles, steel, and automobiles. It perceived the Japanese reliance upon mercantilist protection of its own market from outside penetration, conjoined with governmental support for export growth, as incompatible with the liberal trading order the United States supported. One of the tools the U.S. government used was selective retaliation against sectors of the Japanese economy (such as semiconductors) in a tit-for-tat policy. It is easy to see how a strong economic power like Japan, pursuing mercantilist (realist) economic policies, could engender action-reaction dynamics very reminiscent of arms races, resulting in countries retaliating by closing markets to each other.

It is not only Japan that poses a challenge to the liberal trading order of the post–World War II period. A number of countries have similarly, if more recently, adopted export-promotion policies that seek to strengthen their domestic economies by sharply increasing exports. Some of these, including Taiwan, South Korea, Singapore, and Hong Kong, belong to the set of newly industrialized countries (NICs). Although a few of these countries, most notably Hong Kong, also open their domestic markets to goods and thus act in a manner compatible with a liberal trading order, others have continued the mercantilist practice of protecting domestic markets while aggressively pursuing foreign ones.

The competing causal analyses of liberals and mercantilists give rise to a number of specific questions concerning choice in the face of uncertainty. How actively should countries pursue free markets? To what degree might protectionist measures weaken or help local economies? How do states committed to free trade deal with a state that takes advantage of open markets elsewhere but protects its own?

In response to the increased challenges of foreign trade, leaders in a number of countries look with increasing favor on mechanisms for strengthening their own economies' positions within the struggle. In the United States and Western Europe, proponents of "industrial policy" have emerged. It comes easily to mercantilists to consider increasing domestic investment in infrastructure such as education, roads, ports, and communication systems in efforts to make the economy more competitive in foreign markets. Classical liberals often resist any intervention in the domestic economy, but their recognition of the centrality of capital formation to growth and well-being encourages a greater support for investment-increasing measures than for most other forms of intervention. The difficulty lies in the details: How exactly does one increase investment in infrastructure or private capital formation, particularly if one hopes, as liberals often do, that the private sector can be induced to do the job without direct governmental support? Nonetheless, there does appear to be some common ground between liberals and mercantilists on support for investment.

The advice of the North to the South remains liberalization: entrance into the world economy with as few restrictions on trade and as few domestic market interventions as possible. Needless to say, in light of some of the protectionist tendencies that we have already discussed, such advice can appear rather hypocritical to less-developed countries (LDCs). LDCs often find that when they do substantially increase exports of a class of goods, such as clothing, shoes, or consumer electronics, developed countries begin to put up barriers. A structuralist could reasonably argue that the rich countries support free trade when they have a strong economic advantage but resort to managed trade when they lose their competitive edge, thus rigging the rules of the game. Does free trade benefit the South as much as it does the North?

The South also questions its position in the global division of labor. Although with industrialization southern countries have rapidly become much more than the global hewers of wood and drawers of water (that is, providers of primary goods), they still tend to specialize in goods with limited technical sophistication. As many producers of such goods struggle for declining markets in part abandoned by the more-developed countries, it is common that deterioration in terms of trade (the prices of what they export relative to the prices of their imports) plague the new exporters. Structuralists argue that those at the bottom of the global economy's totem pole constantly face markets that weaken just as they come to dominate them. Even the IMF has calculated that the terms of trade shifted against developing countries at an annual rate of 2.2 percent between 1982 and 1991 (International Monetary Fund, 1990b: 152).[4] What is the trend with respect to terms of trade, and how much impact does it have on developing countries?

Whereas trade issues preoccupy the North, the South devotes much of its attention to financial ones, particularly the resolution of debt burdens that developing countries often initially incurred during the 1970s. LDCs have had a very difficult time repaying their foreign indebtedness. In 1982 the total external debt of LDCs was $836.1 billion; by 1991 that had grown in nominal terms to $1,313.5 billion (International Monetary Fund, 1990b: 184). The debt equaled about 120 percent of exports at both ends of the decade (it peaked at 172 percent of exports in 1986). During the decade, many schemes were devised to relieve the LDCs of some of that burden— by forgiving parts of it, by reducing interest rates or lengthening repayment terms, and even by swapping the debt for environmental preserves or ownership of formerly state-controlled industries. For much of the South, however, particularly countries in Latin America and Africa, foreign indebtedness remains the key international economic issue of the 1990s. Because northern banks and governments hold most of the debt, the North also has an interest in this issue. To what degree would debt relief assist the economies of the South (or the North)?

Neither structuralists nor liberals direct all of their attention in analysis of the problems of LDCs to their interaction with the world economy. Both also point to substantial domestic problems. Liberals point to the heavy hand of governmental intervention in the average developing economy. Structuralists focus on the distortions of the developing economies set up by the coexistence in a **dual economy** of modern and traditional sectors. The modern sector tends to be tied to the world economy, to be industrialized, and often to be relatively affluent. The traditional sector remains predominantly agricultural but also includes traditional handicrafts and light manufacture, and it exists in great poverty with high unemployment and underemployment. Structuralists attribute the desperate status of the traditional sector not just to the continued reliance on traditional production methods but to its inability to compete with more technologically advanced sectors in its own country and abroad.

The division of a less-developed economy into a dual economy creates great disparities of income and wealth. As we saw earlier, these tend to be more substantial than inequalities within developed countries. Whereas liberals expect the processes of growth to spread ultimately to the traditional sector, structuralists remain skeptical that the spread will occur without some social intervention. They therefore place closing the divisions within the societies of the developing countries as high on their agendas as improving the conditions of their relationship with the outside world. How might LDCs narrow those divisions, and what secondary consequences would doing so have?

Liberals, mercantilists, and structuralists bring differing but overlapping agendas to our attention. They offer competing causal analyses of key global processes in support of their respective prescriptions. Once again, it is required that we act in the face of uncertainty.

### THE PURSUIT OF WELL-BEING AND
### EQUALITY: EXPLORATION OF IFs

This section returns our attention to the computer simulation (IFs) for explorations of global political-economic futures. As Chapter 4 emphasized, use of a computer model cannot resolve the problem of the necessity of choice in the face of uncertainty. What interaction with the model can do is to actively involve you in grappling with that problem by providing you with some additional insights into the dynamics of the issues, helping you grapple with value trade-offs, and suggesting the leverage that we might have.

---

**Important Note 4**

Appendix 2 can be very useful in helping you introduce a scenario because it details how parameters work.

---

If you do not remember how to examine results from the model, to change parameters, and to compare results of new runs with the base case, you may wish to review Chapter 3, especially the last section of it. You should keep in mind the availability, as references for your work here, of that chapter and the appendixes on variables and parameters at the end of the book. (Refer to Important Note 4.)

This exploration with IFs begins by considering the issues of greatest interest to liberals and their mercantilist challengers in the North: trade and investment. It then turns to the contemporary issues of central importance to structuralists and the South: the terms of North-South trade and indebtedness.

You may come away from these interactions convinced (as you may already be) that liberals, structuralists, or the mercantilist incarnations of realists have a corner on insight into the workings of the world. You may also come away from them, however, believing that the insights of these groups are somehow additive and interactive. If so, your real challenge will be to determine how to balance, weight, and, insofar as possible, integrate the understandings.

### Markets and Restriction of Them: Trade and State Intervention

Tariffs are taxes on imports and thereby raise the price and reduce the volume of them. Various nontariff barriers to trade, such as quotas or quality restrictions on imports (like health standards on food imports), have the same general effect.

Explore the growth of trade in the base case. Looking at world trade as a percentage of the world economy (WTRADE) will help you do that. In general, the advocates of free and expanded trade argue that continued growth in trade as a percentage of the economy carries with it many benefits. These include faster economic growth, because countries can specialize in what they produce most efficiently. Better economic performance carries a secondary benefit in terms of quality of life.

▶ Does IFs show the benefits of greater trade that liberals claim? To explore this question, manipulate the protection (PROTEC) parameter (you can do that country by country). When the value is 0, there is no change in tariff and nontariff barriers to trade. Positive or negative values increase or decrease the effective price of imports. Thus a value of 1 effectively doubles the world price faced by a region on all of its imports. As the value approaches $-.5$, the price of imports is cut in half (the model will not allow you to reduce prices by more than that).

You might begin by asking about the consequences should the United States move away from free trade, as many suggest is likely (and some say is desirable), in the next decade. For instance, introduce a scenario that effectively doubles the price of goods coming into the United States by ramping PROTEC for the United States from 0 to 1 between 1990 and 2005. What are your expectations? Consider, in addition to the implications for the United States, the possible economic consequences for Japan.

If the global economic impact of U.S. protection is less than you expected, one reason might be that trade protection, like military spending, is often subject to an action-reaction dynamic. As in the case of military spending, it is very difficult for a computer model to forecast the extent of reaction, and therefore IFs does not build in any automatic reaction by other regions to the U.S. protectionist measures. You must do that through your scenario(s).

▶ Introduce proportionate reaction to the increased U.S. protection by all other regions in the system (representing an overall breakdown in the liberal trading order). You can do this by ramping up PROTEC for all regions. Look again at the results for the economies of the world. You might also experiment with a severe global trade war—tariffs of perhaps 300 percent. What does it do to global economic growth?

Almost everyone agrees that trade is beneficial, and the results of these scenarios suggest that the structure of IFs is such as to reinforce that opinion. As we shall see in the next section, however, some argue that countries benefit very unequally from trade and should approach it carefully. It is sometimes the fear of unequal benefits that leads states to restrict trade and that could lead to a protectionist future.

Liberals recognize that the less-developed countries face a particularly demanding world, but they argue that the appropriate response is to use the market fully, not to withdraw from it. They point to the economic success of Taiwan, Korea, and other export-promoting countries as evidence. Go back to the base case and develop a scenario that incorporates an export-promotion policy for the region called "rest of the developed world" (the region that contains many of the NICs, like Taiwan and Korea).

▶ There is an export shift (XSHIFT) parameter in IFs that allows you to "force" exports of countries onto the global market. Values of 0 leave exports unchanged from the base case, but positive values increase exports (a value of 1 would initially double exports, although some other linkages in the model dampen the attempt to dramatically increase exports over a long period). The effects of XSHIFT are cumulative. That is, a value of 0.1 adds about 10 percent to exports for that year and all subsequent years until other factors in the model dampen the increase. Thus it is best to set the value of XSHIFT fairly low (such as 0.1) for all years. Look at the impact your scenario has on exports (X) of the rest of the developed world (or XS for sectoral exports). And then look at economic and quality-of-life indicators. Does it have any effect on other regions?

*How does trade improve economic performance in IFs?* If there were both a high level of sectoral disaggregation and a detailed representation of factor costs in IFs, the benefits of trade from comparative advantage and specialization would be implicit. IFs does not have that level of detail. Instead it relies on a mechanism that relates manufactured imports to the efficiency of production. As the ratio of manufactured imports to the GNP increases, the productivity of production in all sectors increases (this is controlled by the elasticity of productivity with manufacturing imports, PRODME). In essence, this ratio serves as a surrogate for two trade benefits: efficiency gains through comparative advantage and productivity gains through the import of manufactures, especially capital goods that bring advanced technology.

### Fostering Investment

Although liberals devote much of their attention to limiting interventions in interstate trade, they also decry much involvement by governments in their domestic economies. They argue, for instance, that government actions as disparate as price controls, subsidies to inefficient industries, highly progressive tax structures (those that heavily tax the rich), and punitive taxes on business either discourage or render less efficient much of the savings and investment that the economy requires for rapid growth.

A world more to the liking of the classical liberals than the base case would be one in which government actions freed up substantially more savings and created opportunities for investment. On this issue the thought of classical and modern (or compensatory) liberals sometimes converges, because modern liberals also want to see greater investment. They are more likely, however, to argue for government action (such as infrastructure spending) that facilitates that increase.

▶ You can simulate increased investment with the investment shift parameter (ISHIFT). When ISHIFT is zero, the model computes investment according to internal rules. When the value is 0.5, investment would be 50 percent higher than normal; similarly, a value of −0.5 would reduce investment by 50 percent.

Investment shifts (I) come at the expense of, or are made to the benefit of, consumption (C).[5] ISHIFT is a regionalized parameter, so if you want to see an entire world in which investment increases, you will need to change it for all regions. There have, however, been many calls for increased investment in the United States, and you may want to look at the impact in just that country.

**Research Suggestions.** How much benefit do countries gain if they open themselves up to imports? Can one country gain that benefit unilaterally, or must many countries/regions open markets simultaneously? If all countries and regions open markets, do they share equally in benefits? Are the costs of protection comparable to the gains of free trade? Is a country's leverage over economic performance greater with trade or with investment policies?

How much additional economic growth can countries achieve if they either promote exports or increase investment? Because investment increases come at the expense of consumption, can less economically developed countries use this strategy as effectively, or does it have short-term implications for the poorer countries (loss of consumption power, declines in quality of life) that are unacceptable?

### Global Inequalities: International Structures

Although the base case of IFs is in no way a prediction of the future, examine it with respect to the arguments of those who forecast relative or absolute stagnation for the poor. What does the model suggest for the world as a whole? NSGAPA and NSGAPR will again provide some evidence on the absolute and relative gaps between rich and poor. What about specific poorer regions of the world such as Latin America, Asia, and Africa? We visited this issue of economic disparities earlier when we looked at the world through globalist eyes and considered alternative foreign aid scenarios. In general, however, we saw that even substantial volumes of aid would not dramatically narrow the North-South gap. Structuralists generally agree with the conclusion and direct our attention elsewhere.

There are a number of factors that structuralists argue contribute to the maintenance of global disparities. One is the price the South receives for its exports relative to the price it pays for imports—the terms of trade. The argument is that the prices of goods the South sells to the North tend to be lower than the prices of those the North sells to the South. Thus the South must sell more and more just to keep even.

▶ You can explore the terms of trade in the base case, as computed by the model, by looking at the computed variable TERMTR. Does it show a clear trend upward (more relative value for southern exports) or downward (less value for southern exports)? There is a tremendous amount of debate among those who have studied the terms of trade as to whether the trend historically has disadvantaged the South or not. Is there any reason to believe that conclusions might depend on the initial and final year of studies? Why?

In reality it is impossible to force a change in the terms of trade. The South cannot simply begin to charge more for that which it exports and expect thereby to earn more; charging more would dampen demand among northern importers and also elicit competing supply. The net result conceivably could be that the South would earn less. We can see how important the terms of trade are for the South, however, by simulating the financial impact of an improvement in them. The terms-of-trade parameter (TERMX) is a multiplier on the value of southern exports (and proportionately reduces the value of northern exports). If you change it gradually from 1.0 in 1990 to perhaps 1.2 in 2005, you can see the impact that a 20 percent improvement in the terms of trade would have for the South (even if it is not clear what policies might accomplish such a shift).

Run the model with such a change and look at the new terms of trade (TERMTR). You might want to look with special care at a particular southern region such as Africa. What happens to the value of exports (X) and the cost of imports (M)? What happens to the GNP per capita (GNPPC) and the physical quality of life (PQLI) relative to the base case? Does the improvement in export earnings allow Africa to import any more food (AGM)? If so, does that have any effect on potential starvation deaths (SDEATH) in Africa? Overall, how does a change in the terms of trade seem to compare with foreign aid (as explored earlier) in its potential for improving the existence of Africans? Why?

Unfortunately for individual countries and global regions (although fortunately for their trade competitors), states cannot significantly affect their terms of trade, except, perhaps, by consciously shifting their production and exports from goods of less value to those with more value, a strategy that Japan has pursued. There is, however, another international structure upon which states have considerably more policy leverage. Structuralists point out that less-developed countries frequently have foreign debt that accumulates with interest and further restricts their ability to import. Moreover, a considerable portion of that debt, especially for the poorest LDCs like many in Africa, is public debt owed by one government to another. There is, for instance, often a substantial loan component to what is loosely called foreign aid.

▶ The annual international public borrowing of southern countries is computed in IFs as a portion (AIDLP) of the aid they receive. IFs accumulates the foreign debt of governments (GFORDT) at interest (LINTR) and computes the annual repayment of it (LOANR) depending on the portion that must be repaid annually (REPAYR). If the loan portion and interest rate are high enough, the amount that must be repaid annually will eventually come to exceed the amount of new foreign aid, creating an actual net aid outflow from poorer to richer countries (see

AID). Explore the values of these parameters and variables in the base case of IFs. You might focus on Africa.

Compare the condition of Africa, including the prospects of starvation deaths (SDEATH), under one or more scenarios that reduce or eliminate the loan portion of aid (giving it all as grants by setting AIDLP to 0.0) or that effectively forgive the outstanding loan (by reducing the repayment rate to 0.0). How much leverage do these policy variables have to improve the condition of Africans? What if *all* the "aid" came as loans?

## Domestic Structures

We have been looking at selected aspects of the position of the South in international structures: unsatisfactory terms of trade and high debt levels. Structuralists, however, point to yet additional structural constraints, including some evident within LDCs. There is generally a portion of a low-income economy that has close ties to the more-developed world. This could be a geographic enclave, like a mining complex or plantation region that trades almost exclusively with the developed world; or it could be a set of manufacturing elites, concentrated in the major cities of a southern country but tied more to the global economy than to the local one.

IFs does not have a level of disaggregation sufficient to represent such regional or social disparities. It does contain an indicator of income distribution, however, that captures the phenomenon of relatively greater income differentials in poorer countries than one finds in the richer countries. That indicator is the Gini index (GINI). The higher the value of GINI, the greater the income gaps within a society. Because GINI is not currently driven by other variables in the model, it does not capture the dynamics of income distribution; it remains unchanged at the initial conditions in 1990 unless you change it in a scenario.

▶ GINI is also a parameter in the population submodel. Fertility declines are harder to achieve when income is very unequal because the poor will often continue to value large families. You can introduce assumptions of income distribution improvement by gradually reducing GINI. For instance, try gradually reducing the GINI index value for South Asia by one-half between 1990 and 2005. Because income distributions do not change very rapidly in most societies (barring major revolution), such a dramatic reduction is in reality very unlikely. Look at the impact such a change could have on the crude birthrate (CBR) and the number of births (BIRTHS) in South Asia. Would such an improvement in income distribution have any net impact on population growth, GNP per capita, or quality of life? You should keep in mind that improvements in income distribution would also bring better nutrition and health care to the poor and thus have an effect on the crude death rate (CDR) and the total number of deaths (DEATHS) as well. Demographic variables change very slowly. To really see the effect of this scenario, you must run the model for at least 26 years (to 2015).

One of the internal strategies for development that many structuralists propose is to focus attention on the poor by providing for the basic human needs of citizens—needs such as food, education, and health care. You can develop scenarios that devote special attention to the satisfaction of those needs by manipulating government spending on education and health (using GK).

▶ Try shifting resources into these categories (and thereby automatically away from the military) and see the implications. Do not forget also to consider the cost this may or may not have in terms of power. You might continue to focus on South Asia.

**Research Suggestions.** How important is an adverse shift in the terms of trade for Latin America? Could it prevent all growth? If all foreign aid to Africa were in the form of loans with fairly demanding repayment periods (say 10 years), would Africa actually be better off in the long run without the aid?

Look again at the export-promotion strategy favored by liberals (using XSHIFT). Is it able to offset even deteriorating terms of trade?

Try developing some worst-case scenarios for the South. They might involve either high or low aid (depending on what you found about the long-term implications of aid). They might involve an arms race that diverted governmental expenditures to the military, as well as an adverse shift in the terms of trade. They could involve trade wars with high levels of protection.

Compare the results of those analyses with best-case scenarios. These might include reduced arms expenditures (and therefore greater expenditures on health and education), improved terms of trade, more aid, and increased investment. How different are the best and worst cases? How much policy leverage does there appear to be in the system?

Can you see the bases for differences of opinion between liberals and structuralists? In general, the best-case scenarios of the liberals are more optimistic than the best-case scenarios of the structuralists. The former tend to be more nonzero-sum (everyone in society can improve his or her position); the latter are more often zero-sum (benefits for some have costs for others).

## CONCLUSION

This chapter moved us from considerations of peace and security to those of economic growth and equality. Liberals tell us about comparative advantage, division of labor, and the virtue of free trade. They promise some ultimate progress in equality but prescribe attention to economic efficiency. Realists remind us that also in economic affairs states remain central actors and will pursue power and wealth, even at the expense of free trade. Structuralists describe the world in a fashion that perhaps owes more to realists than to liberals, including control by the powerful of the terms of trade, but they prescribe a breaking of concentrated political and economic power.

Different values and understandings lead to primary focus on different issues, and we have examined many of them with IFs. Liberals draw our attention to the dangers of mercantilist protectionism and the virtues of encouraging higher investment. Structuralists heavily emphasize the deterioration of terms of trade, the dangers of international indebtedness, and the way in which domestic structures can reinforce global ones. Once again you are left to draw your own conclusions about the relative or combined merit of the worldviews and the leverage we have with respect to our future.

# SIX

□　□　□

# The Pursuit of Progress
# and Sustainability

We have seen that those who value both security and peace face a dilemma: Should they, as realists counsel, emphasize the maintenance of state power and the protection of state interest, thereby achieving a measure of security but periodically sacrificing peace to do so? Or should they accept globalist advice to direct their efforts into development of global community, trusting that effort ultimately to provide peace and security?

Similarly, in the last chapter we saw that those who simultaneously desire both economic well-being and some degree of equality also face a dilemma: Should they, as classical liberals advise, devote themselves to improving economic efficiency and increasing growth, counting on economic restructuring eventually to deliver improvements in life quality to all? Or does the prescription of structuralists, to emphasize improvements in the condition of the downtrodden, perhaps even better serve their interests in growth?

In this chapter we investigate the dilemma confronting those who value both progress and sustainability. We find again that such individuals receive conflicting advice from two competing worldviews. The first worldview, one that we call ecoholism, holistically portrays humanity as a species within an environment upon which it places demands. Those demands must ultimately respect limits if the environment is to meet them in a sustained manner. The second view, modernism, visualizes humanity as being in a privileged position relative to the environment by virtue of its technological capability. Progress by means of that technology allows the species to exercise considerable and increasing control over its environment, with more and more human demands upon it and no clearly fixed limits.

The two worldviews of this chapter also carry other names. For obvious reasons, Pirages (1983, 1989) calls them "inclusionist" and "exclusionist"; Grant (1982) prefers "Jeremiads" and "Cornucopians." Many others prefer "neo-Malthusians" and "technological enthusiasts."

## ECOLOGICAL SUSTAINABILITY: ECOHOLISM

The central concern of ecoholism is sustainability. All species place demands upon the ecosystem(s) in which they function. Periodically, the numbers of a species grow because their food supply surges or a predator population declines. For nonhuman species such growth is, however, always temporary and limited. Ultimately, the population will bump up against new limits or old ones will reemerge.

Ecosystems are seldom, if ever, in a steady state. Populations of some organisms grow and those of others decline. Cycles of growth often lead a species temporarily to exceed the long-term **carrying capacity** of an environment. For instance, deer protected from their canine and human predators will expand in numbers until they overgraze their environment (they "overshoot" a carrying capacity). After a delay, the despoiled environment will no longer support the overgrazing—in fact, because of destruction to the vegetation it will no longer support even the population that it could once comfortably feed. Therefore, the population of deer will collapse as the animals become vulnerable to starvation in winter and to micropredators in the form of disease. Gradually the vegetation will rebound, and the deer population will begin another cycle.

Figure 6.1 portrays a negative feedback loop that links human population to the environment in roughly the same way. The primary difference is that the demands of humans on their environment are more variable than those of deer on theirs. As humans increase the scale of their economic activities per capita, they multiply their individual demands on the environment—each person demands more water, energy, and other goods. Whereas the demands that most animals place on their environment are limited to food inputs, humans require a variety of energy and mineral inputs as well. In addition, human outputs back to the environment include extensive waste from industrial activities. Both input demands and outputs detrimentally affect the environmental quality necessary to satisfy future human needs.

Negative feedback loops like those of Figure 6.1 often produce cyclical behavior around a target value (in this case the environmental carrying

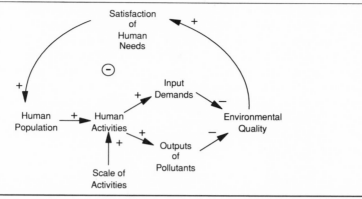

FIGURE 6.1   A simplified model of ecoholism

capacity). In Chapter 4 we discussed a household thermostat as part of a negative loop linking the temperature of a home and its heating system. Although good thermostats maintain temperature within a fairly narrow range, temperature will alternately exceed and fall short of a specific target value.

Historically, human populations have exhibited such cyclical variation in their interaction with the environment. There remains much debate over the causes of collapse in a variety of early Middle Eastern, Asian, and American civilizations. Scholars attribute such collapses to invasion from the outside (potentially a result of the invaders having exceeded their carrying capacity or of the weakening of the invaded as they exceeded their own), to exhaustion of soils or their damage from salts in irrigation water (and therefore to famine), to social breakdown (sometimes a consequence of food shortages), and to a variety of other factors. Clearly, the relationship between humans and their environment has often played a key role.

Obviously, we cannot now know with certainty the distance into a condition of overshoot (use of the environment beyond sustainable limits) humanity has progressed, if at all. Nor can anyone predict accurately when collapse might occur and how severe it could become. Finally, no one can be certain how rapidly humanity might recover from a collapse. Ecoholists emphasize, however, that the costs of recovery can often well exceed the costs of anticipatory and preventative action. For instance, it may be impossible to restore a tropical rain forest once it has been destroyed; one can drive a species to extinction, but we have no means of recovering a lost species. Similarly, heavy soil erosion may leave little choice but abandonment of agriculture over the area involved. In terms of the models of extrapolation we saw in Chapter 2, environmental change can involve threshold changes that we can make in only one direction.

Ecoholists therefore point out that the costs of preventative and ameliorating action are generally small in comparison with the potential costs of inaction.

The concept of carrying capacity is obviously very important to ecoholists. They believe in the existence of reasonably definite limits to the sustainable level of economic activity in the long term, while generally admitting that such limits remain uncertain until activity overshoots them. In their famous computer modeling project, Meadows et al. (1972) produced forecasts suggesting that human population and economic growth face a wide variety of interacting limits early in the twenty-first century. Brown (1981) also sought to specify the limits and argues that the fisheries, cropland, grazing land, and forest area of the world would ultimately sustain only about 6 billion humans. The world population will reach that level near the turn of the century. He argues that substantial parts of the world have already exceeded local limits.

There are by definition limits to what we call the nonrenewable resources of the world, including the mineral wealth and especially the fossil fuels. We saw in Chapter 2 that most of the world's energy now comes from such fossil fuels. Almost no one questions that the speed at which new fossil fuel forms is dramatically slower than our rate of its use. Thus with respect to those energy forms, humanity has already significantly overshot the level of sustainability (although existing stocks may last for many decades).

Yet many ecoholists devote less attention to the limits that affect inputs than to those on outputs. Chapter 2 already documented the increase in environmental pollutants such as CFCs and carbon dioxide. Although collective global action is now rapidly reducing the production and use of CFCs, there is less prospect for substantial near-term reductions in the production of carbon dioxide, in part because fossil fuels have proven to be more plentiful than many ecoholists believed twenty years ago. With respect to problems connected to outputs, global pollution of air and water are now near the top of the list that ecoholists identify; they expect such pollution to increasingly constrain marine and terrestrial production of food and therefore to limit human population.

Ecoholists identify a factor that complicates the relationship of humans and their environment, especially with respect to the outputs of human activity. That factor is the nature of ownership. When individuals control their own environment and can restrict access by others, they have an incentive to maintain it. Unless under great economic stress, ranchers do not build their herds so large as to destroy the vegetation on their own land. When individuals have common access to an environment, however, they have an incentive to derive as much utility from it as possible for themselves, even at the expense of others. Ranchers sharing access to government land have an incentive to add a few additional cattle, even if it reduces the viability of vegetation in the long term and the average weight gain of each animal. Ranchers calculate that they will benefit from their own additional cattle and have little concern with the weight loss of cattle owned by other ranchers. This collective destruction of an environmental area open to many is called the "tragedy of the commons."

Consider another example. Should a single company be given a very long-term lease to the timber rights in a forest area, the company would have an incentive to see that the area continues to produce trees over that long term. Were the government to permit multiple companies periodic access to the same area, each would want to extract the timber as quickly as possible, before its rivals did so. Very long-term leases begin to approximate private ownership and elicit similar concern with longer-term environmental quality.

Many global environments remain open to common use by humans who have no clear ownership. It is impossible to subdivide the atmosphere, and it would be extremely difficult to allocate the deep ocean regions to individuals or countries. Even within countries, most waterways and many forests remain common property.

Although the establishment and enforcement of property rights over grazing land, energy resources, and forests may reduce the rate of their use dramatically, this cannot guarantee that the rate will drop to one that is sustainable in the very long run. Ecoholists see the continued growth of human populations and the scale of individual human activities as severe threats to the environment, whether collectively or privately owned. Given the centrality of population size to the simplified model in Figure 6.1, it should surprise no one that ecoholists place especially great prescriptive weight on slowing or stopping global population growth. Chapter 2 traced the rapidity of growth in both human numbers and economic activity per capita.

Ecoholists worry, however, that the growth in human population has a great deal of momentum and therefore will not cease in the near future. Those who bear children are overwhelmingly in the age categories between 15 and 45. Thus a good predictor of the growth in the population of a country for the next 30 years is the size of the population now under 15 and therefore about to enter the most fertile years. Whereas the population under 15 in more-developed countries averages 21 percent of the total, in less-developed countries that age group constitutes 36 percent of the total (Population Reference Bureau, 1992).[1]

It is often argued that population growth in the less-developed countries will follow the same declining trend as that in the more-developed countries. In the latter, birthrates and death rates were both high at the beginning of the nineteenth century. Death rates declined quite steadily over the next two hundred years, falling at times enough below birthrates to cause population to grow at rates of 0.5 to 1 percent annually. Yet birthrates also declined, and in recent decades they have come again to be so close to much-reduced death rates that overall population growth in many rich countries has virtually ceased.

The movement from high birth and death rates to low birth and death rates, through an intermediate period in which births exceed deaths, is known as the **demographic transition**. It is generally argued that a variety of improvements in the quality of life of Europeans gradually caused them to reduce their birthrates to the level of their death rates. As incomes of societies go up, the costs of raising children climbs, while their contribution to the average family declines. More recently, as opportunities for women in the work force have increased, the costs of forgoing those incomes and staying home with children have climbed quite sharply. Chapter 5 described this logic from the viewpoint of a liberal.

The decline of death rates in poorer countries began largely at the end of World War II and was so sharp that the gap between birth and death rates came quickly to exceed that in rich countries at any time during their demographic transitions (see Fig. 6.2). This led to population growth rates of as much as 4 percent annually; the rate that now characterizes Africa on average is 3 percent (Kenya and Zambia lead with rates of 3.8 percent).

What worries ecoholists is that this rapid growth in Third World population, with less outlet for migration than the European countries had when the United States was wide open for them, may so overwhelm the environment that the economic and social transformations that eventually slowed the birthrate in the developed countries will never occur. If environmental deterioration prevents improvements in income, the poorer countries could find themselves not in a demographic transition but in a **demographic trap** (Brown, 1988)—a situation in which inadequate food supplies and economic opportunities prevent incomes from rising and from slowing birthrates. Continued high birthrates would in turn maintain the pressure on the environment. Figure 6.3 portrays the demographic trap in terms of a positive feedback loop. (Remember in examining any feedback loop first to assess the sign of each individual linkage by asking what happens to the variable in front of the arrow when that behind it increases; after determining the sign of each linkage, characterize an entire loop as positive if the number of negative links is zero or even.)

Even if the developing world, and therefore the world more generally, manages to escape the demographic trap, ecoholists worry about the constantly increasing environmental impact of each individual human being. Figure 6.1 represented this scale-of-activity factor as external, or exoge-

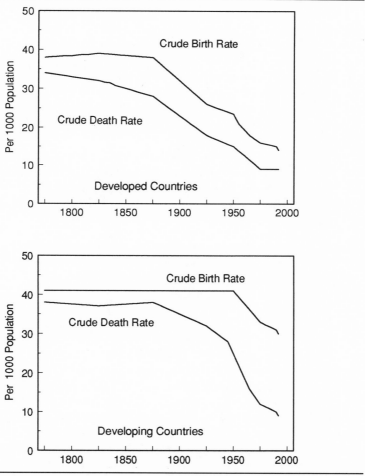

FIGURE 6.2   Demographic transition. *Sources:* Nancy Birdsall, *Population and Poverty in the Developing World,* World Bank Staff Working Paper no. 404 (Washington, D.C.: World Bank, 1980), 4; Population Reference Bureau, *World Population Data Sheet* (Washington, D.C.: Population Reference Bureau, 1986, 1988, 1992).

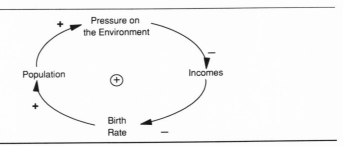

FIGURE 6.3    The demographic trap

nous, to the feedback loop. We know, however, that it is closely tied to economic activity and that it exacerbates the impact of humans on the environment.

Year after year, the average human being places greater demands on the environment. Average calorie and protein consumption continue to climb, and more of the protein comes from meat, thereby requiring still greater increases in agricultural output. Energy use rises, especially in developing countries, and fossil fuels contribute the bulk of the increase. The ecoholist sees in this pattern the near certainty of overshoot and collapse in the relationship of humans to the environment.

Ironically, modernists often look to the same trends in food and energy consumption as strong evidence of progress. They see in these trends increasing human mastery of the environment. We turn to that perspective.

## TECHNOLOGICAL PROGRESS: MODERNISM

The core of the modernist model is technological progress. Figure 6.4 represents that model in simple form. The most important feedback loop in that model is almost certainly the one that links human technological knowledge to itself. The stronger our existing base of understanding, the faster and easier scientists and engineers add still more to that base. This process creates what the discussion of trends in Chapter 2 called exponential and even superexponential growth in knowledge. Modernists frequently point to the facts that more scientists and engineers live today than have lived in all of prior human history and that technical publications continue to proliferate at ever more rapid rates.

Whereas ecoholists place humans squarely within their environment, modernists tend to put humanity in a privileged and superior position relative to it. The body of cumulative human knowledge, efficiently transmitted across generations and augmented in each, allows humans to increasingly control and shape their environment—for instance, to grow

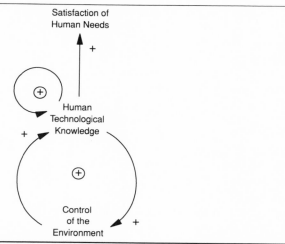

FIGURE 6.4    A simplified model of modernism

more food on a given area of land or to extract more oil from deeper pools. That increasing control in turn allows us to devote ever more resources to building the knowledge base for even greater control. The prospect that humans could actually put a relatively self-sustaining colony on the moon or Mars captures the enthusiasm that modernists often exude.

Note that the dominant loops in Figure 6.4 are positive and represent virtuous cycles of ever greater knowledge and therefore of steady improvements in human welfare. This contrasts sharply with the dominance of a negative feedback loop in the simple ecoholist model (Fig. 6.1).

Modernists frequently acknowledge the concerns that ecoholists have with respect to the steady growth of demands upon the environment. They tend to see that growth not as overshoot of sustainable limits, however, but as the steady pushing back of limits that face other species or that faced humans in earlier eras. Certainly, we now require more food than ever before, as both populations and average per capita consumption grow. Yet the productivity of agriculture in places like Japan, where rice yields are nearly three times those in most of Asia (Hopper, 1976), suggests the tremendous potential for yet greater production. The benefits of the "green revolution" that began in Mexico in the 1950s continue to spread around the world; modernists attribute much of the difficulty that Africa has in meeting its food requirements not to environmental limits but to the lesser impact that the green revolution has had there. Modernists argue that genetic engineering of plants and animals has only begun to push agricultural yields up to an even higher plateau.

Similarly, some generally ecoholistic studies in the 1970s (like *Limits to Growth*) suggested that the world was in imminent danger of exhausting its supplies of fossil fuels. They argued that the oil price shocks of that decade were harbingers of an era of very high prices and increasing scarcity. In fact, global energy production and consumption have continued to increase; natural gas production grew by 65 percent between 1976 and 1991 (British Petroleum, 1992: 21).

Modernists point out that when economists study economic growth, they often initially look for its roots in increasing *quantities* of capital (machines and buildings devoted to production) or of labor devoted to production. What they generally find is that improvements in the *quality* of capital and labor—that is, in technological capability—provide 50 percent or more of gains in production.

Frequently such gains in productivity actually reduce the need for raw material inputs, including energy, and also reduce the outputs of waste to the environment. Consider the rapidly increasing power and capabilities of the personal computers with which most of us now process information. A few years ago the desktop (even laptop) computers that we now use for word processing, information storage and retrieval, and communications would have filled a good-sized room and required heavy-duty air conditioning to cool them.

Aggregate data suggest the scope of improvements already obtained in such material use efficiency. Between 1974 and 1988, the world's economy grew by approximately 52 percent (CIA, 1990b: 36). Over the same period of time, the world's use of energy grew by about 35 percent (Council on Environmental Quality, 1991: 302). These relative growth patterns have broken a longer-term pattern in which there was a nearly 1-to-1 relationship between growth in economies and energy consumption.

Agriculture provides an even more striking example. Between 1950 and 1989, total output in the United States grew by 87 percent. The Department of Agriculture estimates that total inputs to the sector actually decreased by 17 percent. Although chemical inputs increased very sharply during the period, labor requirements dropped rapidly and mechanical inputs stagnated (Council on Environmental Quality, 1991: 339). As a result of productivity increases such as these around the world, the price of U.S. wheat in constant 1980 dollars fell from $296 per ton in 1950 to $91 in 1990.[2]

Modernists anticipate that the long-term trend for many individual human requirements (including food, energy, and minerals) will be downward, reflecting the ever-increasing efficiency with which human technology satisfies needs. This contrasts sharply with ecoholist expectations that such trends will be upward, thereby exerting increasing pressure on the environment.

Julian Simon, an active modernist author, convinced Paul Ehrlich, an outspoken ecoholist, to place a wager on the price trend of commodities during the 1980s. Simon bet that prices would move down and won the wager.[3] In reality, improvement in efficiency of input use has increasingly become an area of some common ground between ecoholists and modernists. The former prescribe such improvements and insist that they are urgent; the latter anticipate that obtaining them will be relatively easy.

Because the output of pollutants back to the environment tends to be highly correlated with the demand for resources from it, modernists expect little difficulty in gradually reducing pollution. They typically point to improvements in air and water quality in much of the United States over the last two decades as evidence for what can and will be done globally. Between 1980 and 1989, the average number of days during which air registered unhealthy levels in 14 major cities dropped from 44 to 21 (Wright, 1991: 534). Over the same period, the Environmental Protection Agency measured declines in national emissions of sulphur oxides, carbon monoxide, and ozone.

Few modernists even attempt to foresee the specific technologies that might arise to augment food production, provide new energy sources, improve the efficiency of commodity use, and reduce pollution. Many would agree with the old saw that "necessity is the mother of invention." Overall the modernist model is much simpler than that of the ecoholists, and many would remain much happier simply extrapolating progress into the future rather than delving into complicated and uncertain causal analyses.

## THE CONTEMPORARY DILEMMA

Once again we see that most participants in the debate between two worldviews actually hold two values; in this instance, they value both progress and sustainability. Few ecoholists prescribe that we move our quality of life back to conditions that prevailed at the turn of the century or early in the industrial revolution. They value the progress that humanity has made with respect to food availability and life expectancy. They want to see all of humanity attain adequate diets and steadily increasing life spans. Their concern is that an emphasis on progress at the expense of sustainability might jeopardize both.

Similarly, modernists do not argue that the environment is irrelevant to the human condition or that we can forever increase our burning of fossil fuels. They recognize that even technological magicians cannot conjure food from thin air or energy from empty wells. Yet they do not wish humanity to repress its talents with respect to innovation and quiescently to accept an equilibrium with the environment that condemns the species to living conditions far below those to which it aspires and which it can reasonably achieve.

How do we combine our yearning for progress with our desire for sustainability? As in previous chapters, the problem becomes one of choosing a mix of actions that can secure an acceptable balance with respect to widely shared values—a choice between the prescriptions of two worldviews that, while sharing values to a considerable extent, offer quite different paths to their attainment.

The dilemma is a real one. In the last two decades, environmental questions have surged upward on national, regional, and even global agendas. We have come to recognize that the current and projected scale of human activities does pose a threat to the long-term availability of food and fossil fuels and to the long-term viability of the oceans and atmosphere as envelopes for life on earth. The 1992 UN Conference on the Environment and Development in Rio de Janeiro issued a call for what is, in effect, a new global environmental order. Such an order might require forgoing the use of some modern technology (6 billion people or more cannot reasonably use automobiles in the way Americans now do). Technological advances have often presented new environmental challenges; the old advertising slogan "better living through chemistry" would now draw as many jeers as cheers.

At the same time, we have witnessed unprecedented technological progress in a variety of fields, including miniaturization of electronics, exploration of space, and understanding of the workings of living organisms. The new technologies clearly promise many benefits for humanity.

Modernism and ecoholism suggest quite different approaches to our search for some balance between progress and sustainability. Their different understandings have significant implications for the new world order now coming into view. The vision of the modernist has much in common with the optimism of the classical liberal. Just as the liberal calls for unfettered markets, the modernist calls for unrestricted opportunities for innovation. The modernist may, however, see a somewhat greater role for governmental assistance than does the liberal. Research and development, especially basic science, require resources that the individual scientist cannot acquire and that many corporations are unlikely to provide. Large-scale projects such as building superconducting supercolliders or mapping the human genome require public support.

Nonetheless, the average ecoholist will normally prescribe considerably more intervention by government than will the average modernist and much more than will the average classical liberal. Like structuralists who identify little hope for resolution of gross inequities except through collective social action, ecoholists frequently regard social action, perhaps voluntary but very often involving regulation, as necessary. Ecoholists see little alternative to regional and global governmental arrangements for protecting the common property resources around the world and for dealing with transboundary flows of pollutants. Ecoholists also argue in favor of governmental action on population control. Many further support collective efforts to lower the use of fossil fuels and other nonrenewable resources.

Throughout the last three decades, the capability of international governance on issues of interest to ecoholists has grown rapidly. Establishment of the United Nations Fund for Population Activities in 1967 and of the United Nations Environment Program in 1973 rank high among the major milestones. Ecoholists urge the establishment and strengthening of such organizations and the drafting of increasing numbers of environmental declarations and treaties.

## SPECIFIC CONTEMPORARY
## ISSUES AND CHOICES

A number of issues appear on the agendas of both modernists and ecoholists. They include dealing with repeated famines in much of Africa and avoiding further energy shocks or crises of the type that the world experienced in the 1970s. Ecoholists bring a number of additional issues to the public stage, formulating recommendations for action against threats to the global atmosphere from both ozone depletion and the greenhouse effect and for action to slow or stop the continued rapid growth of global population. Interestingly, however, it proves very difficult to investigate these issues of relationship between humans and their broader environment and to formulate policy choices unless we also consider the insights that other worldviews—realist, globalist, liberal, and structuralist—add to those of modernists and ecoholists.

Consider famine. Although people in a number of areas of the world still struggle to obtain sufficient food, the problem manifests itself most strongly in Africa. After a long period of stagnation, African food production per capita actually began to decline in the early 1970s (see Fig. 2.4). It is therefore not surprising that the first of several major contemporary famines to strike the continent appeared in 1972–1974. Africa, especially countries of the Sahel (the belt of countries below the Sahara) and the Horn (Somalia, Ethiopia, and Sudan), fought a second bout with famine in the 1984–1985 period (Jansson, Harris, and Penrose, 1987). Still other famines have threatened the region in the late 1980s and early 1990s (including the major Somalian famine of 1992). Food problems in the continent may have moved from being episodic to being endemic.

There are many explanations for recurrent African famine (Hughes, 1991: 451–461) and therefore many prescriptions. In fact, all of the worldviews that this volume considers contribute partial explanations. Focusing here on the countries of the Horn, realists draw our attention to the degree to which power struggles in the region have contributed substantially to food problems. The desire of the superpowers during the cold war for regional client states, or at least to deny those states to the other superpower, contributed to the political tensions and conflicts that drew the attention of both farmers and governments away from food production. For instance, in 1974 civil unrest erupted in Ethiopia and deposed long-time emperor Haile Selassie. A new government declared itself socialist, and in 1976–1977 the USSR abandoned its former client Somalia and threw its support to the new government of Ethiopia. Somalia attacked in 1977, during a period of military transition, in order to reclaim disputed territory into which border raids had begun in 1972. The United States and the USSR continued to support Somalia and Ethiopia, respectively, with substantial supplies of military equipment. The end of the cold war therefore offers some hope for the region.

Those who look at the world in terms of communities, including national and religious ones, identify other problems. Because colonial powers drew most borders of African states with little regard for ethnic groups, political boundaries are notorious for cutting across such groupings. Common ethnic populations have been a primary basis for the conflict between Ethiopia and Somalia. In addition, several ethnic groups unhappily shared the territory of Ethiopia, including the now independent Eritreans in the far North. Similar ethnic divisions, augmented by racial and religious ones, cleave the Sudan. Various groupings have used access to domestic or relief food supplies as a tool in their conflicts.

Liberals direct our attention to the mistakes that governments of the region have made in food and more general economic policy. For example, the Ethiopian government moved to collectivize agriculture and to resettle large numbers of people within the country. More generally, many African governments have dictated food prices at levels that have weakened incentives for farmers to produce it.

Many structuralists explain the intervention of outside powers in terms of the global division between rich and poor and see such involvement as a continuation of the process that brought Italy and Britain to the region earlier. They cite also the continuing diversion of many agricultural resources to the production of crops for export rather than of food for the domestic market.

Modernists note that Africa has invested little in agricultural research or training and that the rest of the world has similarly provided limited support in these areas (Eicher, 1982). The green revolution has yet to come to most of Africa. Ecoholists point to the droughts that have become as frequent in the Sahel and the Horn as has famine and may indicate long-term or permanent climate change. In addition, they note the high growth rate of African populations, the highest in the world today. They identify the overgrazing of common grazing lands in much of the region as yet another example of the tragedy of the commons.

The world has become fatigued by reports of famine in Africa and perhaps even somewhat inured to the sight of starving children on television. The problem has not, however, gone away. Choices, even those to do nothing, must be made. How much aid, if any, should be given? To whom should the aid be given? What conditions might accompany that aid? Would it be preferable to direct support toward agricultural research? Is relief of famine possible without economic reform, or income and wealth redistribution, or population control?

Energy issues also present us with difficult choices. The instability of global energy markets received widespread attention at about the time of the first contemporary African famine, when world oil prices quadrupled in 1973–1974. Although global market prices eroded a bit thereafter, they doubled again in the second oil shock of 1979–1980. They subsequently collapsed in the mid-1980s. They would have risen even more sharply during the UN-Iraq war of 1991 had not Saudi Arabia opened its oil taps.

Explanations for this instability abound. One can look for them in the attempt by the members of OPEC to exercise power over their primary resource and to extract maximum revenues. One can see clear linkages between the first oil shock, in particular, and the ethnic and religious rivalries of the Middle East. One can identify distortions in world oil markets resulting from collusion by the rich and powerful. One can look at the failure of Western oil-importing countries to develop and utilize other energy technologies. And one can emphasize the geologically limited resources of world oil and gas and the inevitability of some supply constraints regardless of political and economic decisions in the region. Again, whatever the predominant worldview basis of explanation, the problem of oil market instability persists and requires attention.

After the 1973–1974 oil shock, oil-importing countries established the International Energy Agency (IEA) to coordinate energy policies. They charged the IEA with working to restrain demand, to encourage alternative energy sources, and to prepare plans for cooperative action should future supply shortages develop. Many question whether governments have pursued such policies with sufficient enthusiasm. Which deserve greatest effort?

Even in regard to many more strictly environmental issues, multiple worldviews assist in explaining the behavior of key actors. The *realpolitik*-based desire of Brazil to strengthen its economic and military potential and to define clearly its borders with other states around the Amazon region, helps explain its long-term pattern of Amazonian development and deforestation. Desires to incorporate indigenous peoples into the larger nation also play a role. Failure to provide sufficiently long leases to timber producers so that they can plan efficiently for long-term renewal is only one market-based explanation for overly rapid rain forest exploitation. Gross inequalities in the distribution of land and other wealth throughout Brazil explains an important part of the pressure upon the Amazon. Neglect of research into alternative uses of rain forests also contributes to their more traditional exploitation for timber and grazing land. Finally, the pressures of population growth and industrialization certainly contribute to the complete picture.

Thus multiple worldviews collectively help us understand issues and thereby present us with a variety of choices concerning action. Is it desirable to pursue development of rain forests and, if so, under what conditions? Or is it preferable to proscribe nearly all conversion of rain forest to alternative uses? If so, what might be the economic costs?

Although ecoholists are especially likely to see the growth of global population as a problem, they are not alone in having something to say about the issue. Realists have long associated numbers with power, and for similar reasons nationalists have long suspected any policies that work to reduce their relative numbers (more than one less-developed country has referred to the North's enthusiasm for their population control as a politically motivated form of genocide). Some classical liberals argue that decisions to have children are largely made by economically rational prospective parents and that larger incomes increase the costs of children and reduce some benefits. Structuralists respond that if higher incomes might alter decision making and family size, policymakers should target the poorest. Modernists can claim that technologies of family planning have already made very important contributions to facilitating freedom of choice on family size. Ecoholists doubt that portraits of individual rationality by liberals or modernists can adequately describe the collective situation, one of individual decisions to exploit the common resources of the earth that result in collective irrationality and overexploitation.

Different definitions and understandings of the situation with respect to regional and global population growth obviously lead to distinctly different prescriptions for choice of action. Should states seek explicitly and actively to control family size? Or should they pursue policies limited to increasing economic growth? Or improving income distribution?

The global issues brought to our attention by modernists and even more often by ecoholists are therefore extremely complex. The problem has, however, not changed. We must still act in the face of an uncertain future. And we must still consider how best to balance a variety of competing values—security, peace, economic well-being, equality, progress, and sustainability. You always have the choice, of course, of leaving the decisions to others, of failing to cast your own ballot or to speak your own mind. Now that you have studied the global trends and the causal logic of six worldviews, however, are you certain that those making the decisions have a better grasp of the key issues than you do? Or that the issues demanding choices are unimportant?

## THE PURSUIT OF PROGRESS AND SUSTAINABILITY: EXPLORATION OF IFs

The IFs computer simulation cannot resolve the tensions between the modernist and ecoholist worldviews. What it can do is to assist you in your own explorations of those tensions. Relative emphasis on progress and sustainability must remain your own choice.

Chapter 3, particularly the final section of it, provided basic information on the use of IFs for any scenario analysis. Return to that chapter if you need your memory refreshed. The appendixes to this volume provide information on both the variables and the parameters introduced throughout this volume and many that it has not discussed. You may need to look at them for a better understanding of additional directions of investigation open to you. (Refer to Important Note 5.)

This section begins by investigating predominantly modernist approaches to agricultural and energy issues. It then moves to largely ecoholistic concerns with deforestation, the greenhouse effect, and overpopulation.

Note as you proceed through this section that the opposition we have set up between modernists and ecoholists is by no means complete. Modernists often apply their technological optimism to the issues that ecoholists have brought to their attention. Ecoholists often look for some technological options in addressing environmental issues. Thus you should not always feel compelled to choose between starkly opposed perspectives; rather you should look to what they jointly bring in understanding of important issues and to the balance you personally wish to strike.

---

### Important Note 5

Appendix 2 can be very useful in helping you introduce a scenario because it details how parameters work.

## Knowledge and Progress:
## The Advance of Technology

The modernist perspective begins with humans as knowledge seekers and describes human history as the steady advance of technology. Many of the forces identified in Chapter 2 create potential problems for the world: overpopulation and associated food shortages, environmental deterioration, energy constraints, and slow economic growth. The modernist is more likely to draw our attention to the positive side: steady improvement in incomes per capita and in life expectancies, global advance in food production per capita, and the integration of the world through advanced communication and transportation technologies. To the extent that problems still remain, modernists look for technological solutions to them, and in this section we will do the same. Some parameters in IFs allow you to reshape the world in a way that will be more compatible with the modernist worldview than is the base case.

Consider agriculture. The base case suggests some regional difficulties, especially in Africa. The citizens of the less-developed regions of the world consume on average fewer calories than they need for good health.

▶ The model contains a parameter called yield factor (YLF) that can be used to introduce assumptions of accelerated technological advance in agriculture. Its normal value is 1, but an increase to 1.1 between 1990 and 2005 would gradually increase agricultural production by 10 percent relative to the base case (with the same inputs). If you believe that rapid technological breakthroughs in crop genetics through biotechnology are probable, this could be an appropriate scenario. Similarly, a decrease to .9 would relatively decrease agricultural production by 10 percent (and might reflect an assumption of severe environmental deterioration). Pick a region and experiment with YLF.

Agricultural breakthroughs could also occur in fish production. The mariculture parameter (MARIC) allows you to increase or decrease exogenous assumptions about the domestic cultivation of fish by region (in million metric tons of fish annually).

Move your attention beyond the regions of the South to the entire globe. A parameter called the world yield factor (WYLF) allows you to increase or decrease global agricultural yield in the same way that YLF does for a region.

▶ Try increasing WYLF by 10 percent over 16 years (to 2005). What impact does this technologically optimistic scenario have on world agricultural production (WAPRO) and price (WAP)? How about accumulated world starvation deaths (WSDACC) or quality of life (WPQLI)? Remember again that the model will to some degree "fight" the change—increases in agricultural productivity will put some downward pressure on food prices and that will in turn shift some resources out of agricultural production.

The ocean fish catch parameter (OFSCTH) similarly allows changes in assumptions about global fish supply. You might consider a scenario in which the global fish catch, which has been relatively stable for some time, increases a third by 2005, perhaps because of improved harvesting or management methods. The regional share in the fish catch (RFSSH) determines the geographic distribution of that catch.

The modernist sees similar scope for technological advance in energy. Energy is said to be the "master resource" because if society has adequate energy supplies it can extract sufficient quantities of any other resource. Go back to the base case and look at the values over time for global oil and gas reserves (WRESER). These reserves peak and begin to fall even before 2005. Because oil and gas tend to be less expensive than other energy forms (such as nuclear, coal, or renewable energy), that puts upward pressure on world energy prices (WEP).

Some modernists argue that pessimists have routinely underestimated the amount of oil and gas in the earth (for instance, by predicting that the United States was running out at the turn of the century, before the discovery of the big Texas fields). Perhaps the assumptions about ultimate oil and gas resources (WRESOR) in the model are too conservative.

▶ You can introduce more optimistic assumptions about world energy resources by changing the value of the resource factor (RESORF), which works as a multiplier on initial conditions. Try doubling it for oil and gas (raising it in 1990 to 2.0). Simultaneously increase the discovery rate of that oil and gas by doubling the initial discovery rate (RDINR). What impact does that have on world reserves and prices? Does it affect world GNP per capita or quality of life?

A modernist might also question the assumptions in the base case of IFs concerning the cost of future production of energy. Technological progress could increase the production of energy with the same investment levels.

▶ The world energy production factor (WENPF) is a multiplier on energy production. Try assuming technological progress that increases production potential (with the same capital level) by 20 percent in 2005 (increase its value gradually from 1.0 to 1.2). What impact does that have on global energy prices and economic output? You might look also at the impact it has (if any) on the relative North-South gap (NSGAPR). Why might global energy production efficiency and the North-South gap be connected? If you are interested, you can explore the implications of decreasing (or increasing) the costs of energy production on a region- and energy-type-specific level. The capital cost in energy parameter (QE) allows you to do that.

Agriculture and energy are only two of the economic sectors in which technological progress could make itself felt. In the base case there are region-specific assumptions about the rate of technological progress in improving the efficiency of overall capital use (RKEF). The same is true with respect to the efficiency of labor (RLEF). Both of these are available to you for scenario analysis. One of the reasons that economic growth rates decline in most regions (and globally) in the base case is that population and labor supply growth is slowing. It might prove that the rate of growth in the productivity of labor would increase to some degree to offset that development (fewer workers could be trained better and longer).

**Research Suggestions.** How might the world of the future look for a modernist? Experiment with a variety of what you consider reasonable assumptions about technological advance and look at how much difference they make with respect to variables such as GNP per capita, life expectancy, and calories per capita. Does the introduction of those asssumptions eliminate starvation in Africa? How convincing are the arguments of the modernist that models like IFs often underestimate the rate of technological advance? Develop a scenario for what you consider to be an optimistic, but still reasonable, future.

### The Constraints of Ecosystems

We have now looked at the world as a collection of states, communities, markets, structures, and knowledge systems. We have not yet considered it as an ecosystem in which the human species is but a small part. Many who adopt this perspective, those we call ecoholists, argue that the rapid growth of human population is putting increasing burdens on both the biological and the physical environments of the world. They see the forces of Chapter 2 almost exclusively in terms of the strains they place on the ecosystem. This section helps you explore the world from the perspective of ecoholists.

Ecoholists frequently argue that much of the regional and global "progress" we have been seeing in previous examinations of the base case and scenarios (especially those of the modernist) is illusory. We have focused our attention heavily on world GNP (WGNP) or GNP per capita (WGNPPC) and on physical quality of life (WPQLI). Ecoholists propose that other indicators suggest such progress may not be sustainable, that humans are living beyond the means of the planet on a long-term basis. Look at some additional indicators from the base case: the amount of global land area covered by forest (WFORST), the oil and gas reserve base (WRESER), the percentage increase in atmospheric carbon dioxide (PERCO2).

An ecoholist notes the deterioration in these sustainability indicators and raises two general questions. First, what would it cost in terms of GNP and quality of life to halt or at least slow that deterioration? Second, how can slowing be accomplished politically, when countries that pay the costs of improving the environment may not reap the benefits (the problem of the commons)?

Let us explore the second question first. What if Latin America were to greatly slow its conversion of rain forest to other uses (including agriculture)?

▶ The target growth in land parameter (TGRLD) controls the percentage increase in cropland (most of which comes from forest). Reduce that parameter to 0.0 for Latin America. Run the model and look at the substantial improvement this makes in the amount of land remaining under forest in Latin America (LD) and even in global forest area. Note that there is no substantial world economic cost to this (look at world GNP). But what cost does Latin America pay? Consider GNP per capita, quality of life, and ability to raise foreign currency by exporting more agricultural products (AGX) than it imports (AGM).

Explore similar scenarios for forest preservation in Africa and South Asia, two other regions in which forest cover is decreasing rapidly. When several southern regions collectively protect their forests, does it affect the North-South gap? Do any northern regions actually benefit by exporting more and higher-priced food to the regions that protect their forests?

Some of the southern regions have argued that if the richer portion of the world wants to protect southern rain forests, it will have to share in the costs of doing so. One possibility would be additional foreign aid; another would be debt relief (swapping forest preservation for debt). These are sometimes called "side payments." Develop what you consider to be some options, and examine whether or not they can provide adequate compensation for the economic losses of the South.

▶ Another side payment might be improved agricultural technology to compensate for lesser amounts of land under cultivation. Were the rich countries to support more research and development (R&D) in agriculture, it might lead to the potential for considerable improvements in agricultural yields in the South. Introduce such improvements through the yield factor multiplier (YLF) that we used for modernist scenarios. Or you might use the world yield factor (WYLF) since the R&D would almost certainly also help regions not making any special effort to protect forests, including the regions of the North. Could a 20 percent improvement in yields in Latin America, Africa, and South Asia compensate for the slower growth in cropland and the protection of forests?

In reality, many of the assumptions of ecoholists are the mirror image of those made by modernists. Food production has managed to stay ahead of population growth in the last four decades only as a result of rapid technological progress known as the green revolution. Instead of an acceleration of such progress, which the base case already assumes will continue at a generally comparable rate into the future, there is the possibility that the growth rate will be slower in the future; environmental damage, ranging from soil loss and desertification through worsened air quality and the spread of pesticide-resistant insects, may contribute to slower growth in yields. The yield multiplier factor (YLF) can simulate such assumptions if you reduce its value below 1.0. And instead of increased ocean fish catch, there is the possibility that overfishing already is depleting stocks of fish and that catches will decline in the future. Consider the possibility that your ecoholist scenarios, instead of compensating for forest protection with improved yields, should combine forest protection with lowered yield forecasts.

The problem of increases in global atmospheric carbon dioxide may be even more difficult to address than that of forest area. We initially tested a possible combination of conservation (saving the forests from the ax) and technological advance (improved agricultural yields) for the problem of global forest area. We can test a similar combination for the problem of carbon dioxide. The primary source of increased $CO_2$ is the burning of fossil fuels (although deforestation also contributes, and other gases add to the greenhouse effect). We will concentrate on the energy connection. Ecoholists suggest that the potentially biggest contribution to addressing both energy and environmental problems lies in the more efficient use of fossil fuels.

▶ The world energy conservation multiplier (WECONM) allows you to explore the leverage of energy conservation (without having to specify exactly how it might come about; it might well involve that nasty word *taxes*). Reducing WECONM from 1.0 in 1990 to 0.8 in 2005 introduces a global reduction of energy demand of 20 percent relative to the base case. Look at world energy production and price (WENP and WEP), the atmospheric carbon dioxide (PERCO2), and world GNP. Are the effects as great as you might have expected? If not, why not?

Remember how the model often "fights" you. In this case, energy conservation may lead to energy price reductions (look at WEP). If so, the normal incentive to conserve energy given by higher prices is reduced in the scenario, and that can offset much of the conservation scenario you added. Consider what might happen if you conserved energy very carefully and this reduced the price of energy for your less environmentally conscious neighbor. Again, we see the problem of channeling the benefits of protecting the environment to those who pay the cost.

Moving beyond conservation to technological advance, another frequent suggestion of ecoholists is that the world rely more heavily on renewable energy. This suggestion is coupled with the argument that government should support more R&D on renewable energy so as to lower its cost.

▶ You can simulate a decreasing cost for renewable energy by lowering the world energy cost multiplier for it (WQEM) from 1.0 in 1990 to perhaps 0.8 by 2005. Since this multiplier controls all costs for production (operating and capital), a 20 percent reduction over 16 years is very optimistic (the cost of solar cells will, however, almost certainly fall much more than that). Does this scenario by itself, or in combination with the conservation scenario, significantly lower the production of global fossil fuels (look at WEP for fossil fuels compared to the base case)? Does it control the growth of atmospheric $CO_2$? You may need to run the model further (even to 2035) to see more meaningful improvement.

Again, however, ecoholists are often somewhat pessimistic and tend not to look for technological fixes to solve problems. The assumptions we have been making to this point could be too optimistic. With respect to energy, it may be that we have overestimated fossil fuel supplies, because as we exploit them, the remaining supplies may become too expensive to extract. Lower values of the resource multiplier factor (RESORF) can introduce more conservative assumptions. And some of the costs of nuclear energy, such as disposal of wastes and decommissioning of old plants, have yet to be borne by many nuclear producers; thus the capital cost of nuclear energy (WQEM) may rise in the future. Both of these possibilities have implications you might want to explore for coal use and carbon dioxide increases; again you may need to look out as far as 2035.

The model also offers a way of investigating possible environmental damage to the agricultural system from the growth in atmospheric carbon dioxide that your scenarios probably failed to stop. You can raise the absolute value of an elasticity of agricultural production with growth in atmospheric carbon dioxide (ELASAC) on a region-by-region basis to posit greater damage (leaving the negative sign intact); lowering it simulates less damage, and a value of 0.0 would turn off the linkage. Positive values represent improvements in agriculture as a result of warming. This elasticity could serve you as a proxy for all forms of environmental damage to agriculture (ozone and acid rain are often caused by some of the same industrial and energy practices that generate carbon dioxide).

Even with conservation and technological advance, it is difficult, if not impossible, to control either deforestation or the increase in atmospheric carbon dioxide. Many ecoholists argue that the rapid ongoing growth of human population, in combination with the efforts we inevitably make to feed, clothe, and shelter ourselves (and maybe even buy a car), inevitably increase the pressure on the environment. Thus, they argue, one of the most fundamental changes we must make is to slow and then halt the growth of human population, to bring it into some kind of balance with the environment.

► In the model, the birth control implementation parameter (BCIMPL) controls the period of time over which the population of a country or region moves toward equilibrium. Ecoholists would like to see that time shortened. Try shortening BCIMPL for all southern regions to 15 years. To see any significant impact of shortening, you will have to run the model 30 years or more (preferably 46), so increase the time horizon when you run the model. This parameter change is quite extreme because it introduces fertility reductions equivalent to those achieved in recent years in China (that country has used considerable social coercion in its program). Look at world and regional GNP per capita, physical quality of life, population growth, and total population.

You will see that even these extreme measures cannot stop southern population growth in 15 years. When fertility equilibrium (two children per family) is reached, the age structure of the population will still be very heavily weighted toward the young and fertile; it will take another generation or two before the population reaches stability or begins to decline.

► Ecoholists sometimes expect that failure to control population voluntarily will lead to undesired increases in mortality as a result not just of starvation but of the spread of disease to weakened peoples (consider the differential impact of both AIDS and cholera on the poor). The mortality multiplier parameter (MORTM) allows you to introduce such assumptions. Its value is 1 in the base case. Were the value to climb to 1.5, it would suggest that annual mortality rates for the specified region had increased by 50 percent. The medical breakthroughs that modernists might anticipate could, conversely, reduce the mortality rate.

Some ecoholists also suggest that modern developed economies are extremely wasteful of energy and other raw materials, simultaneously depleting resource bases and contributing to environmental degradation. They propose slower economic growth rates, concentrating remaining economic growth on true improvements in the quality of life. In fact, it is conceivable that the early post–World War II period was extraordinary with respect to general technological advance and that the period since the early 1970s, characterized by slower growth in productivity and economic output worldwide, better indicates the future. If so, the assumptions in the base case about efficiency improvements in both capital and labor (RKEF and RLEF) could be too high. In contrast to the modernist argument, you may wish to experiment with more conservative assumptions.

You probably have noticed that the position of ecoholists with respect to technology is somewhat ambivalent. Some expect or at least hope that technology will offset the hard choices they prescribe to save the environment. Others see technology as a failed hope and expect little from it in the future.

**Research Suggestions.** How might the world of the future look for an ecoholist? Experiment with a variety of what you consider reasonable assumptions about environmental constraints and look at how much difference they make with respect to variables such as GNP per capita, life expectancy, calories per capita, starvation, and economic growth. How convincing are the arguments of the ecoholist that models like IFs often overestimate the ability of the world to sustain the economic growth patterns of the past? Develop a scenario for what you consider to be an environmentally constrained, but still reasonable, future. Look at the scenario with and without the policy measures proposed by the ecoholists. Do such policies help the world adapt to the constraints, or do they cause additional pain? Remember that it is best to develop scenarios by changing one variable at a time and examining and understanding the impact of that one before adding additional changes.

## CONCLUSION

This chapter has been the third in a presentation and consideration of competing worldviews and the future. Whereas the first contrasted realism and globalism and the second compared liberalism and structuralism, this third chapter in the sequence introduced and investigated modernism and ecoholism. Ecoholists emphasize the value of sustainability. They point to limits in the carrying capacity of ecosystems and to the dangers of overshoot and collapse by species within them unless population control themselves. Modernists respond with both description and prescription of progress in technological capability.

Attention to issues further separates the thinking of modernists and ecoholists. We pursued those differences both in consideration of contemporary issues and with IFs. Modernists, while not ignoring problems in the relationship between humans and their environment, see no problems that technological advance (and reasonable management) cannot resolve, including sufficiency of food and energy supplies. Ecoholists are not at all certain that humanity will successfully address the problem of food availability, much less those of deforestation in tropical regions and of growth in levels of atmospheric carbon dioxide.

To this point we have considered issues of international politics, the global political economy, and the world's environment as if they were largely separable concerns. The next chapter forces us to face the reality that they are very closely linked. Moreover, the chapters of this volume to this point have proceeded on the assumption that we best approach choice in the face of uncertainty by sequentially examining the direction of change, clarifying values, and investigating potential leverage. Although that sequence of steps has been useful, the next chapter reminds us that even after such decomposition of the analysis, we must still ultimately choose without knowing exactly where those choices will lead us.

# SEVEN

□ □ □

# Preferred Futures

We began this volume with the question, What will be the future of human demographic, economic, and political-social systems? The obvious answer to that came quickly: no one knows. That simple answer creates a serious problem. Our actions, even decisions not to act, will affect the human future in potentially very significant ways. We cannot know the future, but we must act as if we did.

It therefore makes sense to improve our understanding of the future as much as possible. We have done so by decomposing the question into three somewhat more manageable ones: Where do current changes appear to be taking us? What kind of future would we like? How much leverage do we have in bringing about our preferred future? Chapters 2 and 3 explored contemporary long-term trends and their apparent directions. Subsequent chapters explored both our values concerning the future and our leverage with respect to it through the lenses of six worldviews. Each of those perspectives emphasizes somewhat different values and provides different causal understandings. They thereby help us transform our general problem into more specific ones, centered on the choice among competing worldviews, each grounded in different units of analysis and guided by differing emphases on competing values.

Having done all of this, we still obviously cannot know the future, and we still have the problem of needing to act in the face of that uncertainty. In this chapter we want to do three things. First, we will reiterate how important choices under uncertainty can be by considering the creation of the world order at the end of World War II. Second, we want to review the character of our contemporary dilemma. Third, we want to put our improved understanding of trends, values, and leverage points to work by forcing ourselves to make some choices.

### THE CREATION OF THE
### POSTWAR WORLD ORDER

In 1945, at the end of World War II, the old world order lay in ruins. Politically that old world order centered on Europe and the balance of power that diplomats at the Congress of Vienna had consciously attempted to establish as long ago as 1815. The Eurocentric balance of power had faced many challenges, particularly World War I, but it continued to function far into the twentieth century. At the end of World War II, however, the armies of two powers from the peripheries of Europe, the Soviet Union and the United States, sat astride the old Europe and made clear the irrelevance of the former intra-European balance.

The colonial empires of the Western and Central European powers had come by the turn of the century to dominate Africa and Asia. Only the Western Hemisphere had freed itself of direct political control. World War II disrupted the long-standing lines of authority between colonial center and colony. The future of those empires posed difficulties for those contemplating the postwar order. Should they be reasserted or disbanded?

At the end of World War I, states had made an attempt to create a security system that would supplement the balance of power that had failed in 1914. The principle of collective security, that all countries would assist any victim of aggression, stood at the heart of the League of Nations. Yet the League took limited action to help China against Japan in 1931 or Ethiopia against Italy in 1935. Although the League officially survived until 1946, it had ceased to be an important part of the world order long before then. Should such efforts be abandoned or strengthened?

The global economic system had also come apart. Its destruction was well underway before the beginning of the war, and its disintegration was, in fact, an important cause of the spasm of global violence during the late 1930s and early 1940s. The old political-economic order had relied upon British economic leadership to maintain relatively free trade throughout the globe and to provide a currency both linked to gold and in relatively plentiful supply. Mercantilist policies of states in pursuit of markets, including the protectionist orientation of the United States, put stress upon that system in the early part of the century. So, too, did the demands of victors for reparations and war repayments after World War I, which stymied the economic recovery of Germany and much of the rest of Europe. During the Great Depression, markets rapidly closed to imports, countries severed the links of currencies to precious metals, and world trade collapsed. What kind of postwar economic order would serve the interests of global economic prosperity?

Even during the war, the leaders of all the belligerents in World War II recognized the necessity of constructing a new world order once the fighting ended. After all, a world war is in substantial part a struggle over the character of such an order. Hitler's Germany and the emperor's Japan offered little but subjugation of defeated powers in the aftermath of the destruction. In contrast, the leaders of the alliance they called the "United Nations," bound together in opposition to the Axis powers by a declaration on January 1, 1942, initially had limited, and very different, concepts of the postwar order. They began quite early, however, to add flesh to their plan for that order.

As early as 1943, China, Great Britain, the United States, and the Soviet Union declared the need for a new international organization to replace the League. They drafted a charter for the new entity at Dumbarton Oaks in late 1944. Fifty-one countries established the United Nations in early 1945, again enshrining the globalist principle of collective security at the institution's core. Recognizing that no collective action against an aggressor was possible without the participation of the Great Powers, however, they established a Security Council charged with maintaining global peace and security and gave each of the five dominant powers a veto. Although a strong belief that traditional balance-of-power politics had failed too often and too catastrophically motivated many of the countries involved in establishing and structuring the UN, they would not ignore the reality of power.

In mid-1944 the United Nations Monetary and Financial Conference convened at Bretton Woods, New Hampshire. The Bretton Woods Conference, as most now call it, established the IMF and the International Bank for Reconstruction and Development (IBRD), better known as the World Bank. Founding countries charged the IMF with promoting international financial cooperation (including reestablishing a gold standard and maintaining relatively stable exchange rates for currencies) and the World Bank with rebuilding Europe. They also agreed upon the establishment of an International Trade Organization, which ultimately evolved into a weaker GATT. The purpose of GATT was to provide a negotiating forum for the reduction of tariffs and other barriers to trade. The efforts at Bretton Woods exhibited primarily liberal concern with free markets and growth but did not entirely ignore new or existing gaps in economic condition.

Thus even before the end of World War II (Japan surrendered on August 14, 1945), the outlines of a new world order had become visible. Countries acted with remarkable decisiveness in the face of great uncertainty. Multiple values and understandings motivated them. Yet the institutions that they created during that period remain fundamentally important in the current world order.

## EARLY CHALLENGES
## TO THE WORLD ORDER

One hope of that period was that the United Nations alliance would continue to function cooperatively after the war. Another was that the institutions created at Bretton Woods would facilitate fairly rapid economic recovery in Europe. Both hopes proved unfounded. Even before the end of the war, the alliance showed signs of stress. The leaders of the United States, the USSR, and the United Kingdom met at Yalta in early 1945 to consider the postwar shape of Eastern Europe, the pursuit of the war in Asia, the status of the new UN organization, and the treatment of Germany after defeat (McWilliams and Piotrowski, 1988: 29–38). The grudging acceptance by Roosevelt and Churchill of Stalin's military domination of Poland and other parts of Eastern Europe, what both saw as a fait accompli, would subsequently create problems. Churchill and Stalin accepted Roosevelt's suggestion of veto power in the UN for five Great Powers (France and China were included in the club), a power Roosevelt believed necessary to rally the American people behind the organization. The three leaders decided temporarily to divide Germany into occupation zones, reserving one also for France.

The seeds for disagreement planted at Yalta germinated rapidly. At Potsdam in mid-1945, after the defeat of Germany, American and British leaders protested the quick establishment of communist governments in Eastern Europe and resisted Soviet demands for $20 billion in reparations from a devastated Germany. The division of Germany became more than temporary.

In early 1947 the ongoing civil war in Greece led President Truman to condemn the Soviets for intervention and to issue a statement, known as the Truman Doctrine, that it was "the policy of the United States to support free peoples who are resisting attempted subjugation by armed minorities or outside pressures" (DeConde, 1978: 219). Britain and the United States began to organize Europe into a coalition to resist the Soviets. In early 1948 Britain, France, Belgium, the Netherlands, and Luxembourg signed the Brussels Pact, with American support. Britain, France, and the United States moved to coordinate policies in their zones of occupied Germany. In June 1948 the Soviets interrupted ground transportation to Berlin in protest of Western currency reform in their zones. The West responded with an airlift that broke the blockade. In April 1949 twelve countries established NATO. The Soviet Union denounced it as hostile to them and incompatible with the UN charter and intent.

One can interpret the events of 1942–1949 as a struggle between the values and understandings of two worldviews. It appeared initially that the globalist view, enshrined in the United Nations and other new institutions, might prevail. There was a widespread desire to break free of balance-of-power politics. Ultimately, the realist view, with its emphasis on balance of power, proved better able to describe the new world order that emerged from the chaos of World War II.[1] There remains a substantial debate over whether the reemergence of politics based on balance of power was inevitable or a result of choices by those who led the superpowers in that period. Nonetheless, the cold war had begun, and no phrase better describes the global political order of the next 40 years.

In addition, all was not completely well with the liberal postwar economic order envisioned at Bretton Woods. Although the USSR attended the Bretton Woods Conference, it opted not to join the institutions created there. More urgently, Western Europe was not recovering economically. In early 1947 the idea of an assistance program for Europe moved rapidly forward and emerged in the form of the European Recovery Program or Marshall Plan. The United States began a pattern of unilateral economic leadership both within and outside of the framework of Bretton Woods.

More generally, the Bretton Woods system has always faced two challenges to its liberal character. The first is from the realists in the form of mercantilism. Given the weakness of European and Asian economies at the end of World War II, the system condoned and actually encouraged certain deviations from free trade. These included the maintenance of undervalued currencies by some of the recovering states. The United States itself maintained a pattern of subsidies to and protection for its agricultural sector, the portion of its economy that had suffered earliest and most in the Great Depression and which continued to be weak. In recent years the mercantilist challenge has grown, and we will return to it in discussion of the contemporary debate over world order.

The second challenge comes from the less-developed countries of the world and has a structuralist character. The Bretton Woods institutions became quickly identified primarily with the economically developed countries of the Western world. The weighted voting of the IMF and World Bank, based upon economic contribution to the institutions and therefore to economic size, reinforced that identification. The GATT demanded adherence to its basic principles as a condition for membership. Those principles include reciprocity in reduction of tariff and trade barriers and nondiscrimination in trade relations.

LDCs believed, however, that they needed access to the markets of more-developed countries while being able to protect their own. From the beginning, LDCs thus felt disadvantaged. Because most either remained colonies or were newly emerged from colonialism, their challenge grew only slowly. In spite of some resistance by the former colonizing powers, by the early 1960s almost all former colonies had become independent and had joined the United Nations. In 1964 the Group of 77 (G-77), consisting of 77 LDC members of that organization (now about 120 states), supported the convening of a United Nations Conference on Trade and Development (UNCTAD). UNCTAD became institutionalized with a permanent secretariat and meetings every four years. It continues to challenge the institutional and philosophical character of GATT.

Through UNCTAD and the UN more generally, the LDCs gradually intensified their challenge to the Bretton Woods system. In the early 1970s, for example, they succeeded in establishing a Generalized System of Preferences (GSP), providing nonreciprocal access to the markets of developed countries in some goods.

A substantial number of principles for reform were put together in 1974 as a call for a new international economic order. These include liberalization and extension of the GSP, implementation of a program for the stabilization of prices and trading in a number of primary commodities, increased access to and easier terms for IMF loans, a comprehensive set of negotiations on LDC debt, more foreign aid to LDCs, and greater and less expensive flows of technology to the poorer countries of the world.

Although the cold war and a new global balance of power came to dominate the post–World War II order, the United Nations has never ceased to exist or to function. The success of some of its technical agencies, including that of the World Health Organization in eliminating small pox from the world, has been notable. Similarly, although the Bretton Woods system continued to organize the international trade and financial relations of the globe, the continuing challenges to that system have changed it considerably. Individuals and organizations have continued to make decisions in the face of great uncertainty about the consequences of those decisions. That need has not ceased.

## THE CONTEMPORARY WORLD ORDER

We would be exaggerating if we identified the contemporary situation with that at the end of World War II. Many similarities do, however, characterize the periods. The world order is almost certainly now going through the greatest and most rapid change it has experienced since the late 1940s.

Most apparent, perhaps, is the breakdown in the global political order of the cold war. On November 11, 1989, the Berlin Wall, the most vivid symbol of the cold war since its construction in 1961, opened to movement of East and West Germans. On November 30 the Czechoslovakian Parliament voted to end the dominant role of communists and to hold free elections. During December the Romanian revolution toppled the communist government there and executed President Ceauşescu. In February 1990 the Soviet communists gave up their complete hold on power. At the end of 1991, the USSR ceased to exist. The new year of 1992 dawned with a Russian flag flying above the Kremlin and Boris Yeltsin, democratically elected President of Russia, inside it.

These domestic changes throughout most of the communist world have changed international relations quickly. In December 1990 the United States offered food and other aid to the USSR. The United States and the USSR signed an agreement during June 1991 limiting conventional forces in Europe and another in July reducing nuclear arsenals. The Warsaw Treaty Alliance, established in 1955 in formal reaction to the creation of NATO, ceased to exist in July. The Baltic Republics of Estonia, Latvia, and Lithuania joined the United Nations as independent states in September 1991. Russia and 14 other newly independent states of the former USSR joined the IMF and World Bank in April 1992.

The changes have potentially revitalized the United Nations. In 1990–1991 all five states with veto power, including the former Soviet Union and China, supported UN Security Council resolutions condemning the invasion of Kuwait by Iraq, imposing sanctions, and ultimately authorizing U.S.-led military action against Iraq. In its first 40 years of operation, the UN sponsored only 13 peacekeeping missions; during the 1989–1991 period alone, it undertook eight more.[2]

The world therefore stands clearly on the cusp of great change with respect to political and security arrangements. On the one hand, there appears to be the prospect of strengthened global community and strengthened institutions of that community. The surprising advances of Western democratic forms, not just in Central and Eastern Europe but in Latin America, Asia, and even Africa, give additional support to those who anticipate a new era of global political relations. On the other hand, there is the possibility that this era is simply another interim period prior to the emergence of a redefined balance of power.

The global political economy is also in a state of transition and accompanying uncertainty. The Third World's demand for a new international economic order remains on the table. The economic success of a number of newly industrialized and export-oriented developing countries has, however, muted much of its force. The decline of the Soviet Union, long a principal advocate of global economic restructuring, has similarly weakened the demands of structuralists for fundamental change in the order of Bretton Woods. Problems of Third World debt have lessened. It would, however, be foolish to dismiss the power of the gap between global rich and poor to mobilize the energies of the poor in mounting renewed challenges to the current order. A variety of economic problems and a general discontent could reemerge with force in the wake of economic downturn.

Nonetheless, the greatest contemporary challenge to the existing economic order appears to be from mercantilism. The United States ran trade deficits of more than $40 billion with Japan for each year from 1986 to 1991.[3] Japanese surpluses with Europe increased steadily in this period. Both the United States and Europe have responded to what they perceive as unfair trade practices by Japan with efforts to protect their own markets. Some of those efforts target Japanese goods specifically. Others have a more general protectionist character.

The United States has been concerned that the movement in the European Community toward greater economic integration and some protection against Japanese goods is creating a Fortress Europe. Canada and the United States agreed on a Free Trade Agreement in 1988 and initiated discussions with Mexico on a North American Free Trade Agreement in 1991. Argentina, Brazil, Paraguay, and Uruguay have targeted elimination of tariffs among them by the end of 1994. Observers of these free-trade agreements debate whether the zones will provide building blocks for renewed attention to free trade within GATT or will close themselves into trading blocs and thereby subvert the liberal principles of the Bretton Woods institutions.

At the end of World War II, environmental issues were essentially absent from the world's agenda. They began emerging in the 1970s. The United Nations Conference on the Human Environment in Stockholm during 1972 was the first major sign of their arrival. That conference created the United Nations Environment Program and set in motion a number of efforts that have continued to grow, including a program to protect the regional seas of the world. During the 1980s, two global atmospheric issues were added to the agenda. The world identified CFCs as a threat to the stratospheric ozone layer and then acted to reduce them with remarkable speed. Twenty-two countries signed an agreement in Montreal during 1987 and have continued to strengthen it since then. The extent of the threat to global temperatures and ocean levels from the buildup of atmospheric carbon dioxide has drawn more debate and less action. The United Nations Conference on Environment and Development (UNCED) in 1992 signaled the arrival of a full range of environmental issues onto the global agenda.

A host of issues now defines an environmental agenda that includes much more than just the quality of global oceans and air. It includes the interaction between population growth and environmental quality, the ability of humanity to feed itself, and even the condition of forests within countries, a debate once confined solely to domestic politics. The future of domestic and international action on such environmental issues remains very uncertain. The Montreal Protocol on CFCs could serve as an exemplar for cooperation on a wide range of issues. On the other hand, international tensions arising from the establishment of a new balance of power could undercut action on all such issues.

## THE INTERACTION OF CHOICES

The simultaneous consideration of environmental and development issues at Rio de Janeiro in 1992 suggests the increasing linkage between those issues on the world agenda, something that extends also to political and security issues. It might be reasonable to hypothesize that during periods of transformation in the world order, issues tend to become fused, much as they did during the building of the postwar economic and security arrangements. When and if power balances reestablish themselves as the dominant character of international politics, renewed global tensions may suppress the linkages and again relegate nonsecurity issues to the domain of "low politics." Do we now find ourselves in a period analogous to 1944–1946, when global resolution of many such issues appeared possible? In 1946 the United States even suggested the Baruch Plan, calling for international control of atomic power. Or are we perhaps about to move into a period like that of 1947–1948, when the two superpowers who dominated the victory of World War II acted to divide the world and consideration of all its security, economic, and environmental issues into two zones?

Up until this chapter, we have largely separated consideration of those issues centering on security and peace from those of growth and equality and in turn from those of progress and sustainability.[4] In reality the issues interact closely, not least in our ability to devote time and financial resources to their attention. In this chapter we have begun to recognize that interaction.

It is therefore time for you to reflect on the interaction of these issues and to begin asking yourself about the comprehensive shape of the world order you wish to see evolve in the next decade. This book leaves you not with a vision but with an exercise. Take some time to describe the world you would like to see in place at the end of 10 years. Where do you believe changes are taking us? What kind of world do you want to see? That is, what do you value? How do you rank security, peace, growth, equality, progress, sustainability, and other values that you hold? What leverage do humans have in bringing about such a world? What specific actions need to be taken and what might be the costs of taking them?

In terms of security arrangements, do you anticipate multipolarity, a renewed bipolarity, or a period of U.S. hegemony? Do you prescribe strengthening the United Nations, the CSCE, NATO, or the defense of particular individual states? In terms of economics, do you anticipate strengthening of free trade, perhaps even the development of a new International Trade Organization (ITO), a struggle to maintain the gains of GATT, or a movement of the world to trade blocs? In terms of the environment, do you foresee increased environmental destruction or the technological redress of multiple environmental problems? Do you prescribe substantial global environmental regulation, national approaches, or sponsorship of technological advance?

The assignment is a difficult one, and you may hesitate to do it. Remember that whether or not you undertake it, others will. Do they share your values? Do they have the same understanding of trends and causal linkages that you have? Is it possible that they do not even fully recognize the significance of addressing the problem of choice in the face of uncertainty?

## CREATING A NEW WORLD ORDER: EXPLORATION OF IFs

You can use the IFs simulation to help you undertake the exercise of this chapter. The model does not, however, allow you to introduce new global or regional institutions with respect to security, economics, or the environment. In that sense, it has a clear bias toward the continuing importance of the existing state system. The bias may not be a significant distortion of reality, since the existing state system appears unlikely to cede its dominant role in policymaking any time soon. Nonetheless, the reliance by IFs and other world models on states as the sole political actors may force you to be creative in your work with them.

What IFs does allow you to do, as we have seen in the preceding chapters, is to introduce a wide range of alternative policy choices and alternative assumptions about causal linkages (parameters). You may have to return to Chapters 4 through 6 to refresh your memory in each issue area. And you can once again turn to the appendixes at the end of this volume for full lists of variables and parameters.

One feature of IFs that we have not yet discussed may help you in this exercise. IFs allows you to select up to 10 variables as "goal variables" and to devote special attention to them across scenarios. For instance, an ecoholist might decide that holding down world population was the single most important goal and so designate it.

You can also combine as many as 10 goal variables into an overall "performance index" by assigning weights to each of them. You access the goal-variable and performance-index features of IFs from the Main Menu with the command GOALS. Inside the submenu you have the options of reviewing or clearing existing settings of goal variables, of setting new ones, and of comparing (via DISPLAY) the performance of your scenarios with respect to individual goals and the overall index. Using the on-line help (with the <F1> key) you should be able to learn about goals and the performance index. These tools are, of course, only useful if you have several files across which you wish to compare model performance.

Whether or not you decide to use these tools of IFs, the place to begin the exercise is by assessing your own values. What features of the world in 10 years hold the greatest importance for you? The next step is to begin considering your leverage points within the base case (which we can temporarily accept as a useful statement of current trends). The easiest way to do that might be to put together two extreme scenarios—the most pessimistic and the most optimistic scenarios about the future that you believe have any credibility. Identify clearly the policy changes and variations in causal understanding (probably based in worldview differences) that differentiate the two scenarios. Your most optimistic scenario should help you identify policies that you would recommend; your most pessimistic scenario will help spot those to avoid.

By now, however, you should have a healthy distrust of all computer simulations or other bases for forecasts of the future. Because no one can know the future, the base case of IFs around which you have undertaken this and earlier analyses is almost certainly wrong. You might wish to map out a scenario with IFs that represents your own current "best guess" with respect to the developments of the next 20 years (or longer, if you wish). That is, you may wish to create your own base case.

Finally, it is time to evaluate IFs with respect to its ability to help you understand the world and represent it meaningfully. What are the major strengths of IFs? What are the major weaknesses? About what do you find yourself most uncertain? How might you gather additional information (facts or theoretical insights) in order to diminish that uncertainty? In short, how can you further develop your own mental model of the world? The author of IFs would be very happy to see your suggestions for improvements of it.

**Research Suggestions.** Before turning to IFs, take some time to describe the world that you would most like to see evolve in the next two to four decades (your optimistic scenario). Identify the kinds of policies and behavioral changes that you believe are both feasible and necessary for movement toward such a world. Introduce those policies and behavioral changes into IFs as fully as possible. Experiment as necessary to improve your future world and to identify the policies that provide you the most leverage. Finally, consider the degree to which you believe IFs fails to allow fully some of the changes you would like to make or correctly to represent the impact of changes you have introduced.

Then develop and explore your worst, or most pessimistic, case. What needs to be done to avoid such a future? Finally, how do you think the future is most likely to evolve? This constitutes your new base case and should help you identify where you think leverage most needs to be applied. At the end of this exercise, you will have attained the objective we identified in the first chapter—to choose and act in the face of uncertainty about the future.

## WHERE TO GO NEXT

There are three directions in which you might wish to go in order to build upon the explorations you have undertaken in this volume and with the IFs simulation. First, you may want more information about the state of the world and major development trends. Second, you might wish to learn more about world modeling and forecasts made with world models. And third, you might want to explore IFs in more detail and even build upon it. This final discussion provides some suggestions in each case.

### The State of the World

The best source of information about the world's physical and biological environment may be the series that the World Resources Institute publishes and titles *World Resources* (World Resources Institute, 1992). In addition, the Worldwatch Institute publishes an annual series that interprets the condition of the environment; it is called the *State of the World* (Brown et al., 1992) and has a distinctly ecoholist viewpoint.

For information on the state of the world's economy, the most useful single source is probably the World Bank's annual series called the *World Development Report* (World Bank, 1992), especially the tables at the end of it. For a somewhat more structuralist counterpoint to the liberalism of the World Bank, see the United Nations Development Programme's *Human Development Report* (UNDP, 1992). For additional information (and some short-term forecasts), turn to the IMF's annual *World Economic Outlook* (1992). And for raw economic data, look to the IMF's *International Financial Statistics* (1990).

Moving to political and social systems, Ruth Leger Sivard's nearly annual series on *World Military and Social Expenditures* (1991) summarizes some of the most important information on state interaction (including war), domestic priorities (including social expenditures), and quality of life. The CIA's annual *World Factbook* (1991) is another very rich source of both political and economic information about states. There are, of course, many sources of data for more specialized interests, including the British Petroleum Company's *BP Statistical Review of World Energy* (1992), the United States Arms Control and Disarmament Agency's *World Military Expenditures and Arms Transfers* (1992), and the United Nations Food and Agriculture Organization's (FAO) *Production Yearbook* (1989).

IFs has drawn heavily on the data sources listed here. Perhaps 90 percent of its data comes from them.

## Models and Forecasts

There have been many models of issues such as world population, the world economy, and the world climate. There are even more models of specific issues that have limited geographic scope (a country or region). Here we will focus only on those models that have global scope and treat the interaction of multiple issues.

The first world model to devote attention to both the environment and the economy was the one used to produce *Limits to Growth* (Meadows et al., 1972), a clearly ecoholist book that received worldwide recognition in the 1970s. The authors have revisited their analysis with *Beyond the Limits* (Meadows et al., 1992). In fact, no model since that time has elicited comparable public interest. The model looked at the world as a whole (no country or regional divisions) and was remarkably simple. Moreover, the documentation for that model (Meadows et al., 1974) is very complete and easy to read. Thus a good place to begin further study of world models would be with the volumes by Meadows and colleagues. That model also uses a modeling technique called "systems dynamics," which facilitates translation of theoretical and commonsense understandings of the world into models, even in the absence of complete data. It builds upon causal-loop diagrams of the kind we have used throughout this book. For more information on the technique, see Forrester (1968).

Several other teams released models in the 1970s. The Mesarovic-Pestel, or World Integrated, Model (WIM) again looked at the environment and the economy but broke the world into 12 regions, much like those of IFs (Mesarovic and Pestel, 1974; Hughes, 1980). In fact, IFs adapted the demographic module of that model and some of the features of the energy and agriculture modules.

The British government sponsored a model called SARUM, which improved the representation of economies relative to earlier models (SARU, 1977). The United Nations sponsored one that became known as the United Nations, or Leontief, model that used a technique called input-output (I-O) matrices as its core (Leontief, Carter, and Petri, 1977). IFs has drawn on both SARUM and the UN model in its representation of economics, combining the general equilibrium structure of SARUM and the I-O structure of the UN model. The Argentine government sponsored a project at the Bariloche Foundation that produced a model with the name of that organization (Herrera et al., 1976). That model had a clearly structuralist bent and influenced the inclusion within IFs of basic human needs and of some structuralist logic.

At the end of the 1970s, the U.S. government commissioned a study of the future that looked to some of these models, to models of particular issues, and to a broad data base for an understanding of probable global developments through the end of the century. Gerald Barney directed that study and produced a three-volume report called *Global 2000* (Council on Environmental Quality, 1981). That study had a generally ecoholist orientation, and its volumes remain one of the best sources for insights into the U.S. government's capability for forecasting.

Although the models of the 1970s combined attention to the environment and the economy with increasing sophistication, they made little or no effort to represent political processes either within states or across them. Karl Deutsch recognized this weakness and initiated a project in Berlin under the leadership of Stuart Bremer that produced a model called GLOBUS (Bremer, 1987; Bremer and Gruhn, 1988). That model was the first to make states (countries) the basic unit of analysis and to represent both domestic and international political processes. In addition, it incorporates state-of-the-art representations of domestic and international economics, making it a unique political-economic world model. Bremer and Hughes (1990) used that model in a study of possible global arms control and global development efforts. IFs incorporates a much simplified political representation based roughly on GLOBUS. For strictly political models, see Bremer (1977) and Cusack and Stoll (1990).

Few of these models are available to you—most were used in scientific studies and have not been developed further. The GLOBUS model is an exception (Bremer and Gruhn, 1988). It is, however, quite a bit larger than IFs and proportionately more difficult to use. In addition, it lacks any treatment of the biological and physical environment (such as agriculture and energy submodels) and has only a rudimentary demographic module. Nonetheless, for those with largely political-economic interests, it is the most sophisticated model available.

**More Information on IFs**

You already know quite a bit about IFs. If you review the information presented about it throughout this book, you should generally understand its structure. Yet this book has stressed several times that the structure and parameters of IFs constitute a complex IF-statement that one should not accept uncritically, and you have seen neither the equations of IFs nor a complete explanation of its structure. Obviously, not everyone will have the technical skills to understand the structure and equations of the model or interest in them, and we will therefore not present them here. Appendix 3 indicates how you can obtain more technical information about IFs and even receive the computer code.

The equations of IFs are both more and less than a set of econometrically estimated equations developed to project the future. They are *more* because they are system- and theory-oriented. IFs is concerned with long-term behavior of global development systems; that concern requires theory and structure, not just the best fit to data. The IFs equations are *less* because the resultant equation structures and decisions on variable inclusion make estimation of parameters very difficult. The overall structure of IFs is a hybrid in terms of modeling style. It maintains an orientation toward the overall system and its closure, even in the face of holes in theory and knowledge, that is characteristic of systems dynamics and that uses some of those techniques. At the same time, as do econometric models, it directs close attention to the data that are available.

World modeling and forecasting with world models began in the early 1970s and have advanced quite dramatically in the intervening years. As this book has stressed, however, one cannot rely upon world models for predictions of the future—they are thinking tools, not crystal balls. Nonetheless, the growing sophistication of the models indicates the degree to which our theoretical understandings of the world and the availability of data about it have grown. Moreover, the development of the models is itself now increasingly contributing to our comprehension of global development processes, to the elaboration of our own mental models. The next generation of world models will draw upon this record of success and will also utilize faster and more powerful computers. The next decade of world modeling should be an exciting one.

## CONCLUSION

This book began by defining a dilemma. We cannot know the future; yet that future is terribly important to us, and we must therefore act in the face of uncertainty as if we did understand the consequences of our actions. The first chapter suggested an approach to reducing (or perhaps more accurately, identifying) uncertainty through the examination of trends and through causal analysis. Ironically, you may actually now feel more uncertain about the future than you did before this discussion and therefore less able to act. If so, this volume has probably added some complexity to your mental model, and your most important need is time for absorption and personal analysis of it. Choice under uncertainty will never be easy. No one can eliminate the uncertainty and make choice substantially easier. We can only hope to define our values, identify important leverage points, and thereby increase the likelihood that our choices will achieve our goals. After all, we do have a world order to create.

# □ □ □

# Appendix 1:
# Glossary of IFs Variables

All of the variables listed in this glossary can be printed out and examined by the user. The types of information provided in the list that follows are:
1. Variable name.
2. Names of the subscript sets that apply to the variable. Set names and members are:

REG (region):
| | | |
|---|---|---|
| US | = | United States |
| EC | = | European Community |
| JAPAN | = | Japan |
| RDEV | = | Rest of Developed World |
| RUS | = | Russia |
| LAM | = | Latin America |
| AFR | = | Africa |
| OPEC | = | OPEC |
| SASIA | = | South and Southeast Asia |
| CHINA | = | China |

SEC (economic sector):
| | | |
|---|---|---|
| AG | = | agriculture |
| EN | = | energy |
| MAT | = | materials |
| MAN | = | manufacturing |
| SER | = | services |

LND (land):
| | | |
|---|---|---|
| CR | = | crops |
| GR | = | grazing |
| FOR | = | forest |
| UN | = | undeveloped |
| URB | = | urban, industrial use |

FTY (food type):
| | | |
|---|---|---|
| CROP | = | crops |
| MEAT | = | meat, fish |

ENE (energy):
| | | |
|---|---|---|
| OILG | = | oil/gas |
| COAL | = | coal |
| RENEW | = | renewable |
| NUC | = | nuclear |

ENS (energy, short list):
| | | |
|---|---|---|
| OILG | = | oil/gas |
| COAL | = | coal |

ENL (energy, long list):
| | | |
|---|---|---|
| OILG | = | oil/gas |

169

|  |  |  |  |
|--|--|--|--|
| | COAL | = | coal |
| | RENEW | = | renewable |
| | NUC | = | nuclear |
| | OILU | = | oil/gas, unconventional |
| GOV (government category): | MIL | = | military |
| | HLTH | = | health |
| | EDUC | = | education |
| | FORA | = | foreign aid |

Variables are accessed only with member names (e.g., MIL), not with subset names (e.g., GOV).

3. Variable and parameter type.

Some variables are internal to the model and cannot be accessed by the model user. Those that can be printed are designated with a "P" on the following list; they include all indicators, initial conditions, and parameters. Only a subset of those that can be printed can also be changed by input. Those are identified in the following list with an "I" and consist of initial conditions and parameters. A further subset can (although they need not) be changed over time. Those parameters are identified with an "S."

4. Units of the variable.

Unit abbreviations include:

|  |  |  |
|--|--|--|
| MMT | = | million metric tons |
| MHA | = | million hectares |
| BBL | = | billion barrels of oil equivalent |
| $10^6$ | = | millions |
| $10^9$ | = | billions |
| $\$10^3$ | = | thousand dollars, constant 1990 |
| $\$10^6$ | = | million dollars, constant 1990 |
| $\$10^9$ | = | billion dollars, constant 1990 |

If no unit is specified, the variable is unitless.

| Name | Subscript(s) | Type | Definition/Units |
|------|--------------|------|------------------|
| A | SEC, SEC | P/I/S | Input/output or A matrix |
| AGCOST | – | – | Agricultural cost parameter |
| AGDEM | REG, FTY | P | Agricultural demand, MMT |
| AGM | REG, FTY | P/I | Agricultural imports, MMT |
| AGON | – | P/I/S | Parameter to turn on economic/agricultural linkages |
| AGP | REG, FTY | P | Agricultural production, MMT |
| AGX | REG, FTY | P/I | Agricultural exports, MMT |
| AID | REG | P | Net foreign aid, $\$10^9$ |
| AIDI | REG | P/I/S | Foreign aid coming from or going to investment |
| AIDLP | – | P/I/S | Loan portion of foreign aid |
| AIDM | REG | P/I/S | Foreign aid donor or recipient mode |
| AIDV | REG | P/I/S | Foreign aid donor or recipient value parameter |
| ALLY | REG | P/I/S | Alliance membership |
| APRAF | – | P/I/S | Agriculture price change parameter |
| BCIMPL | REG | P/I | Birth control implementation period, years |
| BCSTAR | | P/I | Birth control starting year |
| BIRTHS | | P | Births, $10^6$ |

| | | | |
|---|---|---|---|
| BURDF | – | P/I/S | Burden factor for action-reaction process |
| BURDM | – | P | Burden multiplier in action-reaction equation of military spending |
| C | REG | P | Private consumption, $10^9$ |
| CAPACT | REG | P/I | Cumulative capital account, $10^9$ |
| CBR | REG | P/I | Crude birthrate per thousand |
| CDAAG | REG | P/I | Cobb-Douglas alpha for agriculture |
| CDALF | REG | P/I | Cobb-Douglas alpha |
| CDMF | – | P/I/S | Civilian damage factor |
| CDR | REG | P/I | Crude death rate per thousand |
| CIVDM | REG | P | Civilian damage from war; multiplier for population and capital stock |
| CLAVAL | REG | P/I | Annual calories available |
| CLD | REG | P | Cost of land development, $10^3$ per hectare |
| CLNEED | REG | P/I | Annual calories needed |
| CLNF | REG | P/I | Calorie need factor |
| CLPC | REG | P | Regional calories per capita |
| CLSEXP | – | P/I | Starvation from calorie shortage parameter |
| CO2ABR | | P/I/S | $CO_2$ absorption rate, percent of $CO_2$ generated each year that is absorbed by oceans or other sinks |
| CPOW | REG | P | Conventional military power, index |
| CPOW1 | – | – | Conventional power of alliance 1 |
| CPOW2 | – | – | Conventional power of alliance 2 |
| CPOWDF | – | P/I/S | Conventional power damage factor |
| CPOWDM1 | – | – | Conventional power damage from war of alliance 1 |
| CPOWDM2 | – | – | Conventional power damage from war of alliance 2 |
| CPOWF | REG | P/I/S | Conventional power factor; converts military spending to conventional power (higher for labor-intensive countries) |
| CS | REG, SEC | P/I | Private consumption by sector, $10^9$ |
| CSPL | REG, SEC | – | Private consumption shares by sector of origin |
| CWAR | – | P | Conventional war (0=no; 1=yes) |
| CWARF | – | P/I/S | Conventional war factor; converts extra military expenditures into war probability |
| CWARPB | – | P | Conventional war probability |
| CWARSV | – | P/I/S | Conventional war severity parameter, portion of weaponry used |
| DEATHS | REG | P | Deaths, $10^6$ |
| DKL | – | P/I | Depreciation coefficient for land |
| DRCPOW | – | P/I/S | Annual depreciation rate of conventional power |
| DRNPOW | – | P/I/S | Annual depreciation rate of nuclear power |
| DSTL | – | P/I | Desired stock level as percentage of stock base |
| ECF | – | P/I/S | Elasticity of energy capacity utilization |
| EHW | – | P/I | Energy historical weight factor for impact of prices on demand |
| ELASAC | REG | P/I/S | Elasticity of yield with increases in atmospheric carbon dioxide |

| | | | |
|---|---|---|---|
| ELASDI | – | P/I/S | Elasticity of energy discoveries with prices |
| ELASEC | – | P/I/S | Elasticity of exchange rate with capital account/GNP |
| ELASED | – | P/I/S | Responsiveness of labor efficiency to education expenditures |
| ELASFD | – | P/I/S | Food demand elasticity with prices |
| ELASFP | | P/I/S | Food production elasticity with prices |
| ELASHC | – | P/I/S | Responsiveness of mortality to health care expenditures |
| ELASI2 | – | P/I/S | Second-order responsiveness of investment to stocks |
| ELASIN | – | P/I/S | Responsiveness of sectoral investment with stock level |
| ELASIS | – | P/I/S | Elasticity of total investment with stock level |
| ELASIT | – | P/I/S | Responsiveness of total domestic demand to stocks |
| ELASLV | – | P/I/S | Responsiveness of livestock herd growth to stocks |
| ELASS | REG, ENE | P/I/S | Responsiveness of energy investment to prices |
| ELASSU | – | P/I/S | Responsiveness of energy investment to surpluses |
| ELASZS | – | P/I/S | Elasticity of capacity utilization to stock level |
| ELCAVL | – | P/I/S | Elasticity of calorie need with approach to saturation level |
| ELIASP | – | P/I/S | Responsiveness of investment in agriculture split to return rate |
| EMD | – | P/I/S | Responsiveness of import demand to prices |
| ENDEM | REG | P | Energy demand, BBL |
| ENGEL | SEC | P/I | Engel coefficients in LES system for personal consumption |
| ENM | REG | P/I | Energy imports, BBL |
| ENON | – | P/I/S | Parameter that turns on economy link to energy |
| ENP | REG, ENE | P/I | Energy production, BBL |
| ENPRI | REG | P/I/S | Energy price, $ per barrel |
| ENPRR | REG, ENE | P/I | Energy production growth rate |
| ENRGNP | REG | P | Energy demand ratio to GNP, BBL/$10$^9$ |
| ENSHO | REG | P | Energy shortage, BBL |
| ENST | REG | P | Energy stocks, BBL |
| ENTL | REG | P/I/S | Energy trade limit, BBL |
| ENX | REG | P/I | Energy exports, BBL |
| EPRA | – | P/I/S | Energy price responsiveness to shortages |
| EPRAF | REG | P/I/S | Energy price responsiveness to surpluses and exogenous price switch |
| EPRAFS | – | P/I/S | Second-order energy price responsiveness to stock levels |
| EPRODR | REG, ENE | P/I/S | Energy production growth rate |
| EXC | – | P/I/S | Responsiveness of export capacity to prices |
| EXRATE | REG | P | Real exchange rate index, initial year equals 1 |
| FDEM | REG | P | Food demand, MMT |
| FEDDEM | REG | P/I | Feed demand, MMT |
| FPRI | REG, FTY | P | Food prices, per ton |

| | | | |
|---|---|---|---|
| FRQK | – | P/I | Livestock feed requirement coefficient |
| FSTOCK | REG, FTY | P | Food stocks, MMT |
| G | REG | P | Government expenditures, $10^9$ |
| GDS | REG, GOV | P | Government expenditures by destination, $10^9$ |
| GFORDT | REG | P/I | Government foreign debt, $10^9$ |
| GINI | REG | P/I/S | Gini coefficients |
| GK | REG, GOV | P/I/S | Government expenditure shares by destination |
| GLOCOM | – | P/I/S | Global community increase or decrease |
| GNP | .REG | P | Gross national product, $10^9$ |
| GNP1 | – | – | GNP of alliance 1 |
| GNP2 | – | – | GNP of alliance 2 |
| GNPP | REG | P | Potential gross national product, $10^9$ |
| GNPPC | REG | P | GNP per capita, $10^3$ |
| GNPPCF | REG | P/I | GNP per capita threshold for completion of fertility transition, $10^3$ |
| GNPPCM | REG | P/I | GNP per capita threshold for completion of mortality transition, $10^3$ |
| GNPR | REG | P | GNP annual growth rate |
| GS | REG, SEC | P/I | Government expenditures by sector of origin, $10^9$ |
| GSPL | REG, SEC | P/I/S | Government expenditure shares by sector of origin |
| HWF | – | P/I | Historical weight factor for expected economic growth |
| I | REG | P | Investment, $10 |
| IALK | REG | P/I/S | Investment in agriculture, land share |
| IASF | REG | P/I/S | Investment in agriculture scenario factor |
| IDS | REG, SEC | P/I | Investment by destination, $10^9$ |
| IESF | REG | P/I/S | Investment in energy scenario factor |
| IGLNK | – | P/I/S | Coefficient linking tax rate to investment level |
| IGNPR | REG | P/I | Initial economic growth rate, decimal form |
| ILVHRG | – | P/I/S | Livestock herd basic growth rate |
| IMARK | – | P/I/S | Initial price markup over cost |
| INAG | REG | P | Investment need in agriculture, $10^9$ |
| INDEM | REG | P/I | Industrial food demand, MMT |
| INFMOR | REG | P | Infant mortality rate per 1,000 live births |
| INVS | REG, SEC | P/I | Investment by origin sector, $10^9$ |
| IRA | REG | P | Investment to gross domestic product ratio |
| ISFL | REG, SEC | P/I/S | Investment expenditure shares by sector of origin |
| ISHIFT | REG | P/I/S | Shift of consumption to investment, decimal form |
| KAG | REG | P | Capital in agriculture, $10^9$ |
| KCONK | – | P/I | Capital contribution to economic growth |
| KENF | – | P/I | Parameter linking energy prices and economic output |
| KS | REG, SEC | P | Capital by economic sector, $10^9$ |
| LAB | REG | P | Labor, millions |
| LABS | REG, SEC | P | Labor by sector, millions |
| LAPOPR | REG | P/I/S | Labor participation rate |

| LD | REG, IND | P/I | Land, MHA |
|---|---|---|---|
| LDWF | – | P/I/S | Land withdrawal factor with population growth |
| LEFMG | REG | P | Labor efficiency multiplier from government |
| LIFEXP | REG | P | Life expectancy, years |
| LINTR | – | P/I/S | Loan interest rate |
| LIT | REG | P | Literacy, percentage of population |
| LKE | ENE | P/I | Lifetime of energy capital, years |
| LKS | – | P/I | Lifetime of capital, years |
| LOANR | REG | P | Loan repayment amount per year, $10^9$ |
| LOSS | REG | P/I/S | Proportion of food production lost |
| LVCF | – | P/I | Livestock calorie conversion factor |
| LVHERD | REG | P/I | Livestock herd, MMT |
| M | REG | P | Imports, $10^9$ |
| MARIC | REG | P/I/S | Mariculture fish production, MMT |
| MHW | – | P/I | Import historical weight factor |
| MILSP1 | – | – | Military spending of alliance 1 |
| MILSPM2 | – | P | Military spending multiplier of alliance 2 from action-reaction equation |
| MLBURF | – | P/I/S | Military burden factor, portion of increased military spending in arms races coming from investment |
| MORTM | REG | P/I/S | Mortality multiplier |
| MORTMG | REG | – | Mortality multiplier from government expenditures |
| MS | REG, ENE | P/I | Imports by sector, $10^9$ |
| NMILF | REG | P/I/S | Portion of military spending directed to nuclear forces (0 to 1) |
| NPOW | REG | P/I | Nuclear military power, megatons |
| NPOW1 | – | – | Nuclear power of alliance 1 |
| NPOW2 | – | – | Nuclear power of alliance 2 |
| NPOWF | – | P/I/S | Nuclear power factor, megatons/billion $ expenditure |
| NSGAPA | – | P | North-South gap, absolute difference between GNPs/capita in the North and those in the South |
| NSGAPR | – | P | North-South gap, ratio of GNPs/capita in the North to those in the South |
| NSPQLI | – | P | Ratio of North to South PQLI/capita |
| NWAR | – | P | Nuclear war (0=no; 1=yes) |
| NWARD0 | – | – | Nuclear war damage of nonparticipants |
| NWARD1 | – | – | Nuclear war damage of alliance 1 |
| NWARD2 | – | – | Nuclear war damage of alliance 2 |
| NWARF | – | P/I/S | Nuclear war factor; converts conventional war into probability of nuclear war |
| NWARPB | – | P | Nuclear war probability |
| NWARSV | – | P/I/S | Nuclear war severity parameter, portion of weaponry used |
| OFSCTH | – | P/I/S | Ocean fish catch, MMT |
| OILGPR | – | P | Oil proportion of global energy |
| PERCO2 | – | P | Percentage increase in atmospheric $CO_2$ |

| | | | |
|---|---|---|---|
| PF1 | – | P/I/S | Power factor 1; relative contribution of population to power index |
| PF2 | – | P/I/S | Power factor 2; relative contribution of GNP to power index |
| PF3 | – | P/I/S | Power factor 3; relative contribution of conventional military power to power index |
| PF4 | – | P/I/S | Power factor 4; relative contribution of nuclear power to power index |
| PFD | REG, SEC | P | Production for final demand, $\$10^9$ |
| POP | REG | P/I | Population, millions |
| POPR | REG | P | Population growth rate |
| POWER | REG | P | Aggregate power index |
| PQLI | REG | P | Physical quality of life index |
| PRAF | – | P/I | Price adjustment factor with stock level |
| PRI | REG, SEC | P | Prices, index values |
| PRODME | – | P/I/S | Elasticity of production with imports of manufactures (0 to .5) |
| PRODTF | REG, ENS | P/I/S | Minimum reserves to production ratio |
| PROTEC | REG | P/I/S | Increase or decrease in protection of imports |
| QE | REG, ENL | P/I/S | Capital output ratio, dollars/barrel |
| RDI | ENS | P/I | Initial discovery rate, BBL |
| RDINR | ENS | P/I | Discovery rate basic annual increment, BBL |
| RDM | REG | P/I/S | Discovery rate multiplier |
| REACM | – | P/I/S | Reactivity multiplier in action-reaction process |
| REPAYR | – | P/I/S | Repayment rate on loans, portion of outstanding balance |
| RESER | REG, ENS | P/I | Known reserves, BBL |
| RESOR | REG, ENS | P/I/S | Ultimate resources, BBL |
| RESORF | ENS | P/I/S | Resource multiplier |
| RFSSH | REG | P/I/S | Regional fish catch share |
| RKEF | REG | P/I/S | Rate of capital efficiency growth |
| RLEF | REG | P/I/S | Rate of labor efficiency growth |
| RYAL2 | – | – | Economic growth of alliance 2 |
| SAVSPN | – | – | Temporary save of military spending from alliance 2 members in computing action-reaction spending |
| SDEATH | REG | P | Starvation deaths, millions |
| SLR | – | P/I/S | Livestock slaughter rate |
| SMAN | – | P | Southern share of global manufacturing |
| SMILSP1 | – | – | First year military spending of alliance 1 |
| SMILSP2 | – | – | First year military spending of alliance 2 |
| SMMANK | – | – | Initial coefficient of manufacturing imports |
| SQUEEZ | – | P/I/S | Switch for energy shortage economic impact |
| SRYAL2 | – | – | First year economic growth of alliance 2 |
| ST | REG, SEC | P | Stocks, $\$10^9$ |
| SUMDIF | – | – | Sum of difference between normal and action-reaction military spending of alliance 2 |
| SUMMIL | – | – | Sum of military spending of alliance 2 |
| TAXRA | REG | P/I/S | Tax rate |
| TD | REG | P | Trade balance, $\$10^9$ |

| | | | |
|---|---|---|---|
| TERMTR | – | P | Terms of trade, computed (higher is better for South) |
| TERMX | – | P/I/S | Terms of trade multiplier (higher is better for South) |
| TGRLD | REG | P/I/S | Target growth in cultivated land |
| TGRYL | REG | P/I/S | Target growth in yield |
| TMORTR | – | P/I/S | Time-related reduction in mortality |
| WAP | FTY | P/I | World agricultural price |
| WAPRO | FTY | P | World agricultural production, MMT |
| WCLPC | – | P | World calories per capita |
| WCPOW | – | P | World conventional power |
| WECONM | – | P/I/S | World energy conservation multiplier |
| WENP | ENE | P | World energy production, BBL |
| WENPF | ENE | P/I/S | World energy production multiplier |
| WEP | – | P | World energy price, BBL |
| WFORST | – | P | World forest area, MHA |
| WGNP | – | P | World GNP, $\$10^9$ |
| WGNPPC | – | P | World GNP per capita, $\$10^3$ |
| WLIFE | – | P | World life expectancy, years |
| WLIT | – | P | World literacy, percent |
| WM | SEC | – | World imports, $\$10^9$ |
| WNPOW | – | P | World nuclear power |
| WP | SEC | P | World price, index values |
| WPOP | – | P | Global population, millions |
| WPOPR | – | P | Global population growth rate |
| WPQLI | REG | P | World physical quality of life index |
| WPROD | SEC | P | World production by sector, percentage share of total global product |
| WQEM | ENE | P/I/S | World multiplier on energy capital and operating costs |
| WRESER | ENS | P | World known reserves, BBL |
| WRESOR | ENS | P | World ultimate resources, BBL |
| WSDACC | – | P | World cumulative starvation deaths, millions |
| WSTK | FTY | P | World food stock, MMT |
| WTRADE | – | P | World trade as a ratio of world GNP |
| WX | SEC | – | World exports, $\$10^9$ |
| WYLF | – | P/I/S | World agricultural yield multiplier |
| X | REG | P | Exports, $\$10^9$ |
| XHW | – | P/I | Export historical weight factor |
| XS | REG, SEC | P/I | Exports by sector, $\$10^9$ |
| XSHIFT | REG | P/I/S | Proportional increase or decrease in exports |
| YL | REG | P/I | Agricultural yield, tons/hectare |
| YLEXP | – | P/I/S | Exponent in saturating yield function |
| YLF | REG | P/I/S | Yield factor or multiplier |
| ZS | REG, SEC | P/I | Gross production by sector, $\$10^9$ |

□   □   □

# Appendix 2:
# Parameters and Their Use

That there are many types of parameters adds to the complexity of their use. Before providing some information on each major parameter in the model, we outline the major types. Further complicating this discussion is the fact that some parameters have characteristics of more than one of the following types.

Some parameters are **multipliers**. That is, they have a normal value of 1, and to increase whatever they multiply (say, food production) by 50 percent you increase the parameter to 1.5. To decrease it by 25 percent, you would decrease the parameter to 0.75. You will almost always spread such changes out over time, keeping the multiplier's value at 1 in 1990 and gradually increasing or decreasing it over a period of years. You should almost never change a multiplier in 1990 because the model is set up to provide accurate results for that year and will compensate for and thereby offset your change. For instance, if you set a multiplier on food production equal to 1.5 for 1990 and all years thereafter, you might find that the results are no different than the base case. You must instead gradually introduce your change, preserving the multiplier value of 1 in 1990. Examples of multipliers include CLNF, MORTM, PF1–4, RDM, RESORF, WECONM, WENPF, WQEM, WYLF, and YLF.

A few parameters are **additive factors**. Most have a normal value of 0, thereby leaving that to which we add them (it could be food production again) unchanged. How much you would add to achieve a 50 percent increase might depend on the amount to which you added it. Most additive parameters are, however, applied multiplicatively to the quantity they modify (that is, 1 plus the parameter is multiplied times the quantity), thereby scaling the parameter. In that case, the base or normal value of the parameter will be zero, but one can achieve a 50 percent increase in the quantity modified with a value of 0.5 and a 50 percent decrease with −0.5. You will very seldom want to change the 1990 value of additive parameters because that will either incorrectly change model results in 1990 or, more likely, result in model compensation to protect initial model results. Examples of additive parameters are GLOCOM, IASF, IESF, ISHIFT, LINTR, PROTEC, RKEF, RLEF, TERMX, and XSHIFT.

Some parameters are **exponents**. For instance, many "elasticities" raise something to a power. For these parameters, the "normal value" will vary greatly, but they will most often fall between −2 and 2, with many clustering around 0. In most cases it will make sense to change these parameters for all years including the first; generally, the model will not use them in the first year, and they will affect results only in subsequent years. Exponents in IFs include BURDF, ELASS, ENGEL, and PRODME.

A small category of parameters includes **reactivities**. These are factors that relate growth in one process to growth in another. Although many will range between −2 and 2 (with 0 eliminating linkage of the processes), some have very large values. They are very much like elasticities, but the formulations that use them do not have exponential form. Reactivities include: CDMF, CPOWDF, CWARF, KENF, NWARF, and REACM.

177

Another small category of parameters consists of **growth rates**. It is possible to force some processes to grow at specified rates. More commonly, the specified rates serve as targets, and the dynamics of the model often shift actual growth rates somewhat, necessitating experimentation with targets and overcompensation to achieve a desired growth. An example is EPRODR.

**Initial conditions** make up still another type of parameter. Although many initial conditions, like the population of the United States, are sufficiently well known that they should not be changed by model users, others, like the ultimate availability of oil and gas resources, are only reasonable guesses. Thus users should feel free to change some initial conditions based on new data or even simply to test the implications. This category includes LD and RESOR.

The next category of parameter is the **coefficient.** We generally use coefficients in multiplicative relationships with other variables, but they are not multiplier parameters. Instead, they often serve an allocative role. For instance, we can use parameters to allocate governmental spending to health, education, and the military. Allocative coefficients frequently have values between 0 and 1. Again, you should generally not change these parameters in 1990 because the model will often compensate for different values. Instead, change them by series over time. Coefficients in IFs include AIDI, AIDLP, AIDV, CO2ABR, CWARF, DRCPOW, DRNPOW, FRQK, GK, IALK, LAPOPR, LOSS, MLBURF, NMILF, NWARF, REPAYR, RFSSH, and TAXRA.

Still another category should not really be called parameters at all but **variables**. They could be computed endogenously, if the model included the appropriate theoretical structure; in some cases, IFs does compute them, but you can override endogenous computations. Such variables include ENPRI, GINI, MARIC, OFSCTH, and QE.

The ninth and final category of parameter consists of **switches**. These parameters turn something on or off. They generally take on values of 1 (on) or 0 (off) but can have additional settings. For instance, some switches not only turn on some process but set a key value within it (like the level of energy exports). Switches are sometimes on or off for the entire run, but in many cases it makes sense to "throw a switch" in the middle of a run. Switches allow us to fundamentally alter the structure of a model. Switches include AGON, AIDM, ALLY, BCIMPL, BCSTAR, ENON, ENTL, EPRAF, GNPPCF, and SQUEEZ.

The focus here is on exogenous parameters only, on those elements of the model that you can change. Many computed variables are used in the computation of other variables in the same way that parameters are—as multipliers, additive factors, coefficients, and so on. You can display those, but unlike the parameters below, you cannot change them.

AGON            Agriculture switch. This switch turns on or off the linkages between the agricultural submodel and all others, including economics. With the switch off, the economic model would thus rely upon the simpler structure of its own agricultural sector. AGON takes values only of 1 (on) and 0 (off). It is often useful to disconnect submodels while exploring the behavior of any one. The normal value is 1.

AIDI            Aid from investment coefficient. The model adds or subtracts from investment this portion (e.g., 0.25 equals 25 percent) of aid given or received. Positive values increase investment for recipients and decrease it for donors; normally the values are positive for all regions. A negative value would reduce investment for a recipient (implying a perverse effect of aid) and increase it for a donor. The remaining aid portion increases consumption for aid recipients and decreases it for donors. Note on foreign aid scenarios: The initial-year levels of aid receipts or contributions, as a percentage of GNP, are assumed to be already represented in initial investment levels. Thus only changes in aid levels as a percentage of GNP will have any effect on investment, regardless of the value for AIDI.

AIDLP          Aid, loan portion. This coefficient determines the portion of foreign aid that actually constitutes loans. A value of 0 means that aid is all nonrepayable; a value of 1 means that aid is all repayable.

AIDM          Aid mode. A switch determining the mode of foreign assistance behavior, by region. This parameter has only two acceptable values: 1 indicates a donor region, and 2 indicates a recipient region.

AIDV          Aid value. A coefficient of foreign assistance, by region. This parameter is always used simultaneously with AIDM. It is in decimal form and has different meanings for donors and recipients. For donor regions, AIDV specifies the percentage of GNP given in foreign aid (e.g., 0.2 equals 0.2 percent of GNP). For recipient regions, it is the regional proportion of the total global assistance available—in other words, a value of .2 indicates that 20 percent of the aid given by all donor regions is received by the designated recipient. The values for all aid recipients should add to 1. If they do not, however, the model will normalize the values (so that they do sum to 1) and will assure that no more or less aid is distributed than is provided by donor regions.

ALLY          Alliance membership switch. A value of 1 indicates membership in the acting alliance, and a value of 2 indicates membership in the reacting alliance (either alliance can consist of a single country or region). Alliances can form or dissolve over time; membership in alliances can change. None of that will, however, happen endogenously; you must specify alliance structures.

BCIMPL          Birth control implementation period, in years. The number of years before a family planning program (or natural processes of demographic change) results in replacement rate fertility, by region. It is generally unreasonable to assume that a program could be successful in less than 20 years; Indira Gandhi once tried a 20-year program in India, used considerable coercion, and met significant resistance.

BCSTAR          Birth control starting year. The year in which a family planning program begins, by region. If no program is desired, this can be set beyond the time horizon of the analysis, say to 2100.

BURDF          Burden factor affecting action-reaction equation for arms spending. A zero value for this elasticity decouples changes in economic growth rate from arms spending. A positive value reduces military spending when economic growth rates fall, and a value of 1 would reduce military spending by the same percentage that economic growth falls below initial conditions. Negative values could represent an outward direction of frustration by a country when growth falls. Meaningful values could range from $-2$ to $2$.

CDMF          Civilian damage factor. This reactivity parameter links the severity of conventional war and the power of the opposing alliance to civilian damage (both population killed and economic capital destroyed). A value of 0 will decouple conventional war from damage, and a value of 1 will make damage proportional to the war severity and opposing power. There is no comparable parameter for the impact of nuclear war on civilians because the model always assumes civilian damage; in fact, it extends some such damage beyond the regions involved in nuclear war to third-party countries (from fallout and other collateral damage).

CLNF          Calorie need factor. A multiplier on calorie needs, by region. It normally has a value of 1. You can use this multiplier to shift the calories needed by a region up or down to avoid starvation (perhaps in reaction to changing assumptions about food distribution). Setting the value to 0 turns off the feedback between food shortages and starvation for a region.

CO2ABR $CO_2$ absorption rate coefficient. The percent of $CO_2$ generated each year that is absorbed by oceans or other sinks. The value should range between 0.0 and 1.0; a value of 1.0 would mean that $CO_2$ was entirely absorbed by sinks and did not add to the atmosphere (values of less than 0 could simulate other sources of greenhouse gases, and values of more than 1 could represent net reductions in atmospheric $CO_2$).

CPOWDF Conventional power damage factor. This reactivity parameter links the severity of conventional war and the power of the opposing alliance to the losses of conventional power (personnel and equipment). A value of 0 will decouple conventional war from damage, and a value of 1 will make damage proportional to the war severity and power of the opponents.

CWARF Conventional war factor. This is a reactivity parameter that relates additional arms spending of the reacting state or alliance to the probability that war will erupt between acting and reacting alliances. A value of 0 eliminates the possibility of war; a value of 1 creates a probability of war equal to the percentage increase in military spending. By setting the value equal to 100 or more, you can force the model to generate a war.

CWARSV Conventional war severity factor. This coefficient determines what portion of the conventional armament potential will be used when a war erupts. Values should range from 0 (none) to 1 (all).

DRCPOW Annual depreciation rate of conventional power (coefficient). High values could simulate arms control agreements that result in destruction of weapons.

DRNPOW Annual depreciation rate of nuclear power (coefficient). High values could simulate arms control agreements that result in destruction of weapons.

ELASS Elasticity of energy supply with price change, by region and energy type. There is tremendous uncertainty about these numbers. Higher numbers will increase the responsiveness of energy supply to increased prices, and lower numbers will decrease that responsiveness. The elasticities actually work on energy investment and therefore only indirectly (and with a time delay) on energy supply. To completely eliminate investment and therefore to phase out production (for instance, in response to a ban on nuclear energy production), use any negative number.

ENGEL Engel elasticities in the LES system for personal consumption. These are uncertain, and changes in them affect terms of trade and regional development patterns. Values above 1.0 result in personal consumption demand within a sector that is growing faster than total consumption, while values below 1.0 have the reverse effect.

ENON Energy switch. This switch turns on or off the linkages between the energy submodel and all others, including economics. When off, the economic model relies upon the simpler structure of its own energy sector. ENON takes values only of 1 (on) and 0 (off). It is often useful to disconnect submodels while exploring the behavior of any one. The normal value is 1.

ENPRI Energy price in dollars per barrel of oil equivalent, by region. This variable is normally computed endogenously so as to balance supply and demand of energy. If you set EPRAF to 0, you can then specify whatever price pattern over time you wish. You will not normally change the value for the first year, which is based on data. It is also possible to intervene with energy prices only for select years by setting EPRAF to zero only for those years and specifying ENPRI only for those years. You might do this, for instance, to represent a period in which government controls energy prices domestically or a cartel sets them internationally.

ENTL — Energy trade limit in billion barrels of oil equivalent, by region. This parameter works both as a switch and as a numerical value. When the value is 0, no limits to energy exports or imports are specified. Positive values (above .001) limit exports to the value specified. Negative values (below −.001) limit imports to the value specified. For instance, a specification for OPEC of 0 for the first five years, 2 for the next three, and 0 thereafter would introduce a constraint on OPEC oil exports of two billion barrels per year during the sixth, seventh, and eighth years. This would be a *severe* oil embargo.

EPRAF — Energy price adjustment factor, by region. This parameter serves as a switch and must be used in conjunction with ENPRI to set prices exogenously and thereby override the model's computation of energy prices. The nonzero value of the base case is a parameter used in the equation that computes change in energy prices based on the balance between supply and demand; you should not change that to another nonzero value because you would disrupt that mechanism. That is, you should either leave this switch parameter as it is (for endogenous pricing) or set it to zero (for exogenous pricing). In the latter case, see the description of ENPRI.

EPRODR — Energy production growth rate, expressed in decimal form (e.g., 0.035 equals 3.5 percent annual growth), by region and fuel type. This parameter can override endogenous patterns of energy production growth and force a pattern of growth for a specific fuel or set of fuels. Growth rates are, however, constrained in the model by the availability of investment and/or resources and may not be met. Only positive values are allowed. Under most circumstances, the initial value for this variable should be equal to that of ENPRR for the specified region and fuel type, because ENPRR is the empirical initial growth rate.

FRQK — Livestock feed requirement coefficient. This represents the pounds of feed required to produce one pound of meat. Changes might simulate alternative types of animals fed for their meat and thus either increased or decreased efficiency (chickens require less feed than cows for each pound of meat).

GINI — The GINI index. A measure of income distribution that is unitless, by region. The initial value represents the best data available for the region. Thus this variable is usually only changed after the initial year. Realistically, income distribution patterns change very slowly. Lower values indicate more equality, with .2 a reasonable lower limit, whereas higher values indicate greater inequality, with .6 a reasonable upper value.

GK — Governmental spending coefficient. The proportion of total regional governmental expenditures going to each of four categories: military, health, education, and foreign aid. Values range from 0 (no expenditures) to 1 (all expenditures). It is not necessary to assure that the values of GK sum to 1 across expenditure categories; the model will normalize them to 1. Do not use GK to change foreign aid expenditures. Use AIDV instead, and the model will correctly compute governmental expenditures on aid.

GLOCOM — Global community parameter. This additive parameter (multiplicatively applied) simulates the impact that growing global community might have on dampening arms races driven by action-reaction dynamics. A value of 0 leaves the base case unchanged. A value of 0.5 would increase "community" by 50 percent and decrease arms spending of both acting and reacting alliances by 50 percent. A value of −0.5 would suggest a deterioration in global community.

GNPPCF     GNP per capita fertilty factor. The upper income threshold on the fertility transition to replacement rate, in thousands of constant dollars, by region. If this threshold is set below the initial value of GNPPC, income change will have no effect on fertility.

IALK     Investment in agricultural land coefficient. The portion of agricultural investment directed to land development. Gradual changes over time can alter the split of agricultural investment between land development and capital.

IASF     Investment in agriculture scenario factor. An additive parameter, by region, that allows shifts of investment into or out of agriculture to supplement internally generated changes in investment. A value of 0 represents no change, 0.25 represents a 25 percent increase, and −0.25 introduces a 25 percent decrease. This variable should be 0 for the first year and then be changed gradually over time.

IESF     Investment in energy scenario factor. An additive parameter, by region, that allows shifts of investment into or out of energy production to supplement internally generated changes in investment. A value of 0 represents no change, 0.25 represents a 25 percent increase, and −0.25 introduces a 25 percent decrease. This variable should be 0 for the first year and then be changed gradually over time.

ISHIFT     Investment shift. An additive parameter allowing increase (positive values) or decrease (negative values) of the investment level, at the expense of or to the benefit of private consumption, by region. ISHIFT is in decimal form so that, for example, a value of .05 would add 5 percent of GDP to investment (it is multiplicatively scaled) for a given year. Realistically, investment levels change slowly, and values should seldom exceed 1.

KENF     Capital efficiency response to higher energy prices. A reactivity parameter that determines how great the reduction in capital efficiency will be (for instance, from premature obsolescence) in the face of higher energy prices. A value of 0 implies that energy prices have no impact on capital efficiency, whereas a value of −.1 would reduce energy efficiency by 10 percent given a doubling in energy prices.

LAPOPR     Labor to population ratio. A coefficient specifying the labor force as a portion of total population, in decimal form, by region. You should change values only after the initial year. This rate tends to increase as economies develop and populations reach equilibrium, because the labor force participation rate of women increases and a higher percentage of the population falls into working years.

LD     Land in million hectares, by region and land category. You can change this initial condition to represent different assumptions about land availability for agriculture. Only initial values can be changed; the model subsequently computes land by category endogenously.

LINTR     Loan interest rate. This additive parameter (multiplicatively applied) determines the annual interest accumulation on outstanding interstate loans. A value of 0 means no interest. A value of 0.05 would mean 5 percent (real) interest per year. Negative values could be used to forgive loans.

LOSS     Agricultural loss coefficient. The proportion of food production lost before it becomes available for consumption (for example, to pests in the field or to distribution inefficiency and spoilage).

MARIC       Mariculture, in million metric tons, by region. Users can provide assumptions over time about domestic fish production with this parameter.

MLBURF       Military burden factor. A coefficient that determines how much of an increase in military spending resulting from action-reaction dynamics is diverted from other governmental spending; the residual affects investment levels.

MORTM       Mortality multiplier. A multiplier on mortality rates, unitless, by region. A value of 1 implies no change, whereas higher values increase mortality proportionately increase mortality and lower values decrease it. A value of zero turns the variable off and is therefore equivalent to a multiplier of 1. You would introduce an epidemic (like AIDS) that doubled mortality rates for a specific time period with a value of 2 during the period; at other times, the value would stay at 1. Scientific advance that doubled our age spans could be introduced by a value of .5, beginning with the year of a remarkable advance, or could be phased in gradually. Maintain the value of 1 in the initial year.

NMILF       Nuclear military expenditure factor. A coefficient determining what portion of a country's or region's military expenditure is devoted to nuclear weapons, including delivery systems. For instance, 0.1 would result in 10 percent. This can be changed over time and could be used to convert a traditionally nuclear-free region into a nuclear power. Normal values will range from 0 to 0.2.

NWARF       Nuclear war factor. This is a reactivity parameter that relates the severity of a conventional war to the probability that nuclear war will erupt between acting and reacting alliances. A value of 0 eliminates the possibility of nuclear war; a value of 1 creates a probability of nuclear war equal to the severity of conventional war (see CWARSV). By setting the value equal to 100 or more, you can force the model to generate a nuclear war whenever a conventional war erupts.

NWARSV       Nuclear war severity factor. This coefficient determines what portion of the nuclear armament potential will be used when a war erupts. Values should range from 0 (none) to 1 (all).

OFSCTH       Ocean fish catch, in million metric tons. This exogenously specified variable represents the total global ocean fish catch, to be divided among all regions (see RFSSH). Normally you will accept the initial conditions and change only subsequent values.

PF1       Power factor number 1. This is a weighting parameter that determines the importance of population size in the summary calculation of a country's power. Similarly, PF2, PF3, and PF4 weight GNP, conventional forces, and nuclear forces, respectively. Values of 1 would give each element equal weight. A value of 2 on any single element, when others retained values of 1, would weight that element twice as heavily.

PRODME       Production elasticity with imports. The parameter that ties the rate of manufacturing imports as a portion of the GNP to the level of production (because increases in manufacturing imports will bring imbedded technology and therefore efficiency improvements). A value of 0 turns off the linkage. A value of 1 translates a percentage increase in manufactured imports relative to initial levels into an identical percentage increase in production (all sectors).

PROTEC       Trade protection parameter. This additive parameter (multiplicatively applied) increases or decreases the cost of imports, thereby representing the addition or reduction of tariff and nontariff barriers to trade. A value of 0 leaves the base case unchanged. A value of 0.5 would increase effective import costs by 50 percent, whereas a value of −0.5 would decrease them by 50 percent. Reasonable values might range from −0.5 to 5, and the value in 1990 should not be changed from 0.

QE  Capital output ratio for energy, in dollars, per barrel of production capacity, by region and energy category. This exogenous variable represents the cost of energy production. Higher values mean higher costs. Values for oil/gas and coal are computed endogenously (and depend on remaining resources) and should be examined only as indicators. To change the cost pattern for those energy forms, use RESORF and increase or decrease resources. Values for renewable and nuclear energy can be exogenously changed, but you should maintain the initial value of the base case. A series of gradually lower costs could represent technological progress (e.g., in the solar component of renewable). A series of gradually higher costs could represent the impact of environmental factors (e.g., increasing costs of nuclear waste disposal). Higher or lower values will increase or decrease investment in a particular energy category and will affect its production level. You should be aware that investment will respond only to changes over time in QE and not to changes in the initial condition.

RDM  Energy reserve discovery multiplier, unitless. This parameter normally has a value of 1. A value of 1.5 would increase annual fossil fuel discoveries by 50 percent (within the limit of ultimate resources, but without additional investment in energy discovery), whereas a value of 0.5 would decrease it by 50 percent.

REACM  Reactivity multiplier. This parameter determines the magnitude of the defense spending increase in the reacting alliance relative to the spending increase in the acting alliance. A value of 1 means that the percentage increase of the two alliances will be identical. A value of 1.5 means that the reacting alliance will increase its expenditures 50 percent faster than the acting alliance, whereas a value of .5 means that it increases its spending only 50 percent as much as the acting alliance.

REPAYR  Loan repayment rate. This coefficient determines the portion of outstanding interstate loans that must be repaid each year. A value of 0 means no repayment (principal and interest accumulate); a value of 1 would mean that the entire balance is due in a given year. A value of 0.05 would imply that 5 percent is repayable, roughly equivalent to a 20-year loan term.

RESOR  Ultimately recoverable resources, in billion barrels of oil equivalent, by region and fuel. You should change this initial condition as a constant value for all time steps. Although the default values already in the model are reasonable guesses, there is much uncertainty among geologists.

RESORF  Ultimately recoverable resource multiplier factor, by energy type. This parameter allows the user to increase or decrease ultimately recoverable resource values in all regions simultaneously and in identical proportion. A value of 1 accepts the values of RESOR as specified. A value of 1.5 would raise the resource levels for that fuel in all regions by 50 percent. This multiplier is unusual in that *it is only important in the first year*; it should not be changed over time because after ultimate resources are calculated the first year they can only run down (be used up).

RFSSH  Regional share in global fish catch (see OFSCTH). For instance, a coefficient of 0.2 equals 20 percent of global catch. The coefficients should sum to 1 across regions (to 100 percent) because the model will not normalize them.

RKEF  Rate of growth in capital efficiency. This parameter is an additive factor in the production function and represents annual technological progress in the efficiency or productivity of capital over time (the model accumulates this progress). It is in decimal form, so that a value of 0.01 implies a 1 percent annual increase in productivity. The initial value should never be changed, and subsequent values should change slowly and relatively little. There is unfortunately little empirical basis for this parameter, in spite of its importance.

RLEF    Rate of growth in labor efficiency. This parameter is an additive factor in the production function and represents annual progress in the efficiency or productivity of labor over time (the model accumulates this progress). It is in decimal form, so that a value of 0.01 implies a 1 percent annual increase in productivity. The initial value should never be changed, and subsequent values should change slowly and relatively little. There is unfortunately little empirical basis for this parameter, in spite of its importance.

SLR    Livestock slaughter rate coefficient. This is the proportion of the herd slaughtered annually. An increase might reflect a global movement to animals with faster growth rates (such as chickens versus cattle).

SQUEEZ    A switch that squeezes economic production when there are energy shortages (IFs does not force equilibration between energy supply and demand in any given time period but seeks it over time; thus in the case of severe supply constraints, such as export limits by OPEC, actual shortages can appear). A value of 0 turns off the linkage, and the normal value of 1 activates it. Other positive values also turn on the switch. A value of 2 would make the impact of a shortage twice as great as normal, and a value of 0.5 would cut it in half.

TAXRA    The tax rate. A coefficient in decimal form, by region, that determines the portion of the GNP taken by the government. The initial value represents the best data available for the region. Thus this variable is usually changed only after the first year. This variable changes the overall level of government spending; if that goes up, private consumption and investment are reduced accordingly.

TERMX    Terms of trade multiplier. The normal value of this parameter is 1.0, signifying no exogenous shift in the terms of trade between more and less economically developed countries. Relative prices in various sectors, particularly agriculture and energy, will still change endogenously. A value greater than 1.0 additionally improves terms of trade for LDCs at the expense of developed countries. A value of less than 1.0 shifts terms of trade to the benefit of wealthier countries. A value of 1.2 would improve the terms of trade of the very-least-developed countries by about 20 percent. This parameter should not normally be changed from 1 in the initial year. Values should generally range from .5 to 1.5.

TGRLD    Target annual growth rate in cultivated land, by region. This parameter establishes the initial pattern of growth in investment in bringing new land under cultivation. It is used in computation only in the initial year; thereafter the investment pattern changes endogenously in response to changing agricultural prices and costs.

TGRYL    Target annual growth rate in yield, by region. This parameter establishes the initial pattern of growth in production yield. It is used in computation only in the initial year; thereafter the growth in yield changes endogenously in response to changing agricultural prices and costs.

WECONM    World energy conservation mutiplier. This factor multiplies the endogenous computation of energy demand for all regions. A value of 1.0 leaves that computation unchanged. A value of 0.8 would reduce energy demand by about 20 percent. Because energy demand will directly affect prices and prices will in turn affect the endogenous computation of energy demand, a reduction in this multipier over time will lower prices and cause an increase in endogenous demand, thereby offsetting some of the anticipated effect. The value should be 1.0 in the initial year.

WENPF      World energy production multiplier. This factor multiplies the endogenous computation of energy production for all energy types and all regions. A value of 1.0 leaves the endogenous compuation unchanged. A value of 0.8 would decrease energy production by about 20 percent (although energy price changes will cause the model to "fight" this decrease). The value should be 1.0 in the initial year.

WQEM      World production cost in energy multiplier, by energy type. This factor multiplies the total of capital and operating costs for an energy type. A value of 1.0 leaves those costs unchanged. A value of 0.8 would reduce them by approximately 20 percent. Leave the value in the initial year unchanged, and generally make fairly moderate changes over time.

WYLF      World yield factor. A multiplier that allows the user to posit global increases or decreases in yields relative to those computed in the base case. One use is to represent technological change that might allow increased yields with effectively no increase in agricultural inputs. It can also be used to represent periods of bad weather, climate change, or crop destruction by pests (like locusts) during which production drops even without changes in input levels. A value of 1 represents no change, 1.25 represents a 25 percent increase, and .75 represents a 25 percent decrease. This variable should be 1 the first year.

XSHIFT      Export shift. An additive parameter that allows increase (positive values) or decrease (negative values) of exports of materials, manufactured goods, and services, by region. Changes will be offset automatically by changes in private and governmental consumption. This variable can be used to implement export-led growth strategies. The model bases each year's exports on the proportion of its product exported the previous year, so a value of 0.05 would add 5 percent to exports for *that and subsequent years*. Because the impact is cumulative, values should seldom exceed 0.1. The initial values of trade represent data, so XSHIFT should be zero, and it should be changed only after the initial year.

YLF      Yield factor, by region. A multiplier that allows the user to posit increases or decreases in yields relative to those computed in the base case. One use is to represent technological change that might allow increased yields with effectively no increase in agricultural inputs. It can also be used to represent periods of bad weather, climate change, or crop destruction by pests (like locusts) during which production drops even without changes in input levels. A value of 1 represents no change, 1.25 represents a 25 percent increase, and .75 represents a 25 percent decrease. This variable should be 1 the first year.

□ □ □

# Appendix 3: Installation of IFs and Summary Description

## INSTALLATION AND USE

IFs requires an IBM-compatible microcomputer with at least 640K memory. Although IFs will run on a computer with the 8088 processor, the run times are too slow to make the model an effective tool on such machines, unless they have a coprocessor. It is recommended that you use a machine with an 80286 or faster processor, preferably with the support of a mathematical coprocessor. Table A3.1 illustrates run times for various machines. In the course of work with IFs, you could easily make 30 or more runs of the model (most until the year 2005, and a few through 2035).

IFs requires a hard disk. Installation will use a little less than 1.5 megabytes of disk space. Users have the option of saving up to eight files of results, each approaching 0.5 megabytes in size. Thus it is possible that IFs could use about 5 megabytes of disk space, but you can also save the files with results to floppy disks.

You can also install IFs on a network. In that case, individual users will manage their own result files locally, probably with floppy disks.

Installation creates a directory labeled IFS90 and puts the model in that directory. To install IFs, insert the installation disk (or the first installation disk if you have a set of two) in floppy drive A: or B: and type A: or B:, followed by touching <Enter> to make the chosen drive the active drive. Then type INSTALL, again followed by touching <Enter>. Once the model is installed, using it requires only that you type IFS90 from the IFS90 directory, as always followed by <Enter>. The installation process does *not* alter your AUTOEXEC.BAT or CONFIG.SYS file.

If you wish to print any of the graphical output of IFs by using the <Shift>-<PrtSc> key combination (this is optional and you can always print tables), you must install your own copy of DOS graphics before running the model. You can do this by typing GRAPHICS from your root directory before calling up IFs or by adding the line GRAPHICS.COM to your AUTOEXEC.BAT file.[1]

There is no copy protection on IFs. There is also no limit on its distribution, so feel free to make additional copies and pass them on. There are, however, normal copyright restrictions on the reproduction of this volume—you cannot copy or disseminate it. Please support the costs of development and distribution of this volume (and thereby the model) by respecting that restriction.

Some individuals may wish to go beyond model use and to explore or even change the model structure. You will find that you have only the .EXE code for the model on the distribution disk, not the source or object code. In addition, it is necessary to understand the equation structure before attempting to alter or extend the model. The author can provide technical documentation and the source code.[2]

Although IFs can stand alone, it may have additional value when used with the textbook by Barry B. Hughes, *Continuity and Change in World Politics: The Clash of Perspectives*, 2d ed. (En-

187

TABLE A3.1   Run Speed of IFs on Selected Microcomputers

| Computer (IBM or IBM-compatible) | Forecast Horizon (minutes and seconds) | |
|---|---|---|
| | 1990–2005 | 1990–2035 |
| 8088 processor (with coprocessor) | 2' 20" | 6' 35" |
| 80286 processor (without coprocessor) | 3' 36" | 10' 22" |
| 80286 processor (with coprocessor) | 1' 32" | 4' 20" |
| 80386 processor (with coprocessor) | 0' 26" | 1' 12" |
| 80486 processor (33 MHz) | 0' 10" | 0' 28" |

glewood Cliffs, N.J.: Prentice-Hall, 1994). The textbook and this book parallel each other in presentation. If you have any problems installing the disk or accessing the program, phone Barry B. Hughes at 303-871-2560.

## THE BACKGROUND OF IFs

This may not be your first exposure to IFs, and it is therefore useful to place this edition of the model in the context of earlier ones.[3] CONDUIT made available the first version of IFs in 1982 (Hughes, 1982). It ran only on larger computers, and users needed to use a specialized command language to interact with it. A substantially different version of IFs, known as Micro-IFs (Hughes, 1985a), was a considerably smaller subset of the original model and was designed to run on IBM-compatible microcomputers; it incorporated a menu-driven interface.

IFs90, the current version, has the full scale of the initial version plus some additional structural features, but it runs on IBM-compatible microcomputers under a more sophisticated menu-driven interface (and with better graphical output). Among the new structural features are representations of arms races between states or alliances and of the possibility that arms races may lead to war. The initial conditions for IFs90 are from the year 1990. For a detailed elaboration of the structure and equations of IFs, see Hughes (1991).

IFs represents the entire world geographically in ten units. It would obviously be desirable to represent many more countries individually, even to portray all countries. Aggregating countries made it possible to provide more detail in the model structure and also to reduce run time of the model. Trade-offs in modeling are always difficult.

IFs has five modules: demographics, agriculture, energy, economics, and politics. The chapters of this volume, especially Chapter 3, elaborate the following sketch of the structure of each. The population module of IFs maintains 15 cohorts in five-year intervals up to age 70 and represents those aged 71 and above as a sixteenth cohort. Overall fertility and mortality rates change in response to income, income distribution, and family planning programs. The module also computes average life expectancy at birth and literacy rate, and it calculates an overall measure of the physical quality of life. The economic module represents the economy in five sectors: agriculture, materials, energy, industry, and services. It is a general equilibrium model that does not assume exact equilibrium will exist in any given year; the model chases equilibrium over time. International trade utilizes the "pooled" rather than the bilateral trade approach. The energy module portrays production, consumption, and trade of four energy types: oil-gas, coal, nuclear, and renewable (hydro, solar, and wood). It represents known reserves and ultimate resources of the fossil fuels and capital costs of each energy form. The agricultural module incorporates production, consumption, trade, and pricing of two major food types: crops and livestock (fish are represented in less detail). The political module has two primary components. Within countries or geographic groupings, the module represents fiscal policy—taxing and spending decisions. The categories of government spending are military, health, education, foreign aid, and a residual category. Between countries or groupings of countries, the module optionally allows the user to explore arms races and the potential for conflict among countries that results from them. The representation of arms races uses an action-reaction approach. There is also an implicit environmental module distributed throughout the overall model.

There are various "policy handles" scattered throughout all modules. For instance, in the demographic module, the user can hypothesize alternative birthrates (a government might affect those rates through programs of family planning). In the agricultural module, the user can alter land use patterns (a government could change those through tax incentives, zoning, or direct regulation). In the energy module, one can assume different efficiencies in the use or production of energy (again affected by tax incentives or legislation).

IFs is as large and sophisticated as most of the world models used in research over the last two decades (see Chapter 7 for some comparative information). It is unique, however, in its ease of use.

Because they recognize the dangers of prediction, those using models generally produce multiple forecasts. As the acronym IFs suggests, each of those **forecasts** is a highly specific IF-THEN statement. A model, with its causal structure and initial conditions, constitutes an IF-statement. Were we able to accept the accuracy of that IF-statement, we could accept the forecast generated by the model, the THEN-statement, as a prediction. There are, however, two basic weaknesses of most IF-statements.

The first weakness of IF-statements, like those in a computer simulation, is that they almost certainly contain errors. For instance, the IF-statement behind a forecast from a world model like IFs is very complex. It consists in part of the model structure, the formal equations that link variables in the model to each other, and there are thousands of such equations in a model the size of IFs, each subject to error.

Second, IF-statements are inevitably simplified representations of a complex world. They therefore inevitably omit factors and relationships that prove important. For instance, IF-statements almost invariably fail to represent social learning. The way in which France copes with the next energy crisis or a new threat from external aggression may be quite different from the way in which it addressed similar situations in the past; new policies may be no better, but they will be different in response to the knowledge gained from past policy efforts. Similarly, to the degree that models like IFs help the leadership in Egypt understand the economic and social costs of rapid population growth, they may actually influence the policies of that leadership. Therefore, a model can ironically facilitate the social learning that falsifies its own forecasts.

In light of these weaknesses, the most common use of computer models is in making **comparative forecasts** or scenarios. That is, we make an initial forecast with the model, a forecast that we often call a base or reference case. Then we change an assumption (such as a policy preference or a questionable specification of the model) and make another forecast. Comparison of the two forecasts or scenarios provides an estimate of the effect of the changed assumption. Obviously, both the magnitude and even the direction of the effect depend on the accuracy of the model, and we must subject comparative forecasts to the same skepticism with which we approach a prediction. That we are focusing our attention on the effect of a single change, however, allows us to delve much more carefully and deeply into the reasons for the result we discover. Assuming that we make such a careful examination, we can have some confidence in the result. This approach is basic to the use of a model.

In spite of the limitations of all models and forecasts, using IFs will extend your ability to address our questions about the future in several ways.

1. IFs can help you formalize your understanding of the world. We all carry around understandings of the world—mental models of key global processes; interacting with a

formalized model of the world can frequently clarify our possibly murky mental models by drawing our attention to how others understand those processes (a good model carries a considerable amount of collective knowledge). A computer simulation also includes a level of precision that will push you toward becoming comparably careful in specification.

2. IFs can help you expand or stretch your mental map. It is very likely that IFs contains many understandings that will enrich your own mental model. Even its very limitations, if you approach IFs critically, can sensitize you to the factors that both the model and your own mental map of the world fail adequately to treat.

3. Through the technique of comparative forecasts, IFs will allow you to explore the possible consequences of actions and therefore to substantially increase your ability to understand human leverage.

4. The process of exploring the model and consequences of actions can help you undertake your own worldview clarification. You will begin to develop preferred futures and to understand why you prefer them.

□ □ □

# Notes

## NOTES TO CHAPTER TWO

1. The *Washington Post* (March 28, 1992: A16) reported that rate for 1991. The area deforested in that year constitutes about 0.3 percent of total Amazonian forest.

2. *The Economist* (December 21, 1991–January 3, 1992: 25–27) provides these and many other examples.

3. A large portion of that increase in life expectancy is accounted for by a dramatic drop in infant mortality. The growth in life span of those who live through infancy is considerably less dramatic.

4. Deutsch (1988: 313). Cipolla (1962: 116) reported a rate of 56 percent literacy in 1955.

## NOTES TO CHAPTER THREE

1. See, for example, Mesarovic and Pestel (1974); Herrera et al. (1976); SARU (1977); Leontief, Carter, and Petri (1977); Bremer (1987). Those models added geographic differentiation, coverage of additional global issues and forces (such as technological change and politics), and sometimes greater sophistication.

## NOTES TO CHAPTER FOUR

1. Similarly, Gilpin developed a relatively formal but noncomputerized model of state behavior in which he assumed that "once an equilibrium between the costs and benefits of further change and expansion is reached, the tendency is for the economic costs of maintaining the status quo to rise faster than the economic capacity to support the status quo" (1981: 156).

2. Bremer and Hughes (1990: 32–38) review the literature that examines the linkage between arms races and warfare. They find that the empirical evidence is quite mixed.

3. James Lee Ray of Florida State University has tentatively identified a list (unpublished) of 22 potential exceptions, going back to the war between Athens and Syracuse in 415–413 B.C. He is skeptical that any of them truly violate the rule of nonbelligerence among democracies.

4. Military expenditures of Russia differ more from the base case than do those of China, because Russian expenditure growth in the base case was lower than that of China. We have made Russia very sensitive to the Chinese and have forced them to

match the higher growth in Chinese military expenditures. Even in the absence of increased Chinese spending, the sensitivity we created through setting the values of ALLY would have led to substantially higher Russian expenditures.

5. Each time you start IFs, the random number generator will produce the same sequence of numbers. Thus you can control the stochastic element simply by restarting IFs. But if you run the same scenario two or more times within the same session with IFs, the random numbers will change and you will see different results with respect to war.

6. Bremer and Hughes (1990) used the GLOBUS model to explore these proposals in much more depth.

## NOTES TO CHAPTER FIVE

1. For nearly identical estimates in the 1970s and 1980s, see International Monetary Fund (1990b: 123).

2. What we might call the global middle class, including the newly industrialized countries, has grown much faster than either the richest or poorest countries. Inclusion of them in the global South accounts for the stability of the overall income ratio of North to South.

3. Kevin Phillips, a former Republican campaign strategist, documents the growing inequality in the United States (1990) and argues that a backlash against the quite purely classical liberal (modern economically conservative) policies of the 1980s was inevitable.

4. The IMF does report, however, that the terms of trade for LDCs in manufacturing improved by an annual rate of 0.7 percent during the same decade (International Monetary Fund, 1990b: 152).

5. The investment in agriculture scenario factor (IASF) and the investment in energy scenario factor (IESF) similarly allow one to increase or decrease investment in those two sectors (although shifts into or out of either are offset by changes in other investment, not in consumption).

## NOTES TO CHAPTER SIX

1. IFs uses a "cohort-component" approach to representing population growth in which it tracks population in 5-year age categories. It thus captures the momentum that population growth attains.

2. This calculation is based on assorted issues of the World Bank's *Commodity Trade and Price Trends* and on CIA data (1991b: 42–43).

3. Ehrlich would probably argue that the 1980s were atypical in that poor global economic conditions (especially in Latin America and elsewhere in developing countries) suppressed demand.

## NOTES TO CHAPTER SEVEN

1. Hans Morgenthau published a new textbook on international politics in 1948, explicating realism for two generations of American students (1948).

2. *Economist* (November 9, 1991: 11).

3. Walters and Blake (1992: 24) report on the 1986–1990 period; 1991 data is from the *Denver Post* (February 21, 1992).

4. In Chapter 6 we did indicate, however, how multiple worldviews could combine to help us understand issues of progress and sustainability, as we had earlier brought realism (via mercantilism) into a consideration of economic issues.

## NOTES TO APPENDIX 3

1. On many systems this option will not work, and it is impossible to print the graphics of IFs.

2. This volume does not detail the technical structure of IFs. Those who would like to know more about the overall structure of IFs and how it compares with other models might first look to Hughes (1985b). Those who want to see the full equation documentation can request Hughes (1991b). It is also possible to obtain the program code for IFs. To use it, however, requires the purchase of the Microsoft Professional Basic software (version 7.1 or later) and the availability of a computer with extended memory. The cost for either the documentation of equations or the program code is $25. Contact Professor Barry B. Hughes, Graduate School of International Studies, University of Denver, Denver, Colorado 80208.

3. Hughes (1988) presents a more extensive history of IFs. For analyses of the capabilities and limitations of IFs and comparisons with other world models, see Hughes (1985b) and Liverman (1983). For general reviews of world models including IFs, see Siegmann (1985) and Barney, Kreutzer, and Garrett (1991). The current version of IFs has benefited from some of the work done on the GLOBUS world model (Bremer, 1987).

# References

Ayres, Robert U. 1969. *Technological Forecasting and Long-Range Planning*. New York: McGraw-Hill.

Barney, Gerald O., W. Brian Kreutzer, and Martha J. Garrett, eds. 1991. *Managing a Nation*, 2d ed. Boulder: Westview Press.

Bremer, Stuart A. 1977. *Simulated Worlds: A Computer Model of National Decision-Making*. Princeton: Princeton University Press.

_____., ed. 1987. *The GLOBUS Model: Computer Simulation of World-wide Political and Economic Developments*. Boulder: Westview Press.

Bremer, Stuart A., and Walter Gruhn. 1988. *Micro GLOBUS: A Computer Model of Long-Term Global Political and Economic Processes*. Berlin: Edition Sigma.

Bremer, Stuart A., and Barry B. Hughes. 1990. *Disarmament and Development: A Design for the Future?* Englewood Cliffs, N.J.: Prentice-Hall.

British Petroleum Company. 1991. *BP Statistical Review of World Energy*. London: British Petroleum Company.

_____. 1992. *BP Statistical Review of World Energy*. London: British Petroleum Company.

Brown, Lester R. 1981. *Building a Sustainable Society*. New York: W. W. Norton.

_____. 1988. "Analyzing the Demographic Trap." In *State of the World 1987*, edited by Lester R. Brown and others, 20–37. New York: W. W. Norton.

Brown, Lester R., et al. 1992. *State of the World 1992*. New York: W. W. Norton.

Buchanan, William. 1974. *Understanding Political Variables*. 2d ed. New York: Charles Scribner's Sons.

Central Intelligence Agency. 1990. *The World Factbook 1990*. Washington, D.C.: Central Intelligence Agency.

_____. 1990b. *Handbook of Economic Statistics, 1990*. Washington, D.C.: Central Intelligence Agency.

_____. 1991. *The World Factbook 1991*. Washington, D.C.: Central Intelligence Agency.

_____. 1991b. *Handbook of Economic Statistics, 1991*. Washington, D.C.: Central Intelligence Agency.

Cipolla, Carlo M. 1962. *The Economic History of World Population*. Baltimore: Penguin.

Cook, Earl. 1976. *Man, Energy, Society*. San Francisco: W. H. Freeman.

Council on Environmental Quality (CEQ). 1981. *The Global 2000 Report to the President*. Washington, D.C.: Government Printing Office.

————. 1981b (July). *Environmental Trends*. Washington, D.C.: Government Printing Office.

————. 1991. *21st Annual Report*. Washington, D.C.: Government Printing Office.

Cusack, Thomas R., and Richard J. Stoll. 1990. *Exploring Realpolitik: Probing International Relations with Computer Simulation*. Boulder: Lynne Rienner.

DeConde, Alexander. 1978. *A History of American Foreign Policy*. 3d ed. Vol. 2, *Global Power*. New York: Charles Scribner's Sons.

Deutsch, Karl W. 1988. *The Analysis of International Relations*. 3d ed. Englewood Cliffs, N.J.: Prentice-Hall.

Ehrlich, Paul R., and Anne H. Ehrlich. 1972. *Population, Resources, Environment*. San Francisco: W. H. Freeman.

Eicher, Carl. 1982. "Facing up to Africa's Food Crisis." *Foreign Affairs* 61, no. 1 (Fall): 151–174.

Forrester, Jay W. 1968. *Principles of Systems*. Cambridge, Mass: Wright-Allen Press.

Gilpin, Robert. 1981. *War and Change in World Politics*. Cambridge: Cambridge University Press.

Grant, Lindsey. 1982. *The Cornucopian Fallacies*. Washington, D.C.: Environmental Fund.

Gurr, Ted Robert, Keith Jaggers, and Will H. Moore. 1990. "The Transformation of the Western State." *Studies in Comparative International Development* 25, no. 1 (Spring): 94.

Haas, Ernst B. 1990. *When Knowledge Is Power*. Berkeley: University of California Press.

Herrera, Amilcar O., et al. 1976. *Catastrophe or New Society? A Latin American World Model*. Ottawa: International Development Research Centre.

Hopper, W. David. 1976. "The Development of Agriculture in Developing Countries." *Scientific American* 235 (September): 200.

Hughes, Barry B. 1980. *World Modeling*. Lexington, Mass: Lexington Books.

————. 1982. *International Futures Simulation: User's Manual*. Iowa City: CONDUIT, University of Iowa.

————. 1985a. *International Futures Simulation*. Iowa City: CONDUIT, University of Iowa.

————. 1985b. "World Models: The Bases of Difference." *International Studies Quarterly* 29: 77–101.

————. 1985c. *World Futures: A Critical Analysis of Alternatives*. Baltimore: Johns Hopkins University Press.

————. 1988. "International Futures: History and Status." *Social Science Microcomputer Review* 6: 43–48.

————. 1991. *Continuity and Change in World Politics*. Englewood Cliffs, N.J.: Prentice-Hall.

————. 1991b. *International Futures 1990, (IFs90): Equation Documentation*. Graduate School of International Studies, University of Denver.

Information Please Almanac. 1990. *The 1990 Information Please Almanac*. Boston: Houghton Mifflin.

Information Please Almanac. 1992. *The 1992 Information Please Almanac*. Boston: Houghton Mifflin.

International Monetary Fund. 1990. *International Financial Statistics*. Washington, D.C.: International Monetary Fund.

_____. 1990b. *World Economic Outlook*. Washington, D.C.: International Monetary Fund.

_____. 1991. *World Economic Outlook*. Washington, D.C.: International Monetary Fund.

_____. 1992. *World Economic Outlook*. Washington, D.C.: International Monetary Fund.

Jansson, Kurt, Michael Harris, and Angela Penrose. 1987. *The Ethiopian Famine*. London: Zed Books Ltd.

Kahn, Herman, William Brown, and Leon Martel. 1976. *The Next 200 Years*. New York: William Morrow.

Kennedy, Paul. 1987. *The Rise and Fall of the Great Powers*. New York: Random House.

Leontief, Wassily, Anne Carter, and Peter Petri. 1977. *The Future of the World Economy*. New York: Oxford University Press.

Liverman, Dianne. 1983. *The Use of Global Simulation Models in Assessing Climate Impacts on the World Food System*. Dissertation, University of California, Los Angeles.

McWilliams, Wayne C., and Harry Piotrowski. 1988. *The World Since 1945*. Boulder: Lynne Rienner.

Meadows, Dennis L., et al. 1974. *Dynamics of Growth in a Finite World*. Cambridge, Mass.: Wright-Allen Press.

Meadows, Donnela H., Dennis L. Meadows, Jørgen Randers, and William K. Behrens III. 1972. *Limits to Growth*. New York: Universe Books.

Meadows, Donnela H., Dennis L. Meadows, and Jørgen Randers. 1992. *Beyond the Limits*. Post Mills, Vt.: Chelsea Green Publishing Company.

Mesarovic, Mihajlo D., and Eduard Pestel. 1974. *Mankind at the Turning Point*. New York: E. P. Dutton.

Morgenthau, Hans. 1948. *Politics Among Nations*. New York: Alfred A. Knopf.

Phillips, Kevin. 1990. *The Politics of Rich and Poor*. New York: Harper Collins.

Pirages, Dennis. 1983. "The Ecological Perspective and the Social Sciences." *International Studies Quarterly* 27, no. 3 (September): 243–255.

_____. 1989. *Global Technopolitics*. Pacific Grove, Calif: Brooks/Cole Publishing.

Population Reference Bureau. 1991. *World Population Data Sheet 1991*. Washington, D.C.: Population Reference Bureau.

Population Reference Bureau. 1992. *World Population Data Sheet 1992*. Washington, D.C.: Population Reference Bureau.

SARU (Systems Analysis Research Unit). 1977. *SARUM 76 Global Modeling Project*. Departments of the Environment and Transport, 2 Marsham Street, London, 3WIP 3EB.

Shane, Harold G., and Gary A. Sojka. 1990. "John Elfreth Watkins, Jr.: Forgotten Genius of Forecasting." In *The 1990s and Beyond*, edited by Edward Cornish, 150–155. Bethesda, Md.: World Future Society.

Siegmann, Heinrich. 1985. *Recent Developments in World Modeling*. Berlin: Science Center.

Sinsheimer, Robert L. 1980. "The Presumptions of Science." In *Economics, Ecology, Ethics*, edited by Herman E. Daly, 146–161. San Francisco: W. H. Freeman.

Sivard, Ruth Leger. 1991. *World Military and Social Expenditures 1991*. World Priorities, Box 25140, Washington, D.C. 20007.

United Nations Development Programme (UNDP). 1992. *Human Development Report*. New York: Oxford University Press.

United Nations Food and Agriculture Organization (FAO). 1989. *Production Yearbook*. Rome: FAO.

United States Arms Control and Disarmament Agency. 1992. *World Military Expenditures and Arms Transfers 1992*. Washington, D.C.: Arms Control and Disarmament Agency.

Walters, Robert S., and David H. Blake. 1992. *The Politics of Global Economic Relations*. 4th ed. Englewood Cliffs, N.J.: Prentice-Hall.

Watkins, John Elfreth, Jr. 1990. "What May Happen in the Next Hundred Years." In *The 1990s and Beyond*, edited by Edward Cornish, 150–155. Bethesda, Md.: World Future Society.

Wildavsky, Aaron, and Ellen Tenenbaum. 1981. *The Politics of Mistrust*. Beverly Hills: Sage Publications.

World Almanac. 1989. *The World Almanac and Book of Facts 1990*. New York: World Almanac.

World Almanac. 1992. *The World Almanac and Book of Facts 1992*. New York: World Almanac.

World Bank. 1991. *World Development Report 1991*. New York: Oxford University Press.

————. 1992. *World Development Report 1992*. New York: Oxford University Press.

World Resources Institute. 1988. *World Resources 1988–89*. New York: Basic Books.

————. 1990. *World Resources 1990–91*. New York: Basic Books.

————. 1992. *World Resources 1992–93*. New York: Oxford University Press.

Wortman, Sterling, and Ralph W. Cummings, Jr. 1978. *To Feed This World*. Baltimore: Johns Hopkins University Press.

Wright, John W. ed. 1991. *The Universal Almanac 1992*. Kansas City: Andrews and McMeel.

□ □ □

# About the Book
# and Author

What are the prospects that Africa can overcome its long-term food problems? What are the costs and benefits of protecting the South American tropical rain forests from development? What impact might strategic arms treaties have on the economies of the United States and Russia? Will trade among Japan, the European Community, and the United States become the new arena of international competition? In *International Futures*, Barry B. Hughes gives us concrete strategies for thinking about the future and gauging our role in shaping it.

*International Futures* is more than a book—it's a text carefully crafted around a computer simulation designed to survey a wide range of future alternatives in international relations, but at the same time, to zero in on 67 key variables for 10 geographical regions that can be manipulated to produce a limitless number of future scenarios in international security, economics, and the environment.

For the reader, *International Futures* coherently defines and develops key concepts in international affairs and tells the story of their potential application and change in coming years. For the computer user, *IFs* (the computer package accompanying the text) allows the interactive testing of theory and data relevant to our global future.

Taken together, the text and simulation allow students and others to transcend the usual level of speculation about the future in international affairs, moving to an empirically grounded and values-based consideration of issues, strategies, and outcomes.

Liberally illustrated with tables, graphs, feedback loops, flowcharts, and other aids to visualizing future options, the text stands alone as a stimulating overview of global trends. It also offers helpful boxed computer notes, simulation walk-throughs (denoted by ▶), research suggestions, and more for those who want to explore the disk along with the book.

Barry B. Hughes is professor of international relations in the Graduate School of International Studies at the University of Denver. He has authored numerous books and articles, including *World Futures* (1985: Johns Hopkins University Press) and *Continuity and Change in World Politics* (1991: Prentice-Hall). The latter is due out in a new edition in 1993 and makes an excellent companion volume to *International Futures*.

# Index

**BY OPENING THE SEALED COMPUTER DISK PACKAGE IN THE BACK OF THIS BOOK, YOU FORFEIT YOUR OPTION TO RETURN THE BOOK FOR REFUND AND INDICATE YOUR ACCEPTANCE OF THE FOLLOWING LICENSE AGREEMENT:**

(1) GRANT OF LICENSE. You are licensed to use IFs90, the computer software program designed to accompany the book, *International Futures*. This software is provided as an educational tool to enhance learning rather than as a commercial software product. It has been carefully reviewed and classroom tested, but even so certain restrictions, warranty disclaimers, and limitations apply.

(2) OWNERSHIP OF SOFTWARE. As the Licensee, you own the disk(s) on which the software is recorded, but Barry B. Hughes retains title and ownership of the software itself. You may copy your disk(s), but you may not modify, adapt, translate, or create derivative works based on the software.

(3) COPYRIGHT. Both the software and the book are copyrighted. Copyright notice must appear on any copies of the disk(s) you make. You are not authorized to copy any portions of the book without written permission from Westview Press except for your own personal use.

(4) DISCLAIMER OF WARRANTY AND LIMITED WARRANTY. The software and book are provided "as is" without warranty as to performance, merchantability, fitness for a particular purpose, accuracy, reliability, currency, or otherwise. The entire risk as to the results and performance of the software is assumed by you. Westview Press warrants to the original Licensee that the disk(s) on which IFs90 is recorded is free from defects in materials and workmanship under normal use and service for a period of ninety (90) days from the date of delivery as evidenced by a copy of the receipt. Westview Press's entire liability and your exclusive remedy shall be replacement of defective disk(s) returned with a copy of the receipt.

The above are the only warranties of any kind, either express or implied, that are made by Barry B. Hughes or Westview Press regarding the software IFs90. Neither Barry B. Hughes nor Westview Press shall be liable for any direct, indirect, consequential, or incidental damages arising out of the use or inability to use IFs90 software.

**IF YOU DO NOT AGREE TO THESE TERMS, DO NOT OPEN THE SEALED DISK PACKAGE. PROMPTLY RETURN THE UNOPENED DISK PACKAGE AND BOOK TO THE PLACE WHERE YOU OBTAINED THEM FOR A REFUND IF AVAILABLE. BY OPENING THE SEALED DISK PACKAGE YOU FORFEIT YOUR OPTION TO RETURN THE BOOK FOR REFUND.**